中译翻译文库·口译研究丛书

实战交传（英汉互译）
Field Consecutive Interpretation

林超伦　著

中国出版集团
中译出版社

图书在版编目(CIP)数据

实战交传（英汉互译）/林超伦著．—北京：中译出版社，2012.6（2022.1重印）

ISBN 978-7-5001-3375-9

Ⅰ.①实… Ⅱ.①林… Ⅲ.①英语-翻译-研究生-教材 Ⅳ.①H315.9

中国版本图书馆CIP数据核字（2012）第091856号

出版发行 / 中译出版社
地　　址 / 北京市西城区车公庄大街甲4号物华大厦6层
电　　话 / (010) 68359287；68359303（发行部）；53601537（编辑部）
邮　　编 / 100044
传　　真 / (010) 68357870
电子邮箱 / book@ctph.com.cn
网　　址 / http://www.ctph.com.cn

责任编辑 / 范祥镇

排　　版 / 北京竹页文化传媒有限公司
印　　刷 / 北京玺诚印务有限公司
经　　销 / 新华书店北京发行所

规　　格 / 700毫米×960毫米　1/16
印　　张 / 14.75
字　　数 / 261千字
版　　次 / 2012年6月第一版
印　　次 / 2022年1月第七次

ISBN 978-7-5001-3375-9　定价：38.00元

版权所有　侵权必究

中 译 出 版 社

中译翻译文库
编 委 会

顾　　问（以姓氏拼音为序）
John Michael Minford（英国著名汉学家、文学翻译家、《红楼梦》英译者）
黄友义（中国外文局）　　　　　　　　尹承东（中共中央编译局）

主任编委（以姓氏拼音为序）
Andrew C. Dawrant（AIIC 会员，上海外国语大学）　　柴明颎（上海外国语大学）
陈宏薇（华中师范大学）　　　　　　　戴惠萍（AIIC 会员，上海外国语大学）
方梦之（《上海翻译》）　　　　　　　　冯庆华（上海外国语大学）
辜正坤（北京大学）　　　　　　　　　郭建中（浙江大学）
黄忠廉（黑龙江大学）　　　　　　　　李亚舒（《中国科技翻译》）
刘和平（北京语言大学）　　　　　　　刘士聪（南开大学）
吕和发（北京第二外国语学院）　　　　罗选民（清华大学）
梅德明（上海外国语大学）　　　　　　穆　雷（广东外语外贸大学）
谭载喜（香港浸会大学）　　　　　　　王恩冕（对外经济贸易大学）
王继辉（北京大学）　　　　　　　　　王立弟（北京外国语大学）
吴　青（北京外国语大学）　　　　　　谢天振（上海外国语大学）
许　钧（南京大学）　　　　　　　　　杨　平（《中国翻译》）
张高里（中译出版社）　　　　　　　　仲伟合（广东外语外贸大学）

编委委员（以姓氏拼音为序）
Daniel Gile（AIIC 会员，巴黎高等翻译学校）　　蔡新乐（南京大学）
陈　刚（浙江大学）　　　　　　　　　陈　菁（厦门大学）
陈德鸿（香港岭南大学）　　　　　　　陈　琳（同济大学）
傅勇林（西南交通大学）　　　　　　　傅敬民（上海大学）
高　伟（四川外国语大学）　　　　　　顾铁军（中国传媒大学）
郭著章（武汉大学）　　　　　　　　　何其莘（中国人民大学）
胡开宝（上海交通大学）　　　　　　　黄杨勋（福州大学）
贾文波（中南大学）　　　　　　　　　江　红（AIIC 会员，香港理工大学）
焦鹏帅（西南民族大学）　　　　　　　金圣华（香港中文大学）
柯　平（南京大学）　　　　　　　　　李均洋（首都师范大学）
李奭学（台湾"中央研究院"）　　　　　李正栓（河北师范大学）
廖七一（四川外国语大学）　　　　　　林超伦（英国 KL 传播有限公司）
林大津（福建师范大学）　　　　　　　林克难（天津外国语大学）
刘树森（北京大学）　　　　　　　　　吕　俊（南京师范大学）
马会娟（北京外国语大学）　　　　　　马士奎（中央民族大学）

门顺德（大连外国语大学）
牛云平（河北大学）
潘志高（解放军外国语大学）
彭发胜（合肥工业大学）
屈文生（华东政法大学）
邵　炜（AIIC会员，北京外国语大学）
石　坚（四川大学）
宋亚菲（广西大学）
孙迎春（山东大学）
王　宏（苏州大学）
王　宁（清华大学）
王振华（河南大学）
文　旭（西南大学）
肖维青（上海外国语大学）
杨　柳（南京大学）
姚桂桂（江汉大学）
张德禄（山东大学、同济大学）
张其帆（AIIC会员，香港理工大学）
章　艳（上海外国语大学）
郑海凌（北京师范大学）
朱振武（上海师范大学）

孟凡君（西南大学）
潘文国（华东师范大学）
彭　萍（北京外国语大学）
秦潞山（AIIC会员，Chin Communications）
任　文（四川大学）
申　丹（北京大学）
石平萍（解放军外国语大学）
孙会军（上海外国语大学）
陶丽霞（四川外国语大学）
王建国（华东理工大学）
王克非（北京外国语大学）
文　军（北京航空航天大学）
温建平（上海对外经贸大学）
闫素伟（国际关系学院）
杨全红（四川外国语大学）
张春柏（华东师范大学）
张美芳（澳门大学）
张秀仿（河北工程大学）
赵　刚（华东师范大学）
朱纯深（香港城市大学）

特约编审（以姓氏拼音为序）

Andrew C. Dawrant（AIIC会员，上海外国语大学）
戴惠萍（AIIC会员，上海外国语大学）
高　伟（四川外国语大学）
黄国文（中山大学）
李长栓（北京外国语大学）
李亚舒（《中国科技翻译》）
罗新璋（中国社会科学院）
孟凡君（西南大学）
屠国元（中南大学）
王立弟（北京外国语大学）
谢天振（上海外国语大学）
杨　平（《中国翻译》）
杨士焯（厦门大学）
俞利军（对外经济贸易大学）
张　鹏（四川外国语大学）
祝朝伟（四川外国语大学）

柴明颎（上海外国语大学）
冯庆华（上海外国语大学）
胡安江（四川外国语大学）
黄忠廉（黑龙江大学）
李凌鸿（重庆法语联盟）
刘军平（武汉大学）
梅德明（上海外国语大学）
苗　菊（南开大学）
王东风（中山大学）
王明树（四川外国语大学）
徐　珺（对外经济贸易大学）
杨全红（四川外国语大学）
杨晓荣（《外语研究》）
张　健（上海外国语大学）
赵学文（吉林大学）

导　言

《实战交传》是为了培训英汉互译的交替传译（以下简称交传）译员。交传译员的概念及其内涵远远超出交传技能，这个区分十分关键。做好交传仰赖于交传技能。但是要想成为优秀的交传译员，光有交传技能是远远不够的。

本教材的主要目的是交传译员的培训，不是对于交传这种口译形式本身的研究。虽然有时也提及理念上的内容，但是重点在于解释如何理解笔者的看法，而不在于论证。

有关交传的实证研究不多，本书基本上是笔者个人实践、观察和思考的结果，难免失之片面或者看法有误。欢迎读者批评指正，请发邮件给 mail@linchaolun.com，有信必回。

本书各课的概要如下。

第一课提出交传的暂用定义，以此界定本书的范围，同时解释了构成交传定义的各个组成部分的内容。

第二课探讨一个往往被认为是没有什么可谈的概念，即：交传译员译什么。本课的讨论将为此后的论述和培训奠定理念基础。

第三课集中讨论与交传概念和培训直接相关的四大议题。这些议题所涉及的内容对于如何认识交传，如何培训交传技能，如何培养交传译员有重大意义。

第四课讲解交传的任务周期以及构成周期的不同阶段，提出交传任务从接到任务，历经准备、完成任务到完成任务之后的学习为止。

第五课讲解交传的核心技能。这些技能为交传特有，必须构成交传培训的核心内容。

第六课和第七课讲解交传的辅助技能。这些技能都是交传译员所需但又不是交传特有。

第八课讲解笔记的使用，由如何建立笔记体系、如何记录、如何使用这三部分内容组成。

第九课以四段话英译汉为例子，逐点分析交传时如何记笔记，然后如何根据笔记说出译语。

第十课介绍如何培训交传，受益的对象即可以是担任交传培训的老师，也可以是自学交传者。之前讲解过的绝大多数技能都将在本课里逐一介绍在培训时如何操作。

笔者认为交传是最复杂、难度最大的口译形式之一；同时也是最令人振奋、最富有事业成就感的口译形式之一。交传能让译员接触到远远超出个人范围的生活，结识本来只能在想象中见面的人。有些译员在某些特定时刻甚至会给国家、国际或者历史事件带来直接的影响。

希望本书成为您走上这样一种职业发展道路的铺路石。

目　录

第一部分　理念学习 ⋯⋯⋯⋯⋯⋯⋯⋯⋯⋯⋯⋯⋯⋯⋯⋯⋯⋯⋯⋯⋯⋯⋯⋯⋯ 1
　第一课　基本概念 ⋯⋯⋯⋯⋯⋯⋯⋯⋯⋯⋯⋯⋯⋯⋯⋯⋯⋯⋯⋯⋯⋯⋯⋯⋯ 3
　第二课　传译什么？⋯⋯⋯⋯⋯⋯⋯⋯⋯⋯⋯⋯⋯⋯⋯⋯⋯⋯⋯⋯⋯⋯⋯⋯ 13
　第三课　四大议题 ⋯⋯⋯⋯⋯⋯⋯⋯⋯⋯⋯⋯⋯⋯⋯⋯⋯⋯⋯⋯⋯⋯⋯⋯⋯ 21
　第四课　交传任务 ⋯⋯⋯⋯⋯⋯⋯⋯⋯⋯⋯⋯⋯⋯⋯⋯⋯⋯⋯⋯⋯⋯⋯⋯⋯ 32
　第五课　交传技能 ⋯⋯⋯⋯⋯⋯⋯⋯⋯⋯⋯⋯⋯⋯⋯⋯⋯⋯⋯⋯⋯⋯⋯⋯⋯ 45
　第六课　辅助技能一 ⋯⋯⋯⋯⋯⋯⋯⋯⋯⋯⋯⋯⋯⋯⋯⋯⋯⋯⋯⋯⋯⋯⋯ 54
　第七课　辅助技能二 ⋯⋯⋯⋯⋯⋯⋯⋯⋯⋯⋯⋯⋯⋯⋯⋯⋯⋯⋯⋯⋯⋯⋯ 68
　第八课　使用笔记 ⋯⋯⋯⋯⋯⋯⋯⋯⋯⋯⋯⋯⋯⋯⋯⋯⋯⋯⋯⋯⋯⋯⋯⋯⋯ 75
　第九课　笔记演示 ⋯⋯⋯⋯⋯⋯⋯⋯⋯⋯⋯⋯⋯⋯⋯⋯⋯⋯⋯⋯⋯⋯⋯⋯⋯ 88
　第十课　交传的培训 ⋯⋯⋯⋯⋯⋯⋯⋯⋯⋯⋯⋯⋯⋯⋯⋯⋯⋯⋯⋯⋯⋯⋯ 94
　附录一　交传模拟角色说明 ⋯⋯⋯⋯⋯⋯⋯⋯⋯⋯⋯⋯⋯⋯⋯⋯⋯⋯⋯ 106
　附录二　交传考试评分卡（水平考试）⋯⋯⋯⋯⋯⋯⋯⋯⋯⋯⋯⋯⋯ 108

第二部分　交传练习 ⋯⋯⋯⋯⋯⋯⋯⋯⋯⋯⋯⋯⋯⋯⋯⋯⋯⋯⋯⋯⋯⋯⋯ 109
　英译汉 ⋯⋯⋯⋯⋯⋯⋯⋯⋯⋯⋯⋯⋯⋯⋯⋯⋯⋯⋯⋯⋯⋯⋯⋯⋯⋯⋯⋯⋯ 111
　　1. 英中关系 ⋯⋯⋯⋯⋯⋯⋯⋯⋯⋯⋯⋯⋯⋯⋯⋯⋯⋯⋯⋯⋯⋯⋯⋯⋯⋯ 111
　　2. 英中贸易 ⋯⋯⋯⋯⋯⋯⋯⋯⋯⋯⋯⋯⋯⋯⋯⋯⋯⋯⋯⋯⋯⋯⋯⋯⋯⋯ 115
　　3. 英国油气业 ⋯⋯⋯⋯⋯⋯⋯⋯⋯⋯⋯⋯⋯⋯⋯⋯⋯⋯⋯⋯⋯⋯⋯⋯⋯ 119
　　4. 英国宇航业 ⋯⋯⋯⋯⋯⋯⋯⋯⋯⋯⋯⋯⋯⋯⋯⋯⋯⋯⋯⋯⋯⋯⋯⋯⋯ 123
　　5. 英国汽车业 ⋯⋯⋯⋯⋯⋯⋯⋯⋯⋯⋯⋯⋯⋯⋯⋯⋯⋯⋯⋯⋯⋯⋯⋯⋯ 127
　　6. 英国制药业 ⋯⋯⋯⋯⋯⋯⋯⋯⋯⋯⋯⋯⋯⋯⋯⋯⋯⋯⋯⋯⋯⋯⋯⋯⋯ 131

7. 英国创意业	135
8. 英国专业服务业	138
9. 气候变化	142
10. 核不扩散	146
11. 反恐怖主义	150
12. 汇丰银行讲话	153
13. 西门子讲话	157
14. 英国招商	162
15. 伦敦招商	166

汉译英 170

16. 中英关系	170
17. 中英贸易	174
18. 中国电讯业	178
19. 中国汽车业	181
20. 中国建筑业	185
21. 中国家电业	189
22. 中国风电业	193
23. 中国纺织业	197
24. 气候变化	201
25. 能源安全	204
26. 知识产权	207
27. 中航讲话	210
28. 中远讲话	215
29. 青岛招商	219
30. 成都招商	223

第一部分　理念学习

第一课　基本概念

交替传译在本书中除非有特殊需要，否则将一律简称为交传。

笔者对于交传的定义为：交传是在有组织的活动中由讲者、译员和听众这三方通过口译而开展的一前一后两个阶段的互动。三方中的讲者具有双重动机，听众往往多样化，译员总是两种角色。这一组特性共同构成了交传的概念。

本课将逐一讲解这些特性，讨论这些特性是如何共同定义交传，使其不同于笔译以及其他形式的口译。

有组织的活动

交传主要用于在两个组织机构之间举行的会谈或者活动。其主要特征是这种活动往往有双方商定的日程或者框架。这个特征决定了交传的其他一些重要特征，以下将作出详细解释。根据这个特征所定义的交传就和偶尔两人语言不通，不得不通过第三方口译而对话有本质的区别，也不同于西欧国家的公共服务口译（警察局口译、法庭口译、政府服务部门口译和医务口译）。

交传主要用于以下活动：

- 会议
- 会谈
- 谈判
- 演讲
- 演示
- 培训
- 座谈会和研讨会
- 参观或者游览

当然，在一些非正式的场合，或者没有明显组织的活动中也会用到交替传译。那种口译有时也被称为联络口译，不在本书范围之内，也不属于本书概念中的交传。

由于交传使用广泛，交传译员的工作地点也就很多样。以下只是无数地点的一些例子：

- 首相或者总统府
- 政府部门
- 会议室
- 船上酒店大堂
- 教室
- 汽车上
- 监狱（陪同代表团参观）
- 工厂车间
- 组装线
- 森林
- 海滩
- 店铺
- 餐馆
- 旅游胜地
- 医院
- 警察局
- 科学实验室

由于地点多样，而且译员仰赖于听，与同传相比，交传更容易受环境影响。同传译员使用专业设备，只要设备没有故障，讲者使用话筒，在听的渠道上就基本没有问题。交传译员则会受到周围噪音或者与讲者的距离（参观团的某个成员突然向东道主提问）而听不清讲话，听众也会因为类似原因听不见译员讲话。

三方

指讲者、译员和受众。讲者可以是一个人，也可以是不止一个。译员可以是一个，也可能不止一个。比如，政府的双边会谈一般使用自己的译员。受众也是这样，即可能是一个人，也可能是许多人，甚至成百上千。不仅如此，三方的角色也不是固定的，而是会在互动时发生变化。稍后有关互动的讲解中将举例说明。

正式会谈布置基本有两大类型，一是长桌形，二是马蹄形。请看示意图：

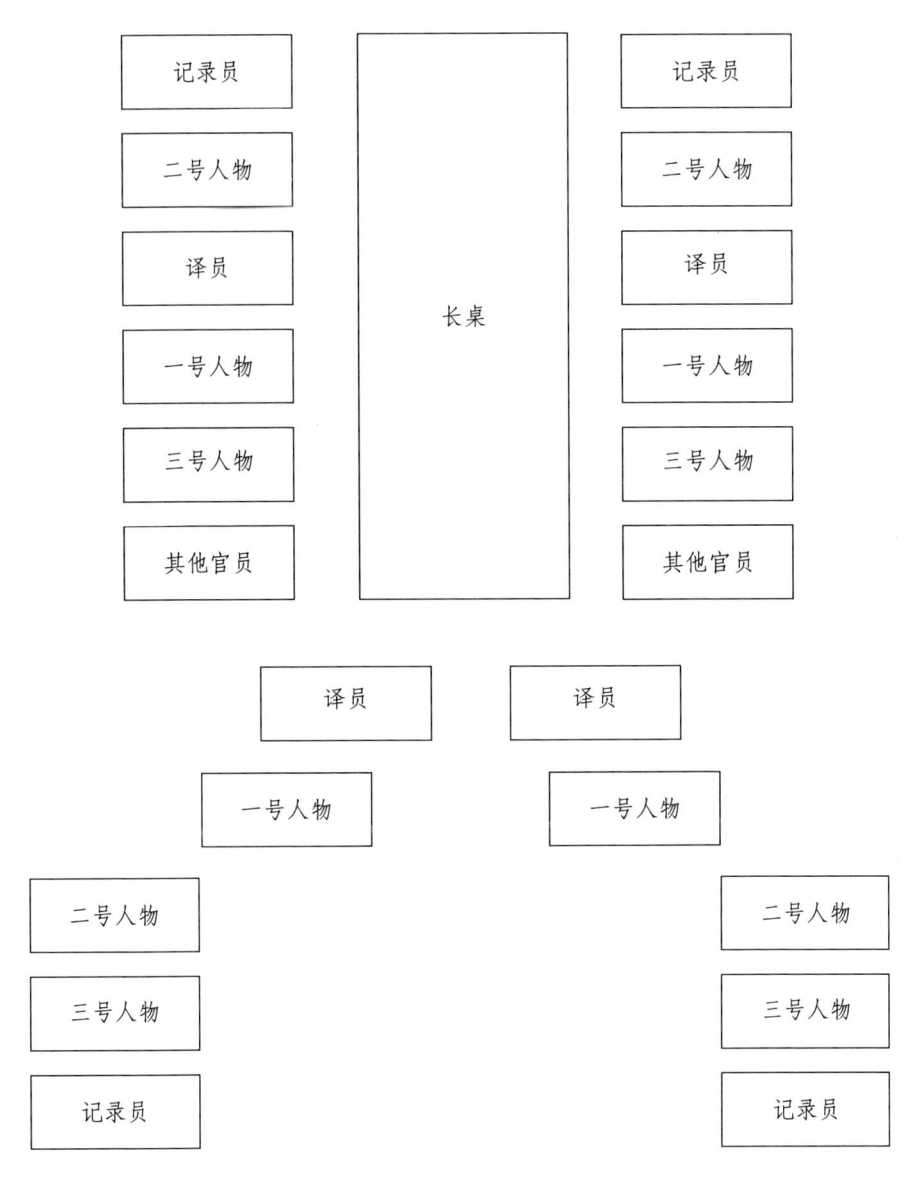

记录员		记录员
二号人物		二号人物
译员	长桌	译员
一号人物		一号人物
三号人物		三号人物
其他官员		其他官员

	译员	译员	
	一号人物	一号人物	
二号人物			二号人物
三号人物			三号人物
记录员			记录员

如果是宴会口译，则基本有两大类型的安排。传统中餐是圆桌，西餐是长桌。但是现在中方宴请有时也会采用长桌的形式。双方译员既可能被安排坐在己方主宾旁边，也可能坐在各自主宾的身后。请看下页的示意图。

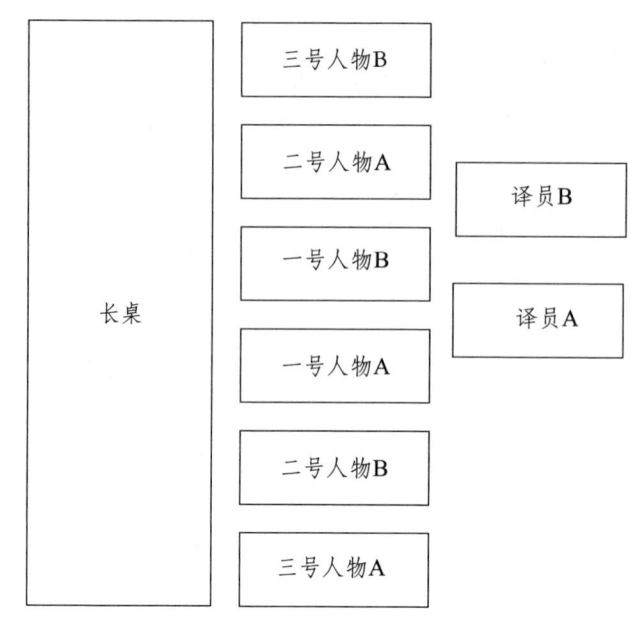

交传里的人际关系虽然最主要的是三方，但是不仅限于三方。

这里的主要原因是每个活动都有双方的不同身份的人参加，他们都会给译员的工作带来影响。比如，双方的礼宾官员或者外事办公室负责人。此外，译员也不一定是双方自己的雇员，中国的自由职业译员队伍不断发展，他们当中有些是直接受聘于活动组织方，有些是通过翻译公司接受口译任务的。如果一家公司举办大型活动，聘用专业公司具体实施，而专业公司聘请译员，这种情况下，交传里的人际关系就更加复杂了。请看以下示意图。

两阶段

讲者说话是第一阶段，译员口译是第二阶段，两个阶段分先后交替发生。需要注意的是，由于三方有可能互换角色，所以两个阶段并不仅限于讲者和译员之间。请看以下的进一步解释。

互动

交传不仅限于讲者说话给译员口译给受众听，而是带有多层次的互动。首先是讲者和译员的互动。这不仅是指讲者和译员交替讲话，而且包括译员向讲者提问，比如澄清是否听错，或者请讲者做出一定的解释。

第二是译员对讲者的影响。由于讲者只有在译员译完之后才能继续讲话，所以译员的讲话速度、声音大小，乃至所站立的位置都会影响到讲者。另外，译员的口译版本，甚至是某个措辞都会影响到讲者接下来要讲的内容和措辞。

第三是译员和受众的互动。比如如果译员成功地把幽默传达给受众，受众就会露出笑容。还有，译员说"接下来休息，外面有饮料"，受众就会起身往外走。

第四是受众与讲者互动。受众向讲者提问就是典型的例子。

最后就是三方角色的转变。如果有受众提问，则受众成了讲者，而讲者成了受众。如果译员在口译时加入自己的解释，那就在一定程度上担当起讲者的角色。如果译员在口译时为了避免暴露讲者的错误，没有把这个错误口译到译入语，那从受众的角度看，译员也是承担了讲者的角色。

讲者以及受众有时也会担当起译员的角色。比如，讲者两种语言都会，发现译员的版本不准确而加以纠正，或者一位受众打断译员纠正译员的口误。此时，受众充当了译员的角色，译员反而成了受众。

讲者双动机：讲者往往不仅是通过讲话提供信息，而且是在影响受众（第二课里将详细阐述）。最典型的例子恐怕就是主旨演讲了，从信息角度看完全可以把讲稿发给受众看了便可。但是现场演讲时，讲者利用声音、语调、目光、肢体语言和个人的感情形成了对受众的超出文字能力的影响。

当然这种影响受众的动机根据讲者的目的和活动的性质不同而不同。主旨演讲、竞选演说、推销演示、谈判都有明显的影响受众的动机在内。这不是说所有交传中讲者都是双动机，而是说在（中国目前情况下）常见的交传中是这样。

受众多样化

交传里受众的人数、身份变化很大。既可以是一对一的会谈，也可以是一个人面对成千的受众；即可以是两位工作人员的交谈，也可以是两国元首的正式会谈。既可以是只懂一种语言，也可能是在译出语和译入语里都有相当的水平。而同传往往用于有一定规模的会议或者活动，极少用于一对一的会谈。

译员双角色

一般概念里译员的角色就是口译，这样理解有失全面。译员的角色应该从宏观和微观两个层面分别来看。从宏观层面看，译员是所参与的有组织活动的一员，其角色是通过自己的工作协助活动进展下去，直至结束。从微观层面看，译员口译时需要尽量准确，使活动能够平稳、顺利地结束。

译员的宏观角色占主导地位，微观角色占次要地位。也就是说，译员的首要任务是保证活动能持续下去，而不是口译的准确。译员追求准确必须以不影响活动的进行为条件，如果为了准确会影响活动的继续的话，就必须牺牲准确。这种情况经常发生，即当译员没有听清讲者的话，或者不理解讲者的意思时，由于不能打断活动的进程而采用补齐句子甚至扔掉不译的办法，而不是打断讲者问清楚之后再译。

另外，越是在正式场合，活动就越是依照事先确定的程序进行。即使译员什么话都没说，活动也会依照程序继续下去。所以，在这种情况下，即如果译员的宏观角色与微观角色之间发生冲突时，必须以让活动平稳、顺利进行为主，口译的准确为辅。

四没

交传有四大障碍，本书称之为"四没"：

- 没听见：根本没听见或者没听清讲者说的是什么
- 没听懂：听见了，但是没听懂讲者说什么
- 没记下：听见了，听懂了，但是等到开始口译时却忘了刚才讲者说什么
- 没思路：听见了，听懂了，记下来了，但就是不知道该怎么译

交传因其上述各种特性而成为与笔译、同传以及其他形式的口译非常不同的双语运用形式，以下以笔译和同传为例，与交传做个比较。

与笔译的区别

第一，来源不同。笔译的来源是文字，靠看。交传的来源主要是话，所以主要靠听。之所以说主要靠听，这是因为如果活动内容是演示或者培训课时，交传译员经常需要参考电脑幻灯投影的内容，不能完全仰赖讲者所说的话。

笔译有上下文，可以看完整篇文章再开始从第一句译起。交传只有上文，没有下文。即讲者说到哪里，译员就必须译到哪里，无法把讲者尚未说出的话考虑在内。这点非常重要，直接影响到交传的理念、做法和培训方法。

第二，要求不同。在笔译中，译者所需的知识是有限的，仅限于需要翻译的文字所涵盖的知识。交传译员所需的知识是无限的，除了所需口译的话题之外，还可能遇到任何一位讲者可能说的任何话，包括与当时的话题完全没有关联的话，或者译员根本不可能知道的事情。

笔译完全是文字工作，单纯得多，主要依靠文字技能就可以完成任务。交传用于有组织的活动，需要与多种人打交道，有周围环境需要应对。交传译员除了语言技能之外，还需要一系列帮助他应对各种讲者、环境、场合和心理的技能。

第三，资源不同。笔译时可以使用的资源远远超过交传，比如可以进行相当量的检索和思考，而交传必须在讲者停顿之后马上传译。虽然有时有问个问题或者稍微思考的时间，但是这种时间很短，一般不能超过两、三秒钟。这在遇到新概念的翻译时尤其突出，笔译时可以推敲，从多种方案里挑选一个译法，可以做了决定之后再修改，而交传时却必须当场决定如何传译。

第四，标准不同。交传时，译员不仅需要当机立断传达讲者的话，而且所传达的内容往往需要超过所采用的文字本身的含义。比如："我很喜欢"即可以出于喜欢而说，也可以改变说这句话时的口气而暗指相反的意思。所以，交传的口语质量不能以笔译的文字质量做标准。

从另外一方面看，人们听话时对准确程度的感受与阅读文字时很不一样。所以，即使是在听交传时感觉相当准确的口译，如果事后把译员的话记录成文字就会觉得准确程度明显不如当时的感觉。这点在第二课里还将举例说明。同样，如果是按照书面文章的文字水准说话，会让人听上去很累，甚至费解。

第五，互动不同。笔译在短期内是没有互动的，只有当译稿被别人看到，甚至出版时，才可能有反馈。交传的互动是当场、当时的。译得好马上见效果，译得不好有可能被当场纠正或者导致受众作出与讲者原话没有关系的反应，这就给交传译员带来了相当大的心理压力。译员必须能够承受这种压力，而且不能让受众的负面反应影响到之后的交传，这是一个做笔译工作时无需面临的局面。

与同传的区别

第一，同传是几个字一译，与讲者同时说话；交传是一段话一译，讲者暂停之后译员口译。

第二，交传的环境因素比同传更加复杂。正式场合，同传译员使用特制的同传设备，与讲者和听众完全隔离，可以集中精力听。而只要设备没有问题，听到讲者就基本没有问题。但是交传译员与讲者和听众之间既没有隔离，也没有相对固定的位置，这就可能因为讲者说话的音量、与讲者的距离、周围的噪音、身边发生的事情而影响听清讲者的话。

第三，总体来说，同传时可以调用的资源超过交传。由于同传译员与受众完全隔离，所以可以在面前摆放资源工具，比如词汇表和手提电脑。由于同传是接力形式，所以在轮休时可以做检索、询问、甚至电话、邮件、短信息求救，这些都是交传译员没有的条件。不过，交传译员也有一个同传译员没有的资源，那就是有时可以向讲者询问，请讲者重复或者请受众帮助解决自己不懂的难题。

第四，交传对准确程度的要求明显超过同传。这里主要有两大原因。首先，同传基本是只能按照讲话的顺序传译，重新调整语序的余地比交传小得多。为此，译员必须断句，每听到几个词就得翻译。断句势必改变句子的结构，改变其重心，而且经常改变词性，并且在哪些话必须译和哪些话由于意思基本到位可以不译上做取舍。这样，即使没有改变原话的大意，也往往是改变了细节和口气。这种程度的改变在交传里即没有必要，也不可取。

其次，同传基本上是听到一组词汇就开始传译。所以，在听到一个多义词时，或者是新概念、新名词时可能不知道应该译成什么，但是又不能等待，只好凭判断译完再说。只是后来由于讲者的解释，或者听过了更多的话，译员才意识到怎样传译更加合适。在交传里，由于译员是听完一段话之后才开始传译，这就减少了不得不译了再说的几率。

第五，由于有些英汉之间的语言现象或者使用不适合于同传，需要有重新组织语言的空间，而这个空间又是同传不允许的，这就导致译员无法按照原话完整译出的结果。这里举两个典型例子，首先是数字，比如亿位数。听到英语 five hundred 时，译员不能马上就说五百，以防讲者接着说 million；听到英语 thirty three point seven eight 时，译员不能马上就说三十三点七八，以防讲者接着说 percent。这样一来，如果讲者连续说一串亿位的数字，每个亿位数字后面再用百分比加以说明（比如谈到双边贸易发展时就经常这样），同传译员就很难面面俱到，不得不在能够传译的信息上做出取舍。其次是职位。英汉之间组织机构职位的顺序恰恰相反，英文里从微观到宏观，中文是从宏观到微观。中文里说：中国社会科学院金融研究所研究员，英文就必须说 Researcher at the Institute of Finance, Chinese Academy of Social Science。如果同传时没有稿子照着读，完全凭借边听边译，则基本可以肯定是无法把所有信息完整地传译到汉语里。但是交传是在讲者说完一段话之后口译，所以就有可能凭借记忆或者笔记比较完整地记录下数字或者头衔，然后逐一复述出来。

第六，由于交传是分成讲者说与译员说这前后两个阶段，所以受众要想判断交传质量比判断同传质量要容易得多，可以先听讲者的话，然后听译员的话，把译员的版本与自己记忆里的原话加以比较。但是如果想确定同传质量，就不仅必须戴上两副耳机，一副听译出语，一副听译员，而且必须自己也会做同传，这样才能把听到的译出语、同传译员的译出语与自己的判断这三个版本做比较。要做到这点很不容易，而且很费脑力。除了非常明显的数字、名称或者意思错误，如果没有相当的同传功夫，如果译员的译入语版本流畅，即使与译出语差之甚远，也很难听出不准确之处。所以，与同传译员相比，交传译员被当场评判、当场纠正的风险远远大于同传译员。

第七，交传是译员与受众的直接互动。优秀译员可以充分利用交传的各种特性，面对目标受众再现讲者在原话中的效果。优秀交传译员可以完整和准确地传译出原语的全部意思，可以传译出讲者的感情色彩和震撼力。相比之下，由于同传所受的固有限制，再优秀的同传译员也难以做到这一点。

但是，优秀同传译员能够在讲者不停的情况下连续传译，使会议、会谈以交传根本无法实现的方式进行。所以，交传和同传目的不同、形式不同、各有长短、各有难点。迄今为止，尚无科学研究表明孰难孰易、孰高孰低。

本课小结

本书里的交传特指在有组织的活动里，讲者、译员和听众三方之间通过口译而展开的互动。讲者往往有双重动机，译员有两种角色，听众则趋于多样化。交传、笔译和同传都是双语技能的应用，但是由于性质不同、形式不同、要求不同，不能以笔译的标准衡量交传或者同传，反之也成立。

工作坊

分小组讨论以下议题：

1. 如果交传译员要想口译准确的话，需要做哪些工作？需要具备哪些具体的技能？

2. 在以下情况里做交传，会有哪些因素影响到译员的表现？

（1）在一个挤满了几百国际宾客的大礼堂里为领导做主旨演讲的交传

（2）在许多 CEO 出席的鸡尾酒会上为东道主的欢迎词做交传

（3）在一间办公室里为两家公司业务主管的谈判做交传

（4）在一个教室里为一名教师讲课时做交传

第二课　传译什么？

本课讲解交传译员应该传译什么？

在第一课给交传下的定义里提到，讲者既提供信息，又施加影响。所以，译员就应该既传达信息，又传达影响。现在逐项讲解。

首先，由于周围环境和讲者的原因，译员可能没有听见或者没有听清。这是口译与笔译的根本区别之一，笔译的来源文是给定的，交传需要译的话是不定的。

其次，中国的绝大多数译员都不是真正的双语者，他们的母语都是汉语，外语的水平都低于母语。在他们相当长的职业生涯里，都会在听外语上遇到困难，增加了交传的不确定因素。

最后，也是最常被误解的因素就是，译员口译的并不一定是讲者的原话，而是对原话的回忆。如果回忆出了问题，口译时就肯定有问题。

讲者说了什么？

这个看似简单的问题却没有简单的答案。请大家做个小实验，由一个人以习惯的声音朗读以下这段话，只朗读一遍，不重复。然后请大家完全凭记忆尽量把原话写下来，接着，请大家把各自写下的文字相互对比一下。很可能出现的局面就是：没有一个人的版本是完全一样的。

"自觉以科学发展观指导各项工作。加大宣教工作力度，进一步凝聚全社会共识，深入动员全系统各级领导干部和广大工作人员，增强责任感、使命感和紧迫感，做科学发展的积极践行者。"

版本不一样的原因在于：首先，环境和讲者干扰可能导致无法每个人都清楚地听到每个字；其次，听话是逐字顺序听的，但是回忆并不是逐字进行，不遵循听的顺序，先说的字后回忆或者后说的字先回忆出来是常见现象；最后，不同人在听到同样的话时会有不同的理解，导致回忆的不同。

因此，除非把讲者的话录下来，重新再听一遍，否则无法客观地得知到底讲者本来说了什么。由于交传时不可能先录下来再口译，所以有关讲者说了什么是没有共识的，译员以及在场的所有听众都有自己的版本，而且译员所翻译的是他对于讲者的话所作的回忆。这点非常重要。

话面意思

话面意思是本书里采用的概念，相当于笔译里字面意思的概念。但是由于在口译里译员是听讲者的话，而不是看讲者讲话的文字稿件，所以需要采用一个适合于口译的概念以示区分。

话面意思是相对话里的含义而言，在交传里常见的有三种情况。首先是修辞手段的采用。比如，"一箭双雕"的话面意思是用一支箭射中两只老鹰，其含义是做一件事情却获得两个结果。其次是抽象概念。比如，在金融术语里有个概念叫"特殊目的工具"，这个工具即可以是公司，也可以是投资基金或者是其他做法或者安排，统称"特殊目的工具"，但是在不同情况下会有不同的含义。最后是陌生信息。这指的是讲者讲的话虽然遣词造句都没有特别之处，即没有修辞，也没有抽象概念，但是所涉及的信息对于译员来说很陌生。虽然译员知道一段话里的每个词，每个句子的话面意思，但是不知道整段话讲的是什么，即不知道其含义。比如，在一次金融培训课将近结束的问答时间，有学员请教员介绍安然公司的诈骗行为是怎么回事。安然曾经是美国最大的公共事业公司，在相当一段时间内采用非法手段隐瞒公司连年亏损的实情。教员说：

> "What Enron did was to create a special purpose vehicle, a separate company. Enron then transferred some assets into this special purpose company and invited external investors to pay for 50% of the equity of this company in exchange for 3% of the shares."

这段话的后半部说投资者投资50%的股权却只得3%的股票，让译员感到困惑。困惑的原因不是译员不懂这段话里的每个词以及由这些词组成的句子，即译员听懂了话面意思，但是没听懂话里的含义。

区分话面意思和话里含义在口译里是一个关键概念，具体运用将在第六课有关交传的辅助技能里举例讲解。

准确幅度

由于上述原因，听众在判断口译准确程度时也是把译员的版本与自己的回忆相比较，不同的听众对于同样的译员版本会有不同的判断结果，没有可以提供实证的客观标准。由于这个原因，交传口译中的准确程度就不是一把所有听众都有共识的尺子，而是在一定幅度内都会有足够多的听众认为是准确的。换句话说，准确不是一根横线，而是在横线上下各有余地的幅度。只要是在这个幅度之内，都会被认为是准确的或者没有错误。本书称之为准确幅度。

交传的准确幅度大于笔译，但是小于同传。这是因为笔译的准确程度可以按单词、单字衡量，用词不同都可能被认为是翻译不准确，所以余地很小，即准确与否的幅度很小。同传由于其特性决定，比如由于顺序驱动的原因不得不重组句子，改变句子重心和用词的搭配等等，根本无法达到交传的准确程度，更不用说笔译了，所以准确与否的准确幅度很大。只要没有明显的事实错误，时不时用词不当，时不时词汇搭配错误，一句话拆成两半，两句话并成一句都可以容忍，甚至时不时句子残缺都无伤大雅。

现在举两个例子比较笔译和交传的准确幅度，做比较的部分以加黑标出。

原 话	交传中，下述版本可能都算准确
Our reputation for engineering excellence has created a sound base for our future business	• 我们在工程方面的卓越名声 • 我们工程卓越的名声 • 我们在工程领域非常卓越的名声
In all areas of our activity, it is our people who make the difference.	• 在我们活动的所有领域 • 我们所作的每件事 • 在我们的所有工作中 • 在我们的所有业务领域 • 我们公司做的每件事

这里需要强调的是，一段话一旦被记录下来阅读，人们就会情不自禁地以笔译的眼光评判，会觉得不够准确，即准确幅度马上缩小。

准确幅度的概念是为了反映口译中的现实，即译员译的是自己对讲话的回忆，受众评判口译质量往往是凭自己对讲者以及译员的话的回忆。所以，讲者的话越长，回忆中的误差越大，准确幅度也就越大。

We provide all the usual local government services, but we also have an important role representing the needs of businesses located here. In elections for other local authorities, the voters are all the local residents; here in the City the voters are a mixture of residents and voters from businesses located in each ward.	(译员笔记)	我们提供地方政府的服务，而且扮演了代表本地公司的角色。 在地方选举中，投票人往往是当地居民。而在我们金融城，投票人既有当地居民，也有公司。

这里举一个实战中的例子说明。左栏是原话，中栏是译员的笔记，右栏是译员的版本。

看文字，译员的版本不够准确，但是如果是当场听译员的口译的话，给人留下的印象则是相当准确。

由于准确幅度比笔译大，交传的受众对于准确程度的评判就比笔译宽松得多。另外，由于受众的回忆也是不准确的，所以只要译员没有犯太大或者太明显的错误，比如只要没有把中国人口说成20亿，受众就不会明显感觉质量不好。这也是交传译员应该注重完成宏观任务，不能过分小心微观准确的重要原因。

目前为止的讨论仅限于讲者的话，如果讲者使用幽默，受众哄堂大笑，而译员把原话传译之后，译入语的受众没有笑，也不算完成任务。讲者的话不是交传的终点，译员还必须再现原话的效果，即让译入语受众经历译出语受众刚刚经历过的体验。

再现原话效果

交传译员为译入语受众再现译出语里的效果，让译入语的受众也得到译出语受众的体验，这是交传的最高境界。如果要达到这种境界，译员不仅要准确地传达讲者的话，而且要完整地再现译出语里产生的效果。而完整地再现效果既包括语言（遣词造句以及语言风格），也包括非语言的因素，比如形体动作和语言之外的表达内容。在交传的最高境界里，译入语的受众已经基本忘了口译的存在，感觉就好像是直接用译出语听讲者一样。

交传里需要再现效果的场合多种多样，常见的有竞选演说、主旨演讲、产品宣传、推介演示。在这些场合中，交传除了传达信息外，还要发挥影响力、从感情上打动受众。

交传里需要再现的效果很多，有些必不可少。如果没有再现，马上就给人留下译员失职的印象；而有些则不太明显，即使没有再现，也不会导致对译员的负面评价。以下讲解交传中最常见效果的三个类型，它们都与再现源语受众的体验直接相关：

- 暗示
- 幽默
- 动作

暗示

当一位英国主人对客人说："房间里有点冷，是吧"，她很可能是在很客气地向客人暗示关窗。要是客人来自中国或者其他必须直截了当提这种要求的国家，就很可能只是回应一声"是有点冷"，而不会问主人"要我把窗户关上吗"。

暗示在英汉交传里是影响受众的一种常见的类型。交传译员不仅需要把讲者的话传译到译入语，还必须把暗示的内容表达清楚，以产生讲者希望获得的影响。

下述例子来自于实战。爱尔兰政府举行爱尔兰音乐舞蹈晚会。招待来访的中国客人。司仪在演出开始前说：

We will demonstrate some typical Irish musical instrument. However, I must stress that mobile phones are not generally considered an Irish musical instrument.

她话音刚落，在场的爱尔兰官员和商界成员一阵笑声，很多人拿出手机关掉。译员碰到了难题。当时，很多中国官员和商界人士还没有关手机的习惯，而且在中文文化里这样含蓄地请客人做某件事也是很少见到。如果按照讲者的原话传译，就有可能达不到目的。但是如果明说了又可能违背讲者不愿意冒犯中国客人的本意。

17

暗示是交传中最难处理情况之一。如果这个暗示是为了在受众身上立即产生同等程度的效果，就更难处理了。

幽默

在交传里，讲者使用幽默是为了产生愉快或者轻松的效果，这有助于讲者和受众建立起沟通的桥梁或者改善讲话可能对受众产生的影响。从语言上看，在幽默里使用的单词或者句子本身往往并没有可笑之处，而是讲者以某种方式使用这些单词或者句子，以某种口气说出这些话时。比如：伴之以表情时，幽默顿然而生。

以下这段话来自于一家跨国公司的人力资源总监，他在一个中国经理人员的培训课开始时做自我介绍：

> When I joined the company, they didn't know what to do with me. So they sent me out to Poland. After three years, they still didn't know what to do with me. They sent me to Slovakia.

由于讲者是大公司的总监级人物，所以，公司招聘他来肯定不会不知道如何安排他；我们知道英国人喜欢正式讲话前先来点幽默是文化习惯；再加上他当时的调侃口气，显然他是在使用幽默。

这句话也是讲者具有双重动机的很好例子，他一方面是提供信息，自我介绍；另一方面是使用幽默以产生轻松的气氛。

在中国文化里，幽默可以说是舶来品，幽默这个词就是音译而来。中文本身的词是开玩笑或者说笑话。由于正式场合不能开玩笑，所以中国人在正式场合很少说能让人发笑的话。由于幽默与文化紧密相关，译员就遇到了挑战。在上面这个例子里，如果只是把原话传达过去而不努力传达幽默的效果，中国听众很可能会从话的表面意思去理解而感到莫名其妙。

由于文化差异，需要超越语言的情况不限于中国和中文。在日本，鞠躬是交谈不可分割的组成部分，鞠躬的深度与双方之间的关系直接相关。而在英文里没有这种文化，交传译员如何传译鞠躬所带来的含义也是一个很大的挑战。

动作

有关幽默的讨论已经触及到了交传的另外一个特点，如果讲者在说话时一挤眼就可能是暗示不可对此言语太认真，因为是在使用幽默。也就是说，译员需要传译的内容可能不仅是从听觉感知的，还需要视觉。为使用 PowerPoint 的讲者做口译就是一个典型的例子，实战中时不时会碰到讲者说这种话的情况：

"If it's this, it'll be this."

如果完全仰赖听觉，译员会莫名其妙。但是如果同时看着讲者就知道他是在指着屏幕上一个地方时说"If it's this"，然后走到屏幕的另一头，指着另外一点说："it'll be this"。如果译员没有在传译时帮助受众了解这两个 this 指的是不同点，就会直接影响到传译的准确性。

译员必须传译话语之外的内容还不限于 PowerPoint 演讲，每当讲者使用肢体语言或者表情时也是这样，常见的一种情况就是讲者正在说明如何操作一台仪器，往往会听到这样的话：

"If you turn here, you'll see it here."

虽然说的都是 here，但是讲者在说话的同时是用手先后指了仪器上的两个不同部位。译员必须在传译的版本里把这两个不同部位表达清楚，如果听众人数比较多，站在外圈的人看不见讲者动作的情况下尤其重要。

道义上的考虑

英文词 ethics 及其形容词 ethical 在中文里尚没有合适的对应翻译，中国比较熟悉的概念是道德。但是道德是全体社会的，道德标准是在社会发展过程里形成的。在交传中可能遇到的部分问题并不是道德性质，所以本书暂且采用道义这个词，并且将其定义为个人在行为上就对错或者合适与否所做的选择。根据这个定义，道义是个人的抉择，所以也可以是个人在与道德相关的事情上所作的选择。

比如，如果邻居想送小孩上个好学校但是经费不够，你没有慷慨解囊，这不能说你是缺少道德，但是根据本课的定义可以说缺少道义。即，从社会角度来看，没有慷慨解囊不是过错；但是从个人角度来看，可帮人而没有帮就是缺少道义。如此定义有点差强人意，但是由于这是个很新的概念，为了能够展开讨论不得不在没有更加合适的词汇之前，暂且先用。

道义考虑特指译员就如何传译或者为谁传译而做出的价值上的判断或者决

定。本书有关交传的讨论都是假设完成口译任务与译员的道义考虑没有形成冲突。但现实里，这种冲突会出现，而且一旦出现冲突，就需要遵循其他原则，本书里所讲解的很多内容，比如再现效果就都不能照搬了。

比如，如果讲者出言不逊，甚至使用脏话，译员就必须决定是否在口译时避免，或者直接向讲者提出这样说话不妥。如果译员服务的对象是战争中的敌对方、宗教里的对立面，就需要决定到底是完成口译任务，还是放弃译员的角色，表示自己的政治或者宗教立场。

比如，如果讲者大谈吃猪肉的好处，而译员是穆斯林；如果唯一能养家糊口的出路是为外国占领军当译员，你是看着全家人挨饿，还是放弃原则为敌人工作。这些局面大多数译员职业生涯里都不会遇到，但是在国际上每年都有译员无法回避这样的尖锐问题。在以色列和巴勒斯坦战争、海湾战争、巴尔干战争以及后来的伊拉克战争里，都有译员碰到了这个尖锐问题。

即使是翻译研究比较先进的欧洲，也对口译里的道义考虑缺少研究。

本课小结

交传译员传译的主要是回忆，回忆的主要内容是讲者的话，但有时还必须包括讲者的表情、肢体语言以及讲者希望给受众产生的影响。

交传译员所需要到达的准确尺度不同于笔译或者是同传，是一个具有一定范围的幅度。只要传译时把握在这个幅度之内，就可以认为达到了准确的要求。

交传译员不仅要传译话语，还必须传达影响力，即必须为译入语受众再现译出语的效果，让译入语的受众得到与译出语的受众同样的体验。能够做到这点的译员为数不多，他们是交传的顶级大师，也是初学者应该定下的宏伟目标。

下一课将讲解如何在译入语里再现译出语里的体验。

工作坊

1. 容忍幅度：由一人阅读一份官方文件，一次念两句。其余的人边听边尽量完整的逐字把原话记录下来。如此听写几次后，分小组比较记录的不同版本，以此认识交传时所面临的准确问题。

2. 讲者的效果：拿一份领导人的讲话，分两人一组，边看边相互指出哪些话属于纯粹提供信息，哪些话包含有领导人希望达到的效果。

第三课　四大议题

本课讨论交传认识的四大议题，这些议题似乎已经达成广泛共识，往往被作为对于交传认识的基础。对于这四大议题的看法直接影响到对交传的认识，影响到对交传培训什么和如何培训的认识与做法。只有对这些议题有了更加深入的了解之后，才能学好、教好交传。

由于有关在交传里知识的作用基本没有实证研究，以下表达的是笔者根据实践经验得出的看法，仅供打开思路、做讨论之用，不可作为教学内容要求培训生掌握。

"必须准确理解"

很多人都认为译员必须准确理解讲者的话才能传译，准确理解是传译的先决条件。这听上去好像很有道理，但是如果深入探讨就会发现，事情没有那么简单。

首先，交传"四没"里的"没听见"和"没听懂"是常见情况。另外，如果深挖"没听懂"的原因，就会发现至少有四个，本书将其归纳为"四不足"。每个不足都影响到译员的理解，当然不一定都会导致错译或者无法传译。"四不足"是：

- 知识不足
- 资源不足
- 输入不足
- 背景不足

知识不足

这指的是译员的知识相对来说不如所需要传译的内容，而且这也是必然现象。这种译员知识不足的情况基本发生在两个层面上：语言、意思。即译员可能听不懂讲者使用的词汇或者句子，也可能听懂了词汇和句子，但是不明白讲者是想表达什么意思。

但是，知识不足并不意味着无法口译。恰恰相反，交传口译的一个主要技能就是在知识不足的情况下准确口译。以下讲解在所需知识不足的情况下如何处理。此外，第四课从交传任务的角度讲解了如何通过充分的准备弥补知识不足；第五课从现场操作的角度讲解了遇到不懂的词汇时如何处理；第六课里介绍了语言运用上的一些应对方法。

以下这段话取自一个有关投资内容的培训课，课上并没有谈到财务内容或者诈骗。但是一位学员在提问时请老师顺便介绍一下有关安然的情况。安然曾是美国最大的公用事业供应公司之一，在公司严重亏损时以诈骗手法瞒天过海，继续经营。在讲到安然的骗局时，教师说：

"What Enron did was to create a special purpose vehicle, a separate company. Enron then transferred some assets into this special purpose company and invited external investors to pay for 50% of the equity of this company in exchange for 3% of the shares."

这段话的后半部分似乎不合常理，外部投资人出资50%却只获得3%的股票。遵循不准确理解就不能或者无法口译的方针，译员就会在这里被卡住。但其实没有必要被卡住，译员只需要照着原话传译就完成了任务。从这个典型的例子里可以看出，译员只要语言听懂了，讲者说的意思不懂仍然可以传译成功。当然，如果不仅语言懂了，而且还理解意思那就更理想。

资源不足

与笔译和同传相比，交传译员是在资源最不足的情况下工作。除了坐在桌前口译时可以在面前摆几张预先准备好的词汇或者清单，绝大多数情况下都必须完全凭借自己的知识和记忆作口译。而同传译员可以查看随身携带的电子工具，比如手提电脑和阅读设备，经常还可以在同传箱里上网检索或者由同伴提示。

不过交传译员也有一个资源是笔译和同传都没有的，这就是能够提问。如果遇到没有听清楚、生词或者意思不明白时，可以询问讲者或者听众。当然，这个资源是有限的，只有在合适的情况下才可以向合适的人询问，而且问了以后可能还是不懂或者在场的人都不懂。

输入不足

一般概念里的知识不足是指译员有所不知，而译员没有听到或者看到需要传译的内容则为输入不足。拿笔译作为比较，在大部分情况下，无论是词汇还是句子都是给定的，白纸黑字。做笔译时可以把需要翻译的文字从头看到尾，然后再开始翻译。笔译有上下文为参照。

交传主要靠听，有时也需要看（比如投影在屏幕上的文字内容）。这就会产生没听见或者没听清（比如讲者口音太重或者讲者没有对着麦克风说话）、没看见或者没看清的情况。如果译员所接收到的内容少于所需，就会给交传带来困难。

交传相当于只有上文，没有下文（以下还将进一步解释）。译员只知道讲者目前为止说了什么，但是往往不知道讲者接着还要说什么。同时，讲者讲话只能顺序说。一旦停顿下来，译员就必须把目前为止的话传译过去。这就经常出现译员没有足够的信息判断某个词汇如何处理或者某句话特指什么的情况。

以下这段对话是中外两位商人讨论一个合资项目。为了展示输入不足的情况，特地提供相当长的内容以为说明，关键词加黑显示。

A　I am very pleased that you can find the time to meet me today. I know you are only passing London.

B　I am very pleased to meet you too. I've been wanting to do this for some time. I was here last month. But I stayed overnight and didn't have time to meet you. I'm sorry about this.

A　No, no. Don't apologise. I totally understand. I've been following your expansion with great interest. I very much hope that we can work together on the project I e-mailed you about.

B　Yes, we are very interested in the idea too. For us, it will be a question of priority. We're looking at a couple of opportunities. We're not yet sure which will be the one to go for.

A　We've had several decades of experience in the sector. Would be very happy to share our expertise with you. I also believe that as your business expands, you'll have an increasingly more important role in the international market. You are number three already, aren't you?

B   That's true. But yours is better **grade**.

讲者突然提到 grade，译员必须根据当时的感觉马上传译，不像现在这样可以白纸黑字看清楚了再说。到目前为止的话里也没有任何线索到底 grade 是指什么。但是，两位商人都知道这里 grade 指的是矿藏的品位，只有译员不知道。

输入不足的情况不限于此，有时讲者使用的词汇或者概念只有他自己知道，译员和听众都不知道，这在培训课里经常出现。往往要到一段时间之后，译员才能从讲者后来的话中判断出意思。有时甚至活动结束之后，译员也还不知道意思是什么。

输入不足有时是讲者故意造成的。有些使用交传有经验的讲者时不时先说个概念，停下来让译员传译，然后接着说 Let me explain。由于交传的特性，译员不得不先传译一个完全陌生的概念，然后才能发现其意思。另外一种情景是讲者使用幽默，先说铺垫部分，停下来让译员传译，然后再像抖包袱一样说出关键词，完全推翻目前为止的所指，引发笑声。

输入不足的另外一个原因是讲者以新颖或者富有创意的方式使用语言，有意延伸某个词汇或者改变了某个词汇使用的背景。而译员已经根据上文判断做出了如何传译某词的决定，形成了回头错的局面，请看下节的说明。

背景不足

这指的是译员只能根据目前为止听到的话而传译，无法得益于讲者还没有说的话。由于口译的这种特性，译员时不时会发现，刚才根据之前讲者的话所传译的版本，在听了后来讲者的话之后变得不合适，甚至是谬误的。以下是件很多人都听说过的事情。

中国政府的一位部长宴请外宾，席间交谈时说："这个问题很简单，小葱拌豆腐一清二白"。译员记得学习翻译时老师讲过要用外宾听得懂的方式，要用地道的英语表达中国文化，于是传译为："The matter is crystal clear"。谁知部长又接着说："你们国家有豆腐吗？"至此，译员已经无法改口，只好迎着头皮说："Do you have crystal in your country?"

由于背景不足而产生的口译谬误叫回头错。回头错在所有口译形式里都会出现，但是在交传里问题最大。有时是因为在正式场合下，译员出错无法自我纠正；有时是因为双方之后的话完全取决于译员对前面的话是如何传译的。

为了避免背景不足所带来的回头错，交传时必须尽量按照原话直译。比如，在刚才的例子里如果直译就能避免麻烦：

部长：这个问题很清楚，小葱拌豆腐一清二白。
译员：The matter is clear, like blending spring onion with bean curd. The white remains white. The green remains green.
部长：你们国家有豆腐吗？
译员：Do you have bean curd in your country?

避免回头错不仅限于延伸原话，凡是讲者采用了修辞手法的话语都会带来背景不足的危险，都要小心。第六课里有对回头错的进一步讲解。

综上所述，交传必须要有对讲者的话的足够理解才能顺利进行，但并不一定需要有准确的理解。由于交传的特性，比如由于上述的四大不足，译员经常需要在没有甚至无法准确理解的时候口译。另外，理解有两种性质。一种是对所用语言的理解，另外一种是对这些语言所表达的意思或者用意的理解。交传时常常出现译员缺少对于所用语言，或者对于所用语言所表达的意思或者意图不够理解甚至完全不理解的局面。所以，交传培训必须包括如何尽量防止这种局面发生，而且一旦发生应该如何应对的技能。

"必须知识广泛"

很多人都认为译员需要广泛的知识，而且这种知识是交传质量的先决条件。这种观点的论据之一是译员需要能够应对不同的话题而且只有知识面比较广的译员才能保证口译质量。因此，追求扩大知识量但同时又发现自己知识量总是不够就成为许多译员和学员的苦恼。

如果要比较正确地认识知识量在交传中的作用，就必须区分一次口译任务所需的知识量和整个口译事业发展中积累起来的知识量。虽然口译界普遍接受知识面的重要性，但是缺少对于每次口译任务所需知识的深度和广度的界定，因此无法为交传译员提供具体的指导。

比如："金融"经常被用在某种知识的统称。但"金融"是个行业名称，在这个名称之下光是大的分类就有银行、保险、再保险、投资、基金管理、金融交易、衍生品、期货期权。每个行业分类以下还有细分的专业内容。这些专业都有自己的一整套特有词汇，有些英文词汇在不同的金融行业里还有不同的意思和中文翻译。即使是对银行业滚瓜烂熟也会在保险方面一筹莫展，俗话叫隔行如隔山。

从原则上看，即使交传任务的主题有限，译员所需的知识也可能是无限的。这是因为讲者不可能仅限于专业术语，其他的话都不说。在金融研讨会上完全有可能出现主持人拿高尔夫球打比方的情况，说"this is really under par"（高尔夫中的意思是没有按照规定的杆数打完，意指水平太低），或者是讲者顺便提及家乡的某件事情。

如果译员所需的知识既需要非常专业，同时又不得不无限广泛，"广泛的知识"这个概念就对译员没有实际的指导意义了。不仅会给译员带来没有必要的沮丧，而且会误导口译的发展，导致口译职业发展过分专业化。结果必然是有多少行业里的专业就需要有多少口译专业，学制造口译的不能译教育，学法律口译的不能译汽车。

大凡经验丰富的译员往往都有广泛的知识，但是广泛的知识是口译事业发展的结果，不能将其作为口译工作的先决条件。所有译员都是从知识相对少到相对多，最后到相当多。

笔者认为，要想为交传实践或者培训提供指导，就需要按照口译任务的时间线把知识划分成以下四种：

预有知识：译员在接受口译任务之前已经拥有的知识
准备知识：译员通过口译任务之前的准备而得到的知识（下一课详细讲解）
现学知识：译员在口译时根据讲者的话马上掌握之前不懂的知识
后续知识：译员通过口译任务以及之后的继续学习而掌握的知识

预有知识非常必要，但在译员职业发展的初期总是不够，总是需要准备知识的补充才能胜任口译任务；在任务期间以及其后继续学习所获得的知识又成为下一次口译任务的预有知识。在这个反复不止的过程中，译员的知识量不断扩大。

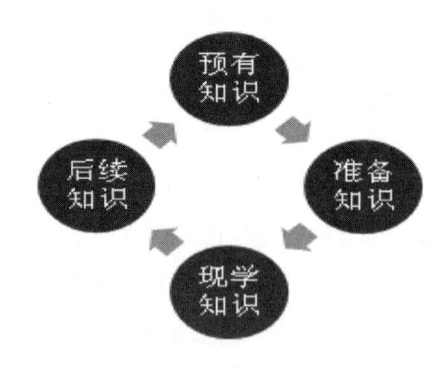

口译职业开展初期，译员的预有知识很有限，获得后续知识的能力很有限，成功主要靠的是准备知识外加现学知识。职业发展到一定阶段时，预有知识相当丰富，获得后续知识的能力大大增强，准备知识和现学知识的作用就明显下降。请看示意图（四者之间的比例是为了说明概念，不是准确地划分）。

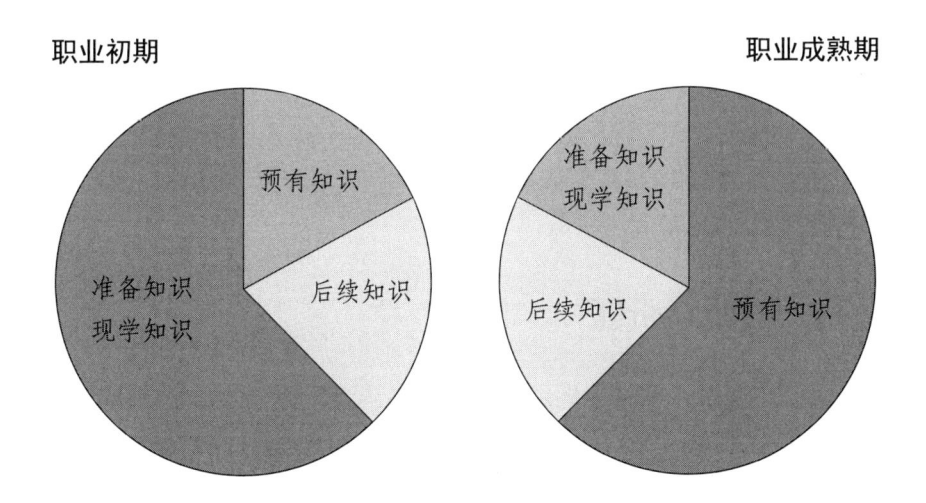

职业初期　　　　　　　　　　　　　职业成熟期

（饼图：职业初期——准备知识现学知识、预有知识、后续知识；职业成熟期——准备知识现学知识、后续知识、预有知识）

如此看来，交传译员所需的知识就是一个不断通过准备、现学以及后续学习不断积累、扩大预有知识的过程。

综上所述，初学交传者不适于以广泛的知识为目标，而是应该根据交传任务的时间线划分所需知识的不同种类，然后根据交传任务的周期特点不断学习、积累。

"必须记忆力强"

交传里所说的记忆，或者短期记忆，其实是两个过程。第一是记，也就是译员边听边记，把听到的内容存储在短期记忆或者笔记里。第二是忆，也就是译员把刚才储存在短期记忆和记录在笔记里的内容回忆出来，然后译成译入语。由于本书的目的是交传培训，不是理论研究，所以暂且把两者统称为记忆。

记忆力在日常交谈里起到重要作用，但是交传的特别之处在于对记忆准确程度的要求高于日常交谈。这就对译员提出了超出日常水准的要求，很多人也因此得出这样的结论：即交传译员必须有超出平常的记忆力。很多交传培训课也从记忆训练开始。

这个问题值得商榷，记忆的准确程度很重要并不等于需要提高记忆力。

二十多岁的年轻人记忆力比四十多岁的人强,这是常识。但是,交传准确度达到近乎完美程度的往往并不是二十多岁的年轻人,反而是三、四十岁富有经验的译员。一些世界顶级的译员在口译以外的短期记忆都不好,他们是靠技能、技巧和阅历达到准确,而不是靠生理上的记忆力。反倒是生理记忆力很强的年轻人在交传时会丢三落四。

所以,交传译员必需的不是超常的记忆力,而是通过职业培训提高对现有记忆力的利用水平。使用笔记就是最重要的技能之一,充分利用现有知识,即长期记忆也是重要因素之一。笔者在实践以及多年的培训中发现,交传培训没有必要从专门培训记忆力开始;正常人的记忆力只要辅助以相关技能,比如笔记的使用,就足以做好交传。

"必须让听众听懂"

交传领域的第四个重大议题就是很多人都认为译员一定要保证让听众听懂,这种看法也值得商榷。

首先,必须区分听懂什么?是听懂讲者的话还是听懂译员的话。如果译员的话准确地反映了讲者的话,则二者为一,否则就会出现两个版本。本课假设译员的话准确地反映了讲者的话,并且将说明为什么在这种情况下听众是否听懂不是译员的责任。

其次,交传译员一般情况下并不知道听众是否听懂了,也无法知道。译员无法每次译完一句或者一段话就问听众是否听懂了,一般情况下都只能根据自己的语言和话题知识对听众是否听懂了自己的传译作出主观的判断。虽然这种判断在大多数情况下是基本可靠的,但是既无法做到、也不可能做到完全可靠。既然如此也就不能作为交传的既定目标,也不能作为衡量交传质量的尺度。

再次,影响听众是否听懂讲者的因素很多,译员传译的准确与否只是其中一个。即使传译准确,听众也还可能因为背景知识不足而听不懂,为专业培训课做交传就是最典型的例子:交传质量越高,越准确,听众就越可能由于培训内容新颖,概念新颖而听不懂或者没听懂。另外,听众也会走神,走神就会没听懂。这些现象都不在译员所能控制的范围之内,不能列为译员的责任。所以,在实践中无法以听众是否听懂作为译员的目标或者交传的质量标准。

最后,"必须让听众听懂"是造成译员超越讲者的主要原因之一。这个概念将在第六课详细讲解,这里仅作简单介绍。超越讲者指的是译员把讲者将在下一段里说的话在上一段里就已经传译了,等到讲者说到时,译员不得不重复自己,或者说:"我刚才已经为各位翻译过了",明显地抢了讲者之先,越俎代庖,违反了口译的根本原则。

现在举一个实际例子说明,有位金融专家在讲解投资手法的时候提到了 Bed and Breakfast 这个概念,而且说完就停顿下来让译员传译。译员传译之后,讲者随之解释 Bed and Breakfast 是什么意思。但是译员由于担心听众听不懂,已经在之前就解释了这个概念的含义,十分尴尬。

讲者　I'm now going to talk about ways to make your investment tax efficient. One of them is Bed and Breakfast.

译员　我现在谈谈怎样才能使投资的税务效率好。方法之一是英文里所称的房间加早餐。这个概念来自于英国很多家庭式的旅馆,他们收取的价格即包括住宿的房间,也包括早餐,所以称之为"房间加早餐"。投资业借用这个概念,指的是在股市交易一天结束之前卖掉持有的股票,然后第二天一开市就再以同样数量买入同样的股票。

讲者　Bed and Breakfast means to sell your shares at the end of a day to buy them all back the following day.

译员　讲者现在说的话我刚才已经翻译过了。

有关超越讲者的害处请看第六课。

交传译员必须负责的首先是让活动顺序进行下去,其次是尽力准确地传达信息和讲者希望传达的效果。如果译员完成了上述宏观和微观任务,就已经完成了交传任务。在上述情况下,听众能否或者是否听懂了讲者的话不是交传译员的责任。

本课小结

对交传的认识里有一些被普遍接受的说法是可以探讨的。由于交传本身的特性,准确理解讲者原话、拥有广泛的知识、拥有超出平常的记忆力、必须让听众听懂讲者的话都只是有助于交传译员成功完成任务,而不是不可或缺的先决条件。交传译员必须通过培训掌握在没有真正理解讲者原话、知识不够、没有超常记忆力并且不知道听众是否听懂讲者的情况下完成口译任务的技能。

工作坊

以下是一名英国政府官员讲话稿的部分内容，请在阅读之后分小组讨论译员需要哪些具体的知识才能够顺利地口译以及需要在任务前的准备阶段采取哪些步骤，如何准备才能确保不会在知识面上出问题？请把讨论的结果用清单的形式列出，而且分类越细越好。比如，不要笼统地称金融知识，而是具体说明金融里的哪个方面或者分类，是银行还是保险。可以考虑一边阅读，一边标出需要某个领域知识才能成功口译的词组。

Your second objective of information sharing reminds me that it is exactly 167 years ago to the day that one Samuel Morse inaugurated the first American telegraph line from Washington DC to Baltimore. Samuel Morse's telegram carried with it a single, biblical, quote from the Book of Numbers. In capital letters no less, it read: "WHAT HATH GOD WROUGHT!"

Bearly a year ago, and over the course of a weekend, the UK had no option but to provide £37bn to both RBS and Lloyds. That was after having already nationalised Northern Rock and Bradford & Bingley. On the domestic scene, the tripartite system proved itself to be wholly inadequate.

The government is therefore putting in place an entirely new regulatory architecture consisting of the Financial Policy Committee and the Prudential Regulation Authority sitting within the Bank of England, and the Financial Consumer Authority. The Interim report provided a valuable contribution to domestic and international debates on capital surcharges for systemically important firms, creditor loss absorption, and protecting retail operations from more risky banking activities.

Whilst supportive of the overall aims of the regulation, the UK was very clear during negotiations that permanent restrictions on the short selling of sovereign debt and related credit default swaps could have potential ramifications for liquid sovereign debt markets. Market making does not increase systemic risk or distort markets. The same arguments apply when we consider issues of High Frequency Trading and Dark Pools in the review of MiFID.

We welcome the G20 agreement to mandate clearing through Central

Counterparties, CCPs, to reduce counterparty risk between institutions. This is an important step forward as the crisis clearly exposed the deficiencies within the over-the-counter derivatives markets: in particular the shortcomings in the management of counterpart credit risk and the absence of sufficient transparency.

The UK's answer is an emphatic no. We must ensure that the clearing obligation and obligation to report trades must apply to all derivatives, not just OTC. On the other hand, there is the widespread concern over the suggestion in the MiFID review to spread transparency in equities markets to other asset classes such as bonds and derivatives.

第四课　交传任务

本课讲解交传任务及其周期，旨在帮助学员建立起完成交传任务的流程和系统，帮助学员从一开始就以职业标准对待每次交传练习，以便在担任第一次交传任务时便马到功成。

交传周期

交传是实践性质很强的职业，学员毕业后需要通过每次交传任务来不断学习、进步，所以必须尽早建立起交传周期的概念。也就是说，不能孤立地看待每次交传任务，而是把每次任务都看做是一个周期里的一个阶段，还需要做好同一周期里的其他工作，才能保证周而复始，不断进步。

交传任务的周期基本上是从接受任务开始，然后是为任务做准备，完成任务，最后以任务后的学习结束（请看右边示意图）。

以下逐一讲解每个阶段的具体内容。

接受任务

接受口译任务是一个相当复杂的工作，牵涉到很多方面，需要建立起一个常用体系，否则容易顾此失彼，直接影响到交传质量以及给客户提供的服务。本课介绍的体系仅作为参考，必须根据个人的具体情况调整使用。

接受任务大致可以分成三个阶段：

1. 查询：客户询问译员是否有空并且愿意承担某项交传任务，收费多少

2. 确认：客户向译员确认任务，形成合约关系
3. 细节：客户向译员提供与任务相关的细节

查询阶段没有合约关系，客户可能是货比三家，同时向多名译员查询，然后确定选择谁承担任务。译员也不受约束，可以在几天后客户确认时说无法承接任务。但是一旦双方确认之后就已经形成合约关系，很多客户往往要求译员签署接受任务的合约，译员处于保护自身利益的考虑也愿意签署合约。

在查询阶段，客户与译员之间必须交换的信息很有限，译员只需要知道是什么形式的口译和日期为几号到几号就可以了。到确认阶段，就必须掌握更多的信息。如果客户在确认阶段无法提供所有信息，则必须尽量在任务日期到达之前向译员提供。有些信息可能直到译员临出发甚至任务开始时都还没有。所以，译员必须非常清楚什么是必需信息，客户必须提前提供；什么信息可以等候。

必须掌握的信息可以根据译员的经验多少而不同：新手应该争取多获得信息，以便有备无患；老手则可以凭借经验而到时随机应变。以下清单一列出的是需要在查询阶段掌握的信息，清单二是在确认时及其后需要掌握的信息，其中很多可以从客户提供的任务日程安排里获得，但是有些需要直接向客户询问。

清单一：
- 日期：几号到几号。
- 地点：在哪个城市。
- 口译形式：由于经常出现客户忘了提、译员忘了问，发现双方各自的预期不一样时已经出现了麻烦。比如，客户要的是同传，你以为是交传。
- 确认：客户大概什么时候可以确认是否需要你提供口译服务

清单二：
- 地点：任务地址以及具体到哪座建筑，哪个房间或者大厅。如果任务是在外地，是否需要提前一天到达。
- 活动形式：是大会还是小型会谈，是正式活动还是非正式交谈，是会议还是演示；
- 口译搭档：如果是同传，搭档是谁？如果是交传，客户使用几名译员？
- 工作时间：几点开始，几点休息，几点午餐，几点结束，这些信息都有助于译员决定如何准备，准备多少，当天如何把握，是否需要自备午餐等等；
- 大概场合：是书记剪彩、还是新闻发布、还是总裁主持鸡尾酒会；是数百

人的活动还是一对一会谈；是全天都在一个楼里还是上午开会，下午外出参观（是否需要带伞或者穿大衣）；
- 主题：是单一主题还是多个话题，什么话题，哪些方面。
- 材料：是否可以提供准备材料，比如讲话稿或者电脑幻灯文件（PPT）？什么时候可以提供？如何提供？
- 有无着装要求
- 食宿：如果是外地或者不止一天的任务，需要了解每天的中饭和晚餐是否自己解决？如果是外地则住在哪里？由谁定房？付费？
- 旅行：是客户购买飞机或者火车票还是译员购买之后向客户报销？

催要信息或者材料的时候也有讲究。客户对于事先提供材料的重要性认识不同，有的很重视，积极配合译员；有的不重视，必须反复催要；有的虽然知道重要性，但是与译员联系的是客户机构里的低级人员，因为不敢向上司说明为什么讨要讲稿而没有这样做。译员需要根据对具体情况的判断决定采取什么行动，总体原则是：礼貌地说明提供材料是客户保证自己的活动能够大获成功的关键环节，不是为了方便译员。

任务准备

对于交传质量而言，任务准备不仅很重要，而且非常关键，对于新手来说尤其如此。需要准备的内容大致可以分成四个领域：

- 任务性质与形式
- 发言人及其组织机构
- 话题与内容
- 旅行、食宿和会务

每次交传任务都有其特别之处，就连同一公司的年会也常常是每年都有新内容、新形式、新活动。所以，每次应该把每次任务都当作是第一次来准备，才能立于不败之地。另外，上述四大领域也会由于不同任务而各有不同。

任务性质与形式。有些任务很简单，就是双边会谈，一天，一个房间，一个话题。但是有些任务就很复杂，可能是持续多天，换几个地点，讨论多个话题。最复杂的交传任务之一就是诸如"领导力培训"或者"全球化培训"这样的高管培训课程，往往是每天4—5个不同话题，各有不同的发言人，除了课堂培训之外，还有公司走访。译员即可能是坐在固定座位上口译，也可能站在发言人身边；即可能是普通教室，也可能是梯形教室；还可能是工厂里、过道里、办公室里；听众即可以是大好几十人，也可能只有两三个。了解任务的性质与形式有利于译员当天比较有信心地完成任务。

以下是译员需要争取了解的内容清单（不详尽，仅供参考）：

- 坐着译还是站着译？
- 听众大约多少人？
- 日程上的休息时间以及中饭时间是否也需要口译？
- 如果中饭需要口译，那么什么时间吃中饭？
- 是否有讲稿或者电脑演示稿？

讲者。如果是大会，则日程安排里很可能提供了所有发言人的名单包括他们的职称。如果是代表团会谈，则译员需要向客户索取代表团成员名单。这里有两大原因，首先，中国译员往往不善于听懂、记录、复述非中文的名字，在任务前熟悉可能需要多次口述的非中文名字就可以避免临场说不清楚甚至说不出来。其次，职称里的信息密集，几乎每个字都不可缺少，而交传笔记跟不上速度，短期记忆也很难回顾准确。最好是手头有名单，一旦知道说谁，马上就照名单念。

知道主要发言人是谁还有一个重要作用，那就是如果客户没有或者无法提供讲稿，译员可以用发言人姓名和发言题目作为关键词上网检索，有时能够找到发言人之前发表的类似文章或者讲话稿。

组织机构的名称也是当场口译很难做好的内容之一，最好是预先列成清单，笔译之后打印出来随身携带。如果是坐着交传，就可以拿出来，放在面前，需要时就照着读。

组织机构除了需要知道其名称的翻译之外，还需要对其性质、工作内容或者业务有个概要的认识。这是因为对发言人所作的介绍往往提及组织机构的性质、工作内容或者业务。由于这种介绍往往说话速度很快，完全依靠笔记或者记忆，很难做好交传。但是预先有了准备，就能减少当场的难度。

话题与内容

这里需要准备的内容基本上可以分为四大组成部分：

- 阅读材料
- 词汇表
- 笔记设计
- 视译练习

最理想的局面是客户提供了所有讲稿和电脑演示文件，这种情况下熟悉所有已经提供的材料基本上就可以了。但是最常见的情况倒是客户提供的材料不全，甚至没有提供。以下讲解如何准备客户没有提供材料的部分。

自我准备时的最大问题是收集什么材料，收集多少？本课介绍两种做法，译员可以根据个人的现有知识和具体口译任务参考使用。一种做法可以称之为全面开花，另外一种可以称为单点深化。顾名思义，前者适用于知之甚少的话题，需要比较全面的阅读某个话题而形成话题知识基础；后者适用于已经拥有相当的话题知识，只是需要在特定题目或者内容上深化知识，补充不足之处。

现在举一个来自实际的例子，假设交传任务是在国际建筑用塔式起吊机（tower crane）协会的年会上担任分会场的交传任务，而且译员过去没有接触过这个话题，这就需要形成有关塔式起吊机的基础知识。由于是业界年会，所以发言人往往从宏观上谈问题，不会在技术细节上太深入，如果时间有限就先覆盖行业的总体信息和最常见的词汇。具体做法是分别用中英文的关键词上网搜索，很快就会发现专业公司的网站和行业的门户网站，网站上的信息可以帮助译员了解该行业（行业现状、走势、主要议题）、主要塔式起吊机的类型与名称及其英中文的词汇对照。

如果任务是行业的技术研讨会，那就需要根据每位发言人的话题深入了解信息，词汇表也必须更加详尽。比如，为年会做准备可能只需要知道塔式吊机的基本原理和主要类型，为技术研讨会做准备就必须掌握塔式吊机的所有主要部件、功能、常见问题、解决方案和市场的最新动态。获得这些信息的渠道往往是行业协会的网站、领先公司的网站、学术论文。

词汇表

词汇表有三大考虑：内容、格式、运用。

内容指的是词汇表必须包括的条目，这里的关键是如果词汇表里的条目不符合要求，则会误导译员，以为准备就绪，其实没有覆盖口译所需。再举上述塔式吊机为例，词汇表必须包括以下三方面内容。

首先是中外与塔式吊机相关的组织机构的名称及其缩写；其次是专业词汇，

即各种塔式吊机的类型及其主要部件的名称，塔式吊机使用中的常用词汇；最后是词汇表的运用，即词汇表必须是英汉对照，最好用 Excel 建立文件，以便增减、编辑、排序、查询。

决定词汇表长短主要有两大因素，首先是话题的复杂程度；其次是译员现有掌握程度。作为参照，1–2 天的行业大会需要上百个词汇是正常情况。

准备好了词汇表才只是准备工作的一半，另外一半是背词汇，译员的一个重要技能就是能在短期内记忆大批词汇。在交传任务的前一天，可以把上百字的词汇表浓缩到最常用，或者译员最担心会反应不过来的 20–30 个，用大字体、大行距打印在一张纸上，便于当天复习或者放在手边随时可以参照。

笔记设计

交传译员没有在任务准备阶段为即将多次听到的词汇设计笔记是个常见错误，熟悉某个词汇的英汉翻译并不等于在听到时就能迅速记下笔记。比如，译员将为国务院发展研究所担任译员，如果没有预先设计好"国务院发展研究所"的笔记方法，猛一听到也会急切之下来不及快速笔记。交传译员必须为上述浓缩词汇设计笔记方式，以便口译时得心应手，无需当场创作。如何设计的具体方法将于第八课详细介绍。

交传视译

很多人都知道视译是练习同传的重要手段，但是很少有人想到视译也是帮助译员做好交传任务准备的重要手段。视译指的是边看来源文，边用目标文口译其翻译。交传视译有两大作用，首先是帮助译员熟悉即将要做交传的内容及其英汉之间的转换，其次是为译员增强成功完成任务的信心。

交传的视译与同传有些不同。同传视译必须严格按照同传的实际情况，每看几个字一译。而交传由于其特性，可以在一定程度上调整词汇甚至分句的顺序。无论怎样，视译都必须是双向练习，既要练英译汉，也要练汉译英，除非客户明确指示口译任务只是单方向，比如只是英译汉。

旅行、食宿和会务

旅行、食宿和会务是很容易被遗忘的事项，但是必须从接受任务开始就应该尽早了解清楚的内容。如果交传任务是在译员所在城市，旅行就比较简单。如果是在另外一个城市，甚至另外一个国家，旅行就会复杂很多。如果需要译员自己购买飞机票或者预定饭店，越早动手越能减少买不到满意的机票或者预定理想饭店的风险。

有时交传任务的地点就是客户安排的下榻酒店，有时是两个不同地点，需要有交通工具。有时客户安排接送，有时译员必须自己解决。有时客户安排译员和与会人员共进午餐和晚餐，有时客户要求译员自己解决。

酒店是否有互联网，多少钱？是否有健身房或者游泳池也是根据译员情况值得了解的内容。这些事情听上去琐碎，但是对于职业译员来说都是不可或缺的。有免费互联网有利于到达后继续准备，有健身设施可以忙里偷闲地锻炼身体。

有关会务事项的最主要内容有三个。首先是客户联系人，有些时候这就是一直与译员联系的人，有些时候当天译员需要向之报到的联系人是另外一位。所以，必须事先了解清楚，旅行是随身携带联系人的电话，如果出现万一而无法提前到达任务地点，就必须在第一时间通知联系人。如果译员顺利到达任务地点，可能需要有联系人带领才可以进入场地。无论如何，译员都必须事先约定报到的大约时间和方式（面对面还是短信息），在到达地点之后向联系人报到，等候任务开始。

其次是工作时间表，再次是餐饮安排。掌握工作时间表才好安排自己不可避免的活动，比如有时上午9点开始交传，11点休息，然后下午3点再开始。这其中会有相当长的空挡，译员需要知道去哪？如何渡过这段时间？上卫生间也是一个很好的例子。由于交传不像同传，往往只有一名译员，上卫生间的时机把握不当，客户需要译员时找不到，很容易产生矛盾。餐饮时间也是同样道理。

总之，客户往往各不相同，要求往往五花八门。译员必须尽量事先了解清楚，以避免误解或者当天无所适从的局面。

这里需要特别说明的是旅行安排，必须门到门，即从出家门开始，直到返回家门为止。如果是上午旅行，下午口译，晚上回家，第二天还有其他任务，这点就更加重要了。比如，家住北京的译员，如果去上海完成交传任务，不能光计划北京—上海之间的飞行时间，还必须计划从家到机场，从机场到市内具体地点的时间。此外，如果是当天旅行，当天口译还必须留出足够的预防万一的时间，防止临时堵车。

完成任务

所有的准备工作都是为了当天顺利完成任务，这里有四大点，提前报到、熟悉环境、建立威信、申请结束。

提前报到：如果客户有具体要求，则按照客户要求的时间到达地点并且向客户联系人报到。如果客户没有要求，则应该以提前半小时到达地点为目标，到达之后马上报到。如果客户联系人尚未到达，则以短消息方式通知对方，然后在约定地点耐心等待。

熟悉环境：如果可能，尽量争取在到达之后前往活动或者会谈地点查看场合的摆设。正式会谈一般有两种座位形式，一种是马蹄形。中国的正式会谈往往是这种形式，另外一种是长桌型，西方会谈往往是这种形式（请参看第一课的示意图）。

用餐或者宴会期间也有可能是在主要人物身后摆放译员的椅子。无论是会谈还是宴会，最好都能提前确定译员的座位，如果客户尚未安排，则尽快提醒客户联系人安排。

熟悉环境还有一个重要内容，那就是麦克风。如果是大场合而且安排了讲者使用的麦克风，译员就必须与客户联系人确认译员用哪个麦克风，是与讲者合用，还是为译员另外安排。客户有时缺少经验会忘记译员也需要麦克风，译员不能假设客户一切安排妥当。恰恰相反，译员应该假设客户没有安排妥当而利用提前到达的机会确保自己的工作环境达到最低要求。

建立威信：资深译员往往带有气场，从与客户见面开始就树立起权威，赢得客户和听众的信任。学员和新手往往既缺少气场，又不知道如何弥补，从见到客户或者听众的那一刻开始就已经给对方留下令人担忧的印象。

建立威信有三个基本环节。第一是着装打扮必须符合职业要求。也就是说无论男女，着装的基本原则是保守，不要采用色彩鲜艳、引人注目的服装或者装饰品。除非客户有具体要求，否则在西方国家现在的普遍做法是男士穿深色西装（深蓝或者深灰为佳），打领带（希望有朝一日，国际着装以中式为准，则可以着中山装）；女士服饰外套也以深色为佳（黑色、深蓝或者深灰），上着西装外套，下着西装裤或者裙子，裙子长度以膝盖为尺度，不要明显短于膝盖。深色外套之下配浅色上衣。如果是正式场合，穿裙子还必须穿单色的长筒丝袜，不要露出腿部。女士头发一定要干净利落；如果是长发，最好在脑后扎起来，成马尾巴式，不要披头散发。

不过也有例外，如果口译是在户外，或者生活水平比较低的地区，由于夏天空调没有保证，男女着装都可能需要根据气温加以调整。

第二个环节是首次见面，无论是见客户联系人、客户主要发言人还是主要听众，都应该稳重地健步向前，认真地握手，然后不慌不忙，口齿清楚地说"您好！我叫……是今天的翻译"。如果客户问及，则充满信心地说"我已经准备好了，请放心"。初入职业的译员必须设计自己的关键对话，避免依靠当场发挥。在缺少经验的情况下,当场发挥不是由于紧张而打磕巴,就是话不从心,总是起到削弱译员权威的负面作用。

第三个环节是见面后找到自己的座位坐下,或者在客户指定的位置站立,保持稳重,不攀谈,安静地等待活动或者会议开始。站立时可以有三个姿势:双手顺势垂放身体两侧,顺势垂下然后在身前交叉(不要像空姐或者公关小姐那样在肚脐下交叉)或者在背后交叉(不要像有些边境检查员那样横背着手)。交传开始之后的姿势将于稍后讲解。

申请结束:任务完成之后,译员应该向为之服务的人物简单道别,然后向客户联系人申请离去:"我的任务结束了吗?可以走了吗?谢谢,再见!"当然需要根据具体情况调整申请结束的话,原则是礼貌到位便可,既不要啰嗦,也不要显得唐突。

后续学习

顾名思义,这指的是完成任务之后的学习,是一个被很多译员忽视的环节。他们完成任务之后就不想了,马上把焦点转到下一个任务或者其他事情上去。后续学习之所以很关键是因为这个时候才知道:

- 自己在准备工作中哪些地方判断准确、用力适当而保证顺利完成了任务;
- 在准备工作中有哪些判断误差或者注意不够而导致执行任务期间力不从心
- 在任务期间哪些地方口译恰当,哪些地方口译不当,本来应该怎样处理更加恰当
- 在任务期间哪些事情处理恰当,哪些事情处理不当,本来应该怎样处理更加恰当

即:既要回顾语言的处理又要回顾事情的处理,把每次任务都作为一次绝佳的学习机会,尽量扩大每次任务的学习量,举一反三,确保每次成功都重复再现,每次错误都永不再犯。

后续学习是交传周期的第四个,也是最后一个阶段。学习之后接受下一个任务,周而复始,不断进步。

交传装备

交传的首要装备是笔记本。交传所需的笔记本有几个特殊的要求,首先必须

带有活页圈，因为交传时先记笔记，然后翻回来口译，所以只有活页圈笔记本才适用。其次，由于译员需要能够站立口译，笔记本最好是能够整个躺在手掌中，而且笔记本的最后是比较硬挺的厚纸板，可以承受译员书写时的压力。如果笔记本背部太软，则不利于流畅地书写。另外，市场上常见的为记者设计的笔记本往往太长，站立口译时，无法用手掌支撑笔记本的下部，需要推一下，这就容易耽误秒秒必争的时间。

再次，交传笔记不是通常意义上的笔记，不是逐行记录，所以带有横杆的笔记本不适用。交传需要的是空白页面，中间一条垂直线，这条线最好是灰色的。这样习惯于笔记较小的译员可以一页分左右使用，习惯于笔记较大的译员可以不理睬灰线而整页使用。目前市场上交传的专业笔记本仍然只有英国 KL Communications 有限公司设计的那一种，不仅满足交传的上述特殊要求，而且分大小两个尺寸，以满足译员手掌大小尺寸不同的需要。

如果是站着口译，则需要用一只手持笔记本，手势与笔记本用法见本课末尾的照片。口译时记完一页，翻过去一页。讲话人收口后，一把将刚才翻过去的几页全部一次翻回来，马上就能找到页面上需要开始译的地方。然后，译一页，翻过去一页。译完后，把翻过去的几页一把压在持笔记本的手掌中。这点很重要。否则，讲话人收口后，译员会急切之下找不到需要译的这段话的开头。

如果是坐在桌前口译，在可以把笔记本放在桌面上。不过也是记完一页，翻过去一页。也千万不要忘记在讲话人开口说下一段之前，把已经翻完的笔记页压到笔记本下。

交传的第二个装备是笔，最好是按压式的。这样，如果是站着口译一手持笔记本，则另一手随时都可以一按就开始记笔记。如果是旋转开盖的笔，则需要两只手操作。如果笔套不紧的，还时不时要掉，很分心。交传译员必须养成常带两支笔的习惯，以免一支笔墨用尽而无法继续笔记。

译员姿势

交传译员最常见的情况是坐译或者站译。顾名思义，坐译指的是译员坐在椅子或者板凳上，可能面前有桌子，也可能没有。站译指的是译员站在受众面前，既可能站在讲者身边，也可能远离讲者，通过麦克风听讲者然后传译。

由于译员直接面对受众，其站坐的姿势能给受众产生下意识的印象。姿势合适有利于传达讲者预期达到的效果，不合适则会有碍于传达讲者预期达到的效果。一般情况下可以遵循下述原则保证姿势合适：两脚八字开（站译），低头不哈腰（坐译）。女译员忌讳在坐译时翘二郎腿。

前者指的是站立时挺胸、收腹、双脚间距同肩膀宽度，脚尖略微朝外。女学生或者女译员尤其需要注意站姿，这有两个原因。第一是因为文化的影响，很多女学生、女译员觉得站立时两脚分开显得不文雅。第二是从来没有被要求站立时两脚分开，由于感觉别扭而两脚紧紧挨着。

需要说明的是，双脚分开站立给人留下稳重，有分量的印象。所以，无论是政界、商界、学界，有身份、有地位，担任领导职务的人，无论是在西方还是在中国，无论男女，大多数都是这样站立讲话。交传译员这样站不仅有利于自身形象，也有利于反映讲者的形象。另外，双脚分开站立便于保持身体稳定。如果双脚并拢，上身容易摇晃，再加上紧张，很容易导致译员摆动不停，给人留下信心不足的印象。

低头不哈腰指的是译员既使是低头记笔记或者看笔记，仍然保持背部直挺，显得精神饱满。而且讲者往往是抬头说话，极少弯背。译员坐姿直挺有助于从外观上反映讲者的形象。请看一组站、坐的照片。

笔记本持法背面 　　　笔记本持法正面 　　　边听边记 　　　笔记本持法背面

第四课·交传任务

| 翻回笔记开始口译 |  译一页，翻一页 |  译完后全部压掌中 |  继续边听边记 |

本课小结

每个交传任务都应该是由四个阶段组成的周期，不仅局限于口译本身。译员需要在每个阶段上都把工作做好，就能够每次都有明显进步。这四个阶段是：接受任务、任务准备、完成任务、后续学习。

工作坊

假设下个月将前往伦敦为国际会议担任交传译员（会议日程如下）。两人一组讨论准备工作需要包括哪些内容，共同起草一份涵盖所有需要准备内容的清单。另外，假设将下榻于假日酒店（地址：Express by Holiday Inn, 106-110 Belgrave Road, London, SW1V 2BJ, UK），制定当天前往会场的旅行方案：几点从哪里出发，乘什么交通工具，于几点到达哪里。如果没有互联网，可以采用自己下榻地的一个合适地点做练习。

EU and UK: Partners in Sustainability
1st December 2008

Venue:
Queen Elisabeth II Conference Centre
Broad Sanctuary
Westminster

London SW1P 3EE

09:45　Registration & Coffee

10:30　Chair's welcome & introduction—the Secretary of State for Business, UK

09:40　"EU and UK: Prospects for the Next Decade", President of the European Commission

10:50　"Rising to the Challenge: the UK's Capabilities in Sustainable Technology and Know-how", UK Minister of State for Trade & Investment

11:00　Coffee Break

11:30　"Global Climate Change—Everyone's Business", Chairman, Confederation of British Industry

12:30　Lunch

13:45　Sustainability Issues at a local level: Panel session joined by—the Mayor of London, Paris, Berlin, Brussels, Madrid, Rome, Warsaw and Prague

15:00　Partnership Sessions—Finance & Economy
Issues for discussion: who should be funding sustainability? How to strike a balance between long-term sustainability and short-term economic growth? Should there be one set of performance indicators for all EU countries?

15:45　Coffee Break

16:15　Partnership Sessions—Energy and Environment
Issues for discussion: Are we in an energy crisis? What are the prospects for a Post Kyoto agreement? Is EU doing enough in its environment policies?

16:45　Closing keynote speech, Chairman, HSBC

17:00　Event ends

第五课　交传技能

本课讲解交传技能的核心技能，第六课和第七课讲解交传的辅助技能。

交传特有的核心技能有四个："使用笔记""四别""三步法""反映讲者"。虽然在其他形式的口译中有时也涉及到上述四大关键技能的部分内容，但是这四大技能在交传里的使用最系统，而且是缺一不可。

交传里对于语言的使用也有其特性，但是这些特性与同传相近，所以在本书里将作为交传的辅助技能在第六和第七课里讲解。由于使用笔记需要掌握的内容很多，所以笔记的演示放在第九课里单独讲解。本课集中讲解"四别""三步法"和"反映讲者"。

交传四别

这四别是：别停下、别露馅、别加快、别拖延。四别既是交传的一组关键技能，需要使用这些技能保证顺利完成任务；又是交传特有的一组衡量标准，以此可以衡量学员的进展和译员的水平。以下逐一讲解。

别停下

别停下指的是译员持续口译，直至完成一段话的口译。如果遇到困难，无论是没听见、没听懂、没记下还是没思路不知道怎么译，都能采用本课稍后讲解的"三步法"，继续口译。这是需要经过培训而发展起来的技能，因为人的本能反应是遇到上述"四没"时就开始想，一想就停止口译；一停止口译，就会出现沉默，讲者等译员，听众等译员，所有的注意力都从听讲话转到了译员本身，整个活动都陷入僵局。

相反，如果译员采用三步法继续口译，讲者继续讲，活动继续进行，译员就完成了任务。没有必要担心漏译甚至错译的发生。首先，译员的水平只能靠事前、事后提高，在口译的当时是无法提高的，能译出来的就译出来了。其次，译不出来的也很难想出来，"四没"里的哪一没都无法靠想解决。最后，听众不是口译考官，而是在参加活动。他们都希望译员不要被卡住，都非常希望活动能继续下去。

别露馅

这指的是遇到"四没"时，译员不显山、不露水，以三步法过关。人的本能反应是在讲话遇到麻烦时会有下意识的表情或者动作，比如：

- 过长的停顿
- 皱眉头
- 脸红
- 干笑
- 喃喃而语
- 搔头
- 托眼镜
- 摸头发
- 以无奈的眼光四下看

露馅有两大害处。首先，露馅清楚地告诉听众，译员遇到麻烦了，即使译对了都可能被怀疑是译错了。其次，露馅是习惯。如果不改掉，即使没有译错，只要译员吃不准就都会下意识地露馅，没有必要地影响听众的信心。

由于露馅是本能反应，要想避免露馅就必须通过反复训练，把露馅的本能改变成越是遇到困难越集中精力持续口译从而不显山、不露水的本能。

别加快

这指的是保持均速。人的本能反应是在听清了讲话，看清了笔记，知道怎么译的时候会自然而然地加快口译速度。这有两个问题。

首先，速度快了不利于译员。交传是个相当复杂的过程，看清笔记，把笔记内容与短期记忆以及译员自有知识结合起来，然后用合适的译入语表述，这一系列过程都需要时间。这个过程对于大多数人来说，在口译内容不是太难的情况下（以英译汉为例）一般速度为每 4–5 个汉字一记。按照这个速度边说、边看笔记、边组织句子就能显得是在持续口译，没有过长的停顿。但是如果说的速度加快了，而其余过程保持原来的速度，就会出现脑子突然空白的情况。为了避免突然空白，就必须加快脑子的处理速度，这等于译员给自己增加口译难度，既没有必要，也难以如愿成功。

其次，加快速度等于失去了喘气的余地，肯定会在口译稍微有点难度的时候马上放慢速度，甚至停顿下来。这个速度反差相当于露馅，让听众知道译员遇到麻烦。如果均速口译，定期自然停顿，不仅能够给自己的大脑留下处理信息的所需时间，而且能够更好地再现讲者预期达到的效果。

别拖延

这指的是译员在讲者停顿之后 3 秒之内开始口译。之所以说 3 秒是因为这是自然停顿的时值，如果超过 3 秒就会觉得停顿了相当长时间，让听众感觉口译出故障了。如果在 3 秒之内开始口译，听上去就会像没有停顿一般，如行云流水，很顺。

要达到这个目标就必须一发现讲者已经停顿，马上结束笔记最后一笔，然后一边让目光回到本段笔记开始处，一边吸一口气，然后开始口译。如果笔记比较长，需要翻页，那也没有关系，只要译员是在操作过程中听众都不会觉得出了问题。

别拖延的难处在于笔记的最后一笔，有时正好赶上讲者说的最后几个字特别不容易记。把笔记记全了可能拖延太久，不拖延太久就可能必须马上停止笔记。由于这个决定很难一概而论，而且可以使用的时间在一秒之内，所以需要在培训中通过摸索掌握好平衡。别忘了，交传是笔记、记忆和知识的互动。笔记来不及就靠记忆补。

三步法

这指的是"问、补、扔"，即如果译员在交传中遇到"四没"必须马上采取的步骤。以下逐一讲解。

"问"指的是通过提出问题解决困难，然后继续口译。既可以问讲话人，也可以问对方译员，或是在场的其他人。问谁比较合适，要看具体情况。如果是没听清楚或者没听懂，应该问讲话人。如果是听到英文的技术词汇而不知道中文翻译是什么，在场懂的人往往能解围。另外，轮到译员开口时，在场人的注意力都会转到译员这里。所以，只要抬起头来，眼中露出询问的目光，就可能会有人提供解决方案。

但是在下述情况里，"问"不解决问题。这既可能是没法问，也可能是不能问。

- 译员不是站在或者坐在讲者身边，而是站在讲台或者坐在长桌的另外一边，无法与讲者直接交谈询问；
- 译员听不懂讲者的整句话，而请讲者解释又不合适，比如为高层人物的主旨演讲做交传就是这种情况；
- 译员问了，但是讲者重复之后还是不懂；
- 多次遇到不懂或者不会译的词或者意思，再问下去成了译员和讲者交谈而不是为听众交传了。

"补"指的是如果问不解决问题，就必须马上走下一步，根据上下文和自己的理解，补齐原话的句子或意思，然后继续往下译。在这种情况下，虽然译文与原话不同，但是没有错误。具体怎么补需要根据当时的情况灵活处理。这里提供几个译员常用的补话表达法：

- 这点……
- 这些……
- 等等……
- 这些人……
- 这些事情……
- 这点很重要
- 这方面的问题

"扔"指的是如果无法或者不能"补"，那就必须马上走最后一步，跳过"四没"之处，从能够译之处继续译下去。

这步听上去简单，做起来不容易。扔必须果断、干净，根据"四别"里"别停下"和"别露馅"的要求，让不懂译出语的听众根本听不出来，即使是双语都懂的听众也觉得一晃而过。这也是需要通过培训而掌握的技能。

反映讲者

这指的是译员不仅传译讲者的话，而且从语气、情感和与听众的互动上也反映出讲者的意图和形象。也即不仅传达讲者的意思，同时还通过反映讲者而实现讲者影响听众的意图。

反映讲者不等于模仿讲者。译员和讲者可能性别不同，身高、长相各异。但是译员可以使用各种技能使听众忘却是在听译员的传译，就好像是在直接听讲者讲话一般。只有成功地反映讲者才能达到再现原话效果的目的。

再现原话效果指的是讲者在译出语里使用幽默之后译出语听众笑了，译入语的听众在听了译员传译之后也笑。再现原话效果要求译员动用一系列技能，请看示意图。

目光交流

译员与听众以目光交流非常重要。虽然译员无法模仿讲者的目光交流次数与时机，但是每15—20秒的一段话里都至少应该有一次目光交流。当然也不能交流太频繁，那样会让听众感到头晕。

目光交流还需要注意场合的大小。如果听众为数不多，译员抬头就能看到整个场面，目光交流时抬头就可以了。但是如果场面比较大，就需要从左到右或者从右到左，每次目光交流的时候面对听众的左、中、右部分，让所有听众都觉得被包括其中。

如果讲者的话中单独提到某人，就应该把目光转向受话人。比如，如果讲者说"我再次对王董事长表示感谢"，而译员能够随即把目光投向王董事长而译出这句话就能为讲者实现意图，让王董事长感受到谢意。

肢体语言

译员无法模仿讲者的肢体语言，但是有三种肢体语言有助于译员反映讲者：

- 手势
- 表情
- 身体动作

讲者随着话语而使用的手势往往比较随意，译员无法也没有必要模仿。但是如果讲者在做电脑演示，指着投影图像的某个部位说"If it's this, it'll be that"，译员就必须也借助手势指着同一部位说："如果是这个，那就是那个"。

一般情况下，译员没有必要模仿讲者的表情，也模仿不上，因为需要低头记笔记。但是在一种特殊情况下需要使用表情，这就是在传达幽默的时候，需要用笑容，略微夸张的表情，向受众表明，刚才的话不可按照原话理解，达到幽默的效果。

当然，幽默与文化紧密相关，译员需要根据自己的两种工作语言的文化来确定是否需要使用表情来协助表达幽默或者其他讲者意图产生的效果。

有关身体动作的要求在目光交流中已经提到，即如果讲者的话是针对某一个人或者会场内某个部位的受众是，译员也应该争取转向具体的个人或者某部分受众而口译。

声音、语调、节奏

交传译员不必也不可能模仿讲者的声音，但是声音的使用有讲究。虽然很多人做交传都是用自己日常生活中的自然声音，但是交传译员应该有自己的职业声音，也就是经过培训在做交传时使用的声音。这个道理和歌唱演员、播音员一样，他们的职业声音也往往不同于日常生活里的声音。

交传培训中的声音基本有两大类型需要注意，一种是有些女性的习惯声音又尖、又细，不适合于使用交传时的场合与客户需要；另一中是很多人习惯于用喉咙以上的部位发声。两种情况都不利于反映讲者，因为尖细或者轻飘的声音缺少交传里很多讲者所拥有的分量。无论中外或者男女，凡是领导人极少有尖细嗓门者，这不是偶然。交传译员应该通过培训，养成使用胸腔共鸣辅助发声的习惯，以此形成自己的职业声音。

由于交传不是歌唱，对于胸腔共鸣的要求不高，所以练习起来也不难。比如，可以先以自然发声拉长音说"啊"，两三秒钟之后努力让声音往喉咙以下走，同时把一只手放在胸脯上感觉震动。感觉到胸腔震动之后，继续"啊"并努力把震动感保持住。接着就是朗读文章，继续努力保持胸腔的震动感。再往下就是说话时也尽量保持胸腔震动。

胸腔共鸣如果通过麦克风传出，效果尤其好。

声音的使用当然会受到文化因素的影响。总体来说，西方女性的声音，包括青年女子的声音都比中国同龄的女性低。在中国以及一些其他亚洲文化里，细声细气被看做是女性的优点，而声音"像男的"是不好的事情。解决的办法就是如同上述，做交传时以胸腔共鸣增加声音的厚度，增加讲话的威力。在个人生活里，想多细就多细，完全是个人选择。

交传译员不必也不可能模仿讲者所有的语调，但是应该争取反映出讲者讲话的总体风格，这是再现效果的一个重要组成部分。当然，讲者也会有例外，也会有毛病，这些个别情况自然不必去反映。

交传译员需要注重的有两大方面，首先是抑扬顿挫。西方领导人，无论是政界、商界还是学界都有个大同小异的演讲风格，相当于汉语里的抑扬顿挫。这是交传译员应该首先掌握的一个技能，需要通过练习汉语朗读来培训。最简单的办法之一就是模仿专业演员或者播音员的朗诵。

其次是特定语调，即讲者在说某个词或者短语时故意加重的语气，译员也应该在传译时同样处理。如果来得及就在做笔记时以自己设计的方式标出，来不及记录就凭短期记忆在传译时在同样的话上加重语气。

最后谈节奏。交传译员不必也不可能模仿讲者的节奏，但是交传有其特定的基本节奏，即："哒哒哒""哒哒哒""哒哒哒"，而且每次"哒哒哒"之后都略微停顿。这个节奏最有利于再现译出语的效果，有利于受众理解、吸收讲话的内容，有利于译员边译边看笔记，边译边想下面如何译。

英语一般讲话速度是每秒三个单词，相当汉语就是 5–6 个汉字，本课称其为标准速度。其中有很重要的心理原因，即一般人在口译时大脑处理信息的速度也同样。如果说话速度超过标准速度，就会出现大脑跟不上嘴巴，已有的话说完之后还不知道接下来说什么，或者按照上一组词造句之后，发现所用之词难以与接下来的话搭配。两种情况下都会导致译员口误或者不得不改口，重新起句。

掌握了哒哒哒的节奏，就能养成说话速度不超过大脑处理信息的速度，保证总是在知道要说什么话之前才开口说，显得胸有成竹。而不是说到一半，戛然而止，无法继续，或者经常改口。

引发动作

反映讲者、再现效果的另外一个重要方面就是要让受众按照讲者的意图行动。在交传中，讲者经常通过话语引发受众的某个行动或者动作，以下是比较常见的一组：

1. 点头赞同
2. 欢呼
3. 微笑或者哄堂大笑
4. 鼓掌
5. 起立
6. 坐下
7. 具体要求：比如关闭手机
8. 举手
9. 推出房间或者会场

在译入语中引发同样的动作在大多数情况下都不难，只要把讲者的原话按照字面传译就行了。需要注意的是如果讲者引发动作的愿望是以间接形式表达，由于两种语言和文化的不同，就有可能由于仅仅是按照原话传译而没有在受众里引发讲者希望看到的动作。第一课里有关暗示的两个例子值得复习一下，这里再举一个。

在一次有一组中国某公司经理参加的培训课上，一位英国教授首先讲解了作为案例的一家英国公司里的情况，然后说：

How do these challenges compare with issues in your company?

说完之后，他坐下来好像讲完了一样。教授当时的意图显然是以这个问题引发各位学员的小组讨论，但是如果完全按照原话传译就有可能处理成：这些挑战与你们公司里的面对的问题有什么不同？这样就有可能出现所有学员都开始自我思考而不是讨论的情况。译员需要把教授的暗示或者说间接的要求在汉语里点明，才能达到实现讲者意图的目的。比如，可以处理成：这些挑战与你们公司里的议题有哪些相似或者不同之处，请大家讨论一下。

本课小结

四别是交传的核心技能。别停下、别露馅、别加快、别拖延从四个方面保证交传的质量，与语言转换本身的质量起到相辅相成的作用。如果"四别"没有做好，即使在语言上没有问题，也会听上去质量不高。但是如果"四别"功夫到家，则能够在语言成功转换的基础上锦上添花。

工作坊

请朗读下面的讲稿（美国时任总统奥巴马的就职演说节选），注意利用停顿来避免口误。反复练习直至可以在没有口误的情况下按限定时间读完。

I stand here today humbled by the task before us, grateful for the trust you have bestowed, mindful of the sacrifices borne by our ancestors. I thank President Bush for his service to our nation, as well as the generosity and cooperation he has shown throughout this transition.

Forty-four Americans have now taken the presidential oath. The words have been spoken during rising tides of prosperity and the still waters of peace. Yet, every so often, the oath is taken amidst gathering clouds and raging storms. At these moments, America has carried on not simply because of the skill or vision of those in high office, but because We the People have remained faithful to the ideals of our forbearers, and true to our founding documents.

So it has been. So it must be with this generation of Americans.

That we are in the midst of crisis is now well understood. Our nation is at war, against a far-reaching network of violence and hatred. Our economy is badly weakened, a consequence of greed and irresponsibility on the part of some, but also our collective failure to make hard choices and prepare the nation for a new age. Homes have been lost; jobs shed; businesses shuttered. Our health care is too costly; our schools fail too many; and each day brings further evidence that the ways we use energy strengthen our adversaries and threaten our planet.

第六课　辅助技能一

交传的辅助技能有两种，一种属于译员作为一名职业人员所必须拥有的，具有普遍性质。这些并不是交传所特有的技能，而是译员在其他工作里或者改行之后可以携带到其他工作领域里的技能。另外一种技能属于交传特有或者在交传里的使用特别突出。

交传的主要辅助技能如下：

1. 自学技能：设定并且实现目标，分析、监测、评估自己的能力和表现，以及相关的组织和计划技能的运用
2. 检索：通过在线、电话、电邮、阅读或者其他手段解决知识上的缺陷
3. 组织技能：善于安排时间、工作量以及自己的活动，善于区分轻重缓急
4. 计划技能：能够策划好行程、时间、交通工具，计划好前往外地担任口译任务所需的物品、行装
5. 使用技术：能够使用技术，比如电脑、话筒以及其他口译技术设备
6. 自身保养：妥善安排饮食起居，保证总是处于最佳生理和精神状态
7. 人际关系：善于应对各种人和要求，其中包括其他译员、翻译公司、公关公司等
8. 商业运作（仅适用于自由职业译员）：设计口译服务项目、定价、宣传、报价、确认预定、收款、做账、税务管理等
9. 演讲技能：善于在大庭广众面前发表即席演讲
10. 语言的处理：交传在语言的运用上有不同于其他语言运用形式的特性
11. 人称的使用：使用人称的特性
12. 与讲者的关系：掌控讲者的说话时间
13. 如何使用讲稿：利用得到讲稿的好处，避免使用不善带来的麻烦
14. 如何应对听众挑战：指听众纠正译员时应该如何应对

15. 控制紧张：过度紧张阻碍正常发挥，而且是学员和新手面临的普遍问题

上述1—6属于通用职业技能，不局限于交传。本书由于篇幅有限，不做讲解。而7和8，即：人际关系和商业技能在笔者的《实战口译》一书里已经讲解过，欢迎参阅《实战口译》。上述9—15的内容与交传直接相关。比如，虽然顺序传译是同传里必须掌握的关键技能，但是在交传里也应该有相应程度的使用。再如，虽然如何控制紧张情绪不限于交传，但是对交传译员的挑战尤其突出，所以需要单独讲解。

由于辅助技能很多，所以分成两课讲解。本课讲解与语言使用相关的内容，其余在下一课里讲解。

交传里英译汉时对于语言的使用有四大手法：采用缺省、传译话面、顺序传译、传达效果。这四大手法都很关键，熟练掌握之后能解决很多常见的问题。但是由于这四大手法都与很多人的理念，尤其是与有些流行的翻译理念格格不入，所以需要对交传的性质和实际操作有清楚地认识才能体会四大手法不可缺少的原因，并且熟练使用。

交传里汉译英时对于语言的使用有三大手法：减字增时、跳词组句、译所指而非所言。以下对总共七大手法逐一讲解。

采用缺省

"缺省"是借鉴了电脑行业的概念发展而来，指的是没有任何线索时的译法。采用缺省指的是在听到一个词汇时，既使没有任何背景，或者与此前的话语中没有任何明显的线索（即笔译里的所谓上下文），译员也能马上传译。这就要求译员必须通过培训或者自我学习，为所有英语词汇确定缺省译法。

缺省译法应该是什么并没有非黑即白的划分，也没有权威版本参照。缺省译法不是指为每个词汇挑选一个最不容易出错的译法，而是译员自我确定在听到一个词汇而又没有线索的情况下如何传译这个词汇。译员没有不译的选择，而且经常需要在没有线索的情况下传译。

这听上去很简单，但却是很多译员的一大难关。绝大多数的译员都是从笔译开始学习翻译，然后学口译。就连整个英语学习从一开始也都是根据上下文判断词义，这种理念和习惯根深蒂固。每听到一个不熟悉的词汇就停下来思考上下文，或者没有清楚的背景就完全不知道应该译成什么乃至无法继续。这也是同传初学者的常见问题。

现在举个实际例子，两位采矿业的商人正在通过交传译员探讨合资的可能性，其中的中国人突然说了"品位"这个词，此前没有明显线索。

英国人　I am very pleased that you can find the time to meet me today. I know you are only passing London.

中国人　我也很高兴，一直希望能够当面谈谈。我上个月还来过伦敦，实在对不起。

英国人　No, no. Don't apologise. I totally understand. I've been following your expansion with great interest. I very much hope that we can work together on the project I e-mailed you about.

中国人　对，我们也很有兴趣。对于我们来说，这是个先后顺序问题。我们正在同时考虑几个机会，现在还没定先做哪个。

英国人　We've had several decades of experience in the sector. Would be very happy to share our expertise with you. I also believe that as your business expands, you'll have an increasingly more important role in the international market. You are number three already, aren't you?

中国人　对，但是你们的品位比较好……

中国商人本来就有比较浓厚的地方口音，在说"品位"两个字时声音还比较低，而且发言不清楚。现在回头看似乎可以说既然两位都是采矿业的，这里"品位"基本上可以断定是指矿物的品位。但是这属于事后诸葛亮，双方对话到目前为止都没有关于矿物的内容，光是凭着两位讲者的背景及其谈话的目的是不足以判断词义的。

再比如，在金融研讨会上，讲者会突然拿高尔夫球打比方，说出："this is really under par"。Under par 在高尔夫术语里指的是没有按照规定杆数打完，是表达业务表现不够好的意思。再如，讲者在开场白里突然与当时的话题以及场合完全没有联系的事情。由于口译的对象是讲者，这种突然转换背景，转换话题，使用的词汇此前没有线索的情况经常发生。只有培训出无论听到什么词汇都有缺省译法的本领才能保证译员立于不败之地。

传译话面

有关话面意思的概念在第一课里已经讲解过了，这里不重复。如果说缺省译法是解决单词或者表达法的问题，那么传译话面就是解决整句或者整段话不甚理解的解决办法。传译话面指根据讲者原话的表面意思传译，而不考虑话里的含义。传译话面可以解决交传里常见的四大问题：没有线索、不懂含义、超越讲者、回头错。没有线索刚才已经讲解过，现在讲解其他的三个问题。

不懂含义。交传里不懂含义的常见情况有三种：修辞手法、抽象概念、陌生信息。第三课里小葱拌豆腐的例子就是修辞手法应该按照话面传译的很好例子。有关抽象概念的例子有比如 special purpose vehicle，听到这个英文词汇就传译成"特殊目的工具"就完成了任务，不必考虑这个工具在当前的语境里到底是指公司、基金还是做法。

第二课在讲到传译什么时就举过陌生信息的例子，说的是在一次金融培训课将近结束的问答时间，有学员请教员介绍安然公司的诈骗是怎么回事。教员说：

"What Enron did was to create a special purpose vehicle, a separate company. Enron then transferred some assets into this special purpose company and invited external investors to pay for 50% of the equity of this company in exchange for 3% of the shares."

这段话的后半部说投资者投资 50% 的股权却只得 3% 的股票，译员听懂了话面的意思，但是不懂话里的含义，因为有悖常理。如果按照很多人所说"必须听懂了再译"，译员就有可能因为不懂其含义而被卡住，或者不得不请讲者解释之后再译。两者都不可取。其实，译员根本不必听懂含义，只需要听懂了话面意思，然后按照话面传译便可：

"安然的做法是建立一个特别目的工具，一个单独的公司。安然把一些资产转移到这个特别目的公司里，然后邀请投资者投资购买公司 50% 的股权以换取 3% 的股票。"

口译里译员只要通过对语言的掌握，听懂了话面意思，即使没有听懂话里的含义，也可以成功地传译。不仅如此，译员还经常应该在仅仅听懂了话面意思就传译，在传译时还经常应该仅仅传译话面，不要也不能增加自己的解读或者解释。

超越讲者

这指的是译员把讲者将在下一段里说的话但是尚未说的话在上一段里就已经传译了。等到讲者说到这段话时，译员不得不重复自己，或者说："我刚才已经为各位翻译过了"，明显地抢了讲者之先，越俎代庖，违反了口译的根本原则。

造成译员超越讲者的一个重要原因是口译里的一大误区，把受众是否能听懂讲者的话当作译员的责任。第三课里已经从理念上说明了这种理念的谬误和害处，这里再举一个实际例子。有位英国教授在向中国学员讲解兼并与收购的时候说了这句话之后停顿下来让译员传译：

"There are three ways one can defend against a bid. Voting restriction, Ownership restrictions and Sale of crown jewels"

这句号里的"crown jewels"指的是公司业务里的最佳部分。如果按照笔译概念里应该用对方听得懂的方式，就很可能会选用地道的译入语处理成"最佳业务"。那样就可能出麻烦，因为讲者接着说："But we had nothing that could be considered a crown jewel. Indeed, not any jewels"。由于译员改变了比喻的内容，听到讲者后来的话就会无法在译入语中自圆其说。

这种讲者先提概念，然后解释的情况在培训课或者是带有解说性质的交传任务里经常发生。如果译员听到概念后在译入语里采用了加以解释的处理，接下来讲者开始解释时，且不说译员正常情况下不应该越俎代庖说讲者还没有说的话，而且会极其尴尬，不得不说："我刚才已经译过了"或者"他（指讲者）就是再解释了一遍我刚才已经说过的话"。

由于超越讲者是由译员说了讲者没有说的话，这违反了交传的基本原则。不仅如此，还为译员带来三大风险，首先是译员自己可能理解错误，因而所加的解释也是错误的。这样当讲者解释之后，听众会以为讲者前后矛盾，甚至自打嘴巴。其次是在高层会谈时，比如为政府或者跨国公司领导人做交传时抢先说讲者尚未说的话非常不合适。比如，你要是为政府首脑做交传时超越了讲者，然后说"他的话我刚才已经译过了"会十分不合适，甚至不成体统。再次，如果会谈内容敏感时，或者讲者有意不把话说明时，如果译员自以为是，认为应该帮助听众听懂，就会把讲者有意隐晦的意思挑明。这不仅会造成违背讲者原意的问题，甚至还可能引起双边关系上的严重问题。

回头错

回头错指的是译员在前一句里的传译方式听上去挺合适，但是讲者接下来说的话使之前的传译方式变得很不合适，甚至谬误。第四课里小葱拌豆腐的例子就很典型。

在交传里犯回头错的风险很大，构成风险主要有两大要素。一个是修辞性质的语言使用，其中包括成语、谚语、固定表达法。另外一个是讲者灵活运用成语、谚语或者固定表达法。这两个要素加在一起就形成了交传的陷阱，只要译员按照传统翻译理念的指导努力让听众听懂而改变原话里的成语、谚语或者固定表达法，就很容易落入回头错的陷阱。

之前有关"crown jewels"的例子也很常见，如果译员按照该表达法的含义传译，就会给自己埋下犯回头错的地雷。如果讲者在下一句里灵活使用这个表达法，说："But if you don't have crown jewels, only inexpensive jewellery, you'll have one way less to play with."译员就会被炸得粉身碎骨。请看以下对比，左边是按照传统翻译理念所作的处理，右边是传译话面的结果。

	传统理念		传译话面
讲者	There are three ways one can defend against a bid. Voting restriction, Ownership restrictions and Sale of crown jewels	讲者	There are three ways one can defend against a bid. Voting restriction, Ownership restrictions and Sale of crown jewels
译员	抵抗兼并要约有三种方法：投票限制、拥有限制、出售最佳业务。	译员	抵抗兼并要约有三种方法：投票限制、拥有限制、出售王冠珠宝。
讲者	But if you don't have crown jewels, only inexpensive jewellery, you'll have one way less to play with.	讲者	But if you don't have crown jewels, only inexpensive jewellery, you'll have one way less to play with.
译员	（但是，如果没有王冠珠宝可言，只有廉价首饰，那么可以使用的方法就少了一个。）？	译员	但是，如果没有王冠珠宝可言，只有廉价首饰，那么可以使用的方法就少了一个。
评论	前面的话里没有任何与珠宝相关的内容，后面突然冒出珠宝、首饰，令听众丈二和尚摸不着脑。	评论	由于传译的是话面，所以可以跟着讲者沿用同一比喻，天衣无缝。

以下再举两个例子：

	传统理念		传译话面
讲者	Our first quarter turnover was 50 million. They say this is under par.	讲者	Our first quarter turnover was 50 million. They say this is under par.
译员	我们第一季度营业额是5千万。他们说这是业绩不良。	译员	我们第一季度营业额是5千万。他们说这像是高尔夫球里杆数打得过多。
讲者	I say this is only the first hole. Too early to say.	讲者	I say this is only the first hole. Too early to judge.
译员	（我说这才是打完第一洞。现在判断为时过早。）？	译员	我说这才是打完第一洞。现在判断为时过早。
评论	前面说营业额，后面要是说打完第一洞会，期间没有铺垫，没有明显联系，令听众丈二和尚摸不着脑。	评论	由于传译的是话面，所以可以跟着讲者沿用同一比喻，天衣无缝。

	传统理念		传译话面
讲者	I'm now going to talk about ways to make your investment tax efficient. One of them is Bed and Breakfast.	讲者	I'm now going to talk about ways to make your investment tax efficient. One of them is Bed and Breakfast.
译员	我现在谈谈提高投资税务效率的几种办法，其中之一就是晚卖早买。	译员	我现在谈谈提高投资税务效率的几种办法，其中之一就是床加早餐。
讲者	This is an analogy taken from the travel industry. There are many small hotels whose room charge includes breakfast the following morning. Hence the term.	讲者	This is an analogy taken from the travel industry. There are many small hotels whose room charge includes breakfast the following morning. Hence the term.
译员	这是一个来自旅游行业的比喻。有很多小旅店的价格既包括住宿，也包括第二天的早餐，所以叫床加早餐。	译员	这是一个来自旅游行业的比喻。有很多小旅店的价格既包括住宿，也包括第二天的早餐，所以叫床加早餐。
评论	前面说晚卖早买，后面说床加早餐，自相矛盾，令听众丈二和尚摸不着脑。	评论	由于传译的是话面，所以可以跟着讲者沿用同一比喻，并且为之解释，天衣无缝。

交传里必须避免回头错，要想避免回头错就不能拿笔译的概念指导交传，而是必须根据交传的性质和需要尽量保留原话的修辞，按照原话的话面传译。

顺序传译

这指的是在交传时应该尽量争取按照讲者说话的顺序传译。虽然在交传里，译员有时间也能够像在笔译里那样重新调整句子结构，但是重新调整应该仅限于词汇的搭配和修饰，应该避免重新调整句子结构。这样做有两个原因。首先，交传的笔记是按照讲者说话的顺序记录的。如果一段话跨了两页，重新调整势必导致译员来回翻笔记本，看上去像是出了麻烦一样，影响口译的速度，影响听众的信心。

其次，译员做交传时是一边看笔记，一边把笔记、短期记忆和自己的知识结合起来然后转换出译入语，本来用脑量就很大。如果还要再加上重新组织句子结构，容易产生没有必要的疲劳。

顺序交传需要借用同传的顺序驱动（也称断句）技巧，不过由于交传时毕竟时间由译员掌握，所以不必像同传那样必须是几个字一译。而是利用顺序传译的技巧减少重新组织句子的次数，在不影响口译质量的同时减轻对大脑的压力，延长准确交传的持续时间。

以下讲解顺序交传里可以采用的三个技巧：介词译动、重复谓语、反话正说。

介词译动指的是在遇到介词状语时把介词处理成动词，这样就可以避免在中文里把状语提前到谓语之前。需要掌握的是能够根据前面的谓语动词，迅速选用一个同义词或者能够表达类似意思的词作为动词。请看以下三个例子的比较，相关词加黑作为说明。

英语原话	笔译版本	交传版本
Throughout the Asian financial crisis, China provided financial leadership **in** the region.	在整个亚洲金融危机期间，中国从金融上为该地区提供了领导力。	在整个亚洲金融危机期间，中国提供了金融上的领导力，**引领**整个地区。
China's continued economic stability will be critical **to** the region.	中国持续的经济稳定对于整个地区来说很关键。	中国持续的经济稳定很关键，**影响到**整个地区。
We're particularly proud **of** the recommendation from our customers.	我们对于我们顾客的推荐尤其感到自豪。	我们尤其感到自豪的**是**我们顾客的推荐。

重复谓语指的是为了避免把状语提前,在交传时先译谓语,遇到状语时再译状语,然后重复谓语。重复谓语的负面后果是听上去比较啰嗦,应该作为后备手段。即:如果已经出口说了谓语才看到状语的笔记,而急切之下又想不出把介词处理成动词的好办法时采用。请看刚才的三个例子的后备方案(关键词加黑以为说明):

英语原话	首选版本	备份版本
Throughout the Asian financial crisis, China provided financial leadership **in** the region.	在整个亚洲金融危机期间,中国提供了金融上的领导力,**引领整个地区**。	在整个亚洲金融危机期间,中国提供了金融上的领导力,**在整个地区提供了**领导力。
China's continued economic stability will be critical **to** the region.	中国持续的经济稳定很关键,**影响到整个地区**。	中国持续的经济稳定很关键,**对整个地区都很关键**。
We're particularly proud **of** the recommendation from our customers.	我们尤其感到自豪的**是**我们顾客的推荐。	我们尤其感到自豪,我们**对顾客的推荐尤其感到自豪**。

反话正说指的是把英语句子里的谓语否定式处理成汉语里的谓语肯定式,然后相应调整,把否定式用在稍后的动词上。请看以下三个例子:

英语原话	笔译版本	交传版本
I never ceased to be amazed at the scale of construction in Shanghai.	我对上海的建筑规模无法不感到惊愕。	我总是惊愕上海的建筑规模。
You won't be able to start unless you're ready.	除非你做好了准备,否则无法开始。	要想开始就必须做好准备。
It's not in our interest to argue about details before we've discussed the principle.	在没有讨论原则之前就争辩细节,这不符合我们的利益。	要符合我们的利益,就不要争辩细节,要先讨论原则。

同传里的顺序译技巧不少,由于本书重点是交传,这里只是举几个典型例子作为说明,希望能有助于打开思路。有意者可以参阅《实战同传》和《实战视译》,把顺序译又不影响译语质量的技巧尝试用于交传。

另外,本书附带的练习中,经常采用顺序译的手法来减低交传时在英汉两种语言之间颠倒句子顺序的必要。由于交传的准确幅度超过笔译（请看第二课的讲解），顺序译不会影响到交传的质量。

传达效果

这指的是为了在译入语里再现译出语里的效果，译员调整遣词造句的方式。这种调整在笔译里往往会被认为是翻译不准确。第二课里有个很好的例子，爱尔兰政府为到访的中国客人以及当地的中国机构与公司举办爱尔兰音乐、舞蹈晚会，演出前司仪为了暗示观众关手机，说了下面的话：

> "We will demonstrate some typical Irish musical instrument. However, I must stress that mobile phones are not generally considered an Irish musical instrument."

他话音刚落，在场的爱尔兰官员和商界成员一阵笑声，很多人拿出手机关掉。如果仅仅是按照原话传译，就有可能因为太含蓄而无法为讲者实现中国观众关掉手机的意图。在这种情况下，译员必须在遣词造句是稍加调整，比如说："但是，我必须强调，手机恐怕不算是爱尔兰乐器。所以，能否请各位留意一下？"

再举一例。为了说明，以笔译处理作为对比。

英语原话	笔译版本	交传版本
Mr President, if you want to find friends of China, you could do no better than looking among your audience today.（听众掌声一片）	主席先生，如果您要找中国的朋友，最好是在今天在场的听众中找。	主席先生，要想找中国的朋友，除了今天在场的听众之外，别无他处。

如果按照笔译的惯例，译员很难传达原话的效果，因为中文里的句子没有在句末形成高潮。如果按照交传的要求，就必须从遣词造句上加以调整。虽然这样如果写成文字，显然是翻译不准确。但这不是笔译，而是交传。语言调整之后，只要译员在句末加重语气，提高声调，就几乎肯定能提醒听众鼓掌，传达原话的效果，高质量地完成交传任务。

哪个版本？

交传时难免遇到笔译和同传都会遇到的一个问题，那就是一个表达法或者意思可以有几种不同的处理方式，需要译员当场决定采取哪种方式。在传译比较敏感或者可能有争议的词汇时，这个问题会显得特别突出。

比如"改革开放"这个词，目前国内的政府版本是 the Reform and Opening Up。这是为了更加准确地反映原文的意思而部分牺牲英文的质量，因为英文里并没有一个与在"改革开放"里的这个"开放"完全对应的单词，而且 opening up 不是名词。所以，汉译英时至少可以有三种处理方法，一是完全按照政府版本；二是加 movement 后英语里成为 Opening Up Movement，听上去比较工整（不过用 movement 译"开放"是否准确会有争议）；三是借助定冠词的作用只译 the Reform，让"开放"也包括其中。这第三种处理方式符合英语的习惯，但也会有人说不够准确，因为没有像原话那样直接说出。

口译时采用哪个版本需要根据为谁译、给谁听、为何效果的原则做出抉择。如果你是中国政府译员，为中国政府官员的正式讲话口译，恐怕按政府版本处理是必须的。如果你是自由职业者，哪怕是为政府官员口译，也有比政府译员更多一点的空间，可以处理得稍微灵活一些，更加接近英语习惯一些。如果你是英方的译员，就可能可以更加灵活一些，更多地照顾英方的理解和英语的习惯。这个理念在笔者由外研社出版的《实战笔译》里有详细的论述。

减字增时

"减"指的是在汉译英时，先决定哪些汉字不必翻译，然后把剩下的汉字翻译成英文。我把这种手法简称为减字，也就是减少汉语原话里需要译入英语的字数。

汉译英必须减字有数个原因。首先，相对英语而言，汉语里重叠、重复表达的现象很多，往往是为了强调或者表达清楚。由于英语里不用这些方式，所以，如果按照汉语全部译入英语，在英语听上去就会显得多余、累赘。

中文原文	建议译作	一般不译作
重点强调	Stress	emphatically stress

（续表）

不断深入	Deepen	continuously deepen
再次重复	Repeat (doing it twice)	Repeat once again (doing it three times)
持续扩展	Expand	continuously expand

其次，如果中心动词已经意思到位，就不必译汉语里起到加强语气作用的其他修饰词。

中文原文	可以译作	不必译作
奠定了获得救灾全面胜利的基础	lay the foundation for disaster relief	lay the foundation for the comprehensive victory of disaster relief
富有勇气的决策	A courageous decision	A decision full of courage
合家团圆的幸福夜晚	A family evening	The happy evening when the whole family gathered

最后，不必译"总结词"。这指的是用一个词总结前面已经详细说过的英语时，只要把前面的具体内容译出来就足够了。

中文原文	建议译作	不必译作
从而形成了人人参加全球化讨论的局面	Everyone is involved in the discussion of globalisation	The situation of everyone being involved in the discussion of globalisation
消费量在过去几年中连续上升的趋势	Consumption increased in the past few years	The trend of consumption being increased in the past few years
明确规则产生了改善业绩的效果	Clarification of rules led to improvement of performance	Clarification of rules created the effect of improved performance

增时指增加时态，由于本教材的练习单元里时态的使用比较简单、明了，所以不在此具体讲解。

译所指而非所言

指的是汉译英时在很多情况下都不能按照汉语的字面传译，而必须根据汉语词汇所指含义处理。

原话	译作	不译作
裸婚	No frills wedding (or for love only)	Naked wedding
给力	fantastic	give power
吸引眼球	Eye-catching	Catching eye-balls
有意见请向我们反映	If you have a different view, please tell us.	Please reflect your view to us if you have one.

跳词组句

这个理念与之前的减字理念相通，但是应用范围更加广泛，泛指在汉译英时选择部分汉字组成相当于是简化后的句子，然后把简化后的句子译成英语。由于本书范围所限，无法详细讲解，只是根据交传汉译英的常见需要说明一种语言现象的处理，这就是汉语里的词组。这即可以是成语及其类似语言现象，也可以是多个汉字组成的固定表达法。

采用跳词组句的理念也就是说汉译英时不必，有时还不能，单独地考虑某个汉语表达法如何译成英语，而是要把之前的话——也包括之后可能说的话——通盘考虑之后，决定如何处理。既有可能按照汉语词组的原意处理，也有可能减去该词组里的部分汉字，甚至整个词组都减去不译。

比如，如果单独看"微不足道"，不译成 too minute too mention 就有不准确的感觉。但是这句话"世界市场很大，我们的份额微不足道"口译成英语时就可以说 The world market is very big. But our share is insignificant。

再如，如果单独看"强国建设"，不译成 development to strengthen the nation 就有不准确的感觉。但是这句话"我们行业已经进入了强国建设的关键时期"口译成英语时就可以说 Our industry has already entered a key phase in the development of a powerful nation，甚至可以说 Our industry is now at a critical juncture of national development。同传时出于顺序译的需要，还可以处理成 Our industry is helping to build a strong nation. We're at a critical juncture。

本课小结

交传里语言处理方面的主要手法根据语言方向不同而分别是：采用缺省、传译话面、顺序传译、传达效果（英译汉）和减字增时、跳词组句、译所指而非所言（汉译英）。英译汉的四个手法为的是帮助译员在上下文不清楚甚至没有上下文的情况下仍然能够继续口译；译员在特定情况下按照话面用词译可以避免回头错或超越讲者；译员采用个别同传的技巧可以避免过多地颠倒句子结构；交传译员应该注意在需要时传达讲者希望通过讲话所造成的效果。汉译英的三个手法是跨越汉英两种语言文化差别的桥梁，能够有效地提高口译的准确程度以及在英语里的译语质量。

工作坊

请按照本课讲解的理念，决定如果在交传时猛然听到下列英语成语将如何处理以避免回头错或超越讲者。

- A chain is only as strong as its weakest link
- A dog is a man's best friend
- Bad news travels fast
- Business before pleasure
- Children should be seen and not heard
- Don't throw the baby out with the bath water
- Don't try to walk before you can crawl
- Enough is enough
- Failing to plan is planning to fail
- First thing first

第七课　辅助技能二

前一课讲的是辅助技能里与语言使用相关的内容，本课讲解：即席演讲、如何处理人称、译员与讲者的关系、如何处理讲稿、应对听众的挑战、控制紧张情绪。

即席演讲

很多人在练习交传之前基本没有在大庭广众面前发表即席演讲的经历，更不用说接受这方面的培训了。往往到交传时才第一次面对听众，难免感到非常紧张。在听众面前发表即席演讲是交传译员不可缺少的技能，也是交传培训不可缺少的内容。

之所以如此强调即席演讲有两个原因。首先，即席演讲要求讲者具有边说、边组织思路的能力。这与交传译员边看笔记，边组织思路，边口译的情况很相近。其次，即席演讲者在面对一组听众时所承受的心理压力与交传译员很相近。

即席演讲最难的恐怕就是马上组织思路，边说边想，但是在听众看来好像是有稿子一样，所谓出口成章也。以下简要介绍如何采用"三"的概念培训快速构思的能力，在培训中如何操作将在第十课里讲解。

用"三"快速构思指的是知道话题后，马上就告诉自己需要谈三个要点或者三个方面。然后在说第一个要点或是方面的时候想第二个要点或方面，说第二个要点或方面的时候想第三个要点或方面。现在用例子来说明，首先看连续使用三个词组成句的做法：

- We need more doctors, nurses and hospitals.
- You've run out of steam, run out of ideas and run out of time.
- 我非常喜欢我的母校，师资优秀、设备精良、学生勤奋。
- 英国早期有莎士比亚，后来出了湖畔诗人，如今的是杰基·罗兰。

现在看借助"三"构思三个要点或者三个方面内容的例子：

- I plan to do three things. I'll start with my analysis of the cause of the problem. I'll then focus on one particular area of pain. Finally, I'll offer a few thoughts on how the problem may be resolved.
- If you look round the globe, you'll see three different pictures. The EU is unlikely to see growth of any significance. The US is showing signs of recovery. The emerging markets are continuing their boom.
- The success of the project depends on three sources of input. The senior management needs to guide the project design. The project team needs to conduct thorough research. Individual members of the team need to be idea generators.

"三"的概念渗透在文化中，无论是讲英语的西方世界，还是中国都有很多"三"的运用和利用。有限于本课主题，不做更多描述。有兴趣者可以通过本课结尾的工作坊进一步探讨。

如何处理人称

交传里除非有特殊情况，否则应该使用第一人称，即以讲者的身份说话。比较常见的特殊情况是译员同时为多名讲者口译，而且每人的话都不长。这时就需要采用第三人称以清楚地表明是谁在说哪段话。

第一人称里有复数，交传时能有三大用途。第一是以"我们"代替一个组织的名称，即如果讲者就是该组织的代表或者成员。也就是说，如果讲者是美国政府官员而且原话是"The US government…"，译员也可以将之处理为"我们……"。比如，在会议或者其他活动的问答时间段里，提问者往往需要自报家门，这时经常听到译员不熟悉的名字，如果使用第一人称复数往往能以"我们"化险为夷。

第二是如果讲者所代表的组织机构名称是缩写字面的话，由于不熟悉的缩写名字很难做好笔记，译员可以用第一人称复数给自己解围，不必按照原话把缩写名称说全。

第三是听到英语里"there is"和"there are"这种结构时，也可以用第一人称解围。比如，如果讲者说："there are 500 staff in our company"，译员可以将之处理为"我们有500名员工"。

交传里也有需要采用第三人称的时候，这往往发生在译员需要在一个时间段里为不止一位讲者口译的情况下。这种情况的发生往往是第一位讲者说完之后译员尚未来得及口译就有第二位讲者插了几句话，译员在传译时不得不采用第三人称区分译出语来自于两位不同讲者。

与讲者的关系

译员与讲者之间不是简单的"你说我译"这种被动关系，而是互动。虽然译员是在为讲者服务，但是要想达到服务的高质量，译员就必须学会什么时候需要掌控讲者以及如何掌控。

大多数讲者都没有受过如何使用交传译员的培训，许多人不是忘了译员而说个没完，就是过分小心，一次只说半句话，给译员准确把握讲者的意思带来困难。在这两种情况下，译员都必须告诉讲者如何行事。前者必须打断，后者必须告诉讲者至少把一句话说完，当然需要注意礼貌。

口译领域常常听说某某前辈或者大腕在讲者连续讲了10几分钟之后仍然能保证交传质量。因此，有些口译培训课也努力训练学生能够在没有笔记的情况下连续交传7–10分钟的能力。这种做法值得商榷。

首先，讲者讲话时间过长，势必给译员的记忆带来过分压力，导致交传的准确程度不可持续。其次，交传里无法打断讲者的情况是例外，不是惯例。在大多数情况下，译员都可以打断讲者。部长可以打断，总理、总统也不是绝对不可以打断，更不用说董事长和总裁了。

总之，能否打断，什么场合可以或者不可以打断是个需要根据具体情况做出的判断，不是个绝对可以还是不可以的问题。虽然打断领导不合适，但是没有准确地传达领导的意图更不合适。这是个把握平衡的问题。没有非黑即白的答案，需要在可以打断的前提下注意不可打断的例外。

既然不可打断是例外，把例外作为惯例来培训，甚至在口译培训的初期就如此要求有点像要求刚学游泳的人就能够一口气游很长距离一样。

如何处理讲稿

事先获得讲稿既可能起到帮助作用，也可能适得其反。从理论上说，译员应该总是争取事先拿到讲稿，但是口译时不能依赖讲稿。

首先，很少出现讲者完全按照稿子逐字朗读的情况。通常情况下，讲者都会在念稿的同时增加临时想起的话，或者跳跃式地使用讲稿。这就给译员使用讲稿带来极大的困难，因为译员不知道讲者什么时候脱稿，也不知道讲者什么时候重回讲稿以及回到哪里。如果译员翻找讲稿，就无法保持笔记，而笔记不全就很有可能导致口译信息不全的结果。

译员得到讲稿可以有两种处理方法，如果是很早就拿到讲稿，可以把讲稿分割成自然段，打印出来贴在笔记页上，每页只贴一段，而且是贴在上半页，留出下半页可以在讲者加字的时候补充笔记。这样每页一段，很容易判断讲者是否脱稿。而且如果讲者跳跃讲稿，译员也能快速翻页跟上。

如果拿到讲稿之后没有时间贴页，最好是采用视译的方法。时间够就视译到熟练，时间不够哪怕视译一遍也能减少口译时的难度。

应对听众的挑战

面临听众当场挑战是交传独有的特性，同传没有这种局面。听众挑战既可能是良性的，也可能是恶性的。良性的挑战是听众以善意纠正译员或者为译员做出提示，对于译员来说很有帮助。恶性挑战的目的是为了贬低译员在听众面前的形象，扰乱译员的阵脚。恶性挑战无论是否合理都会给译员带来很大困难。

挑战译员的听众有两种，一种是"守门人"，另外一种是"敌对者"。前者往往是会议或者活动的具体负责人，他们要为当天会议或者活动的成功担负个人责任，所以对交传质量产生了过分的要求。

所谓过分要求指对于译员的准确程度要求超过了交传本身的特性。比如，讲者说"good morning"，译员说："大家早"，听众打断译员说："不准确，应该译成早上好"。虽然译员的传译没有达到精确的水准，但是不会有误解，无伤大雅，没有必要纠正。

最常见的"守门人"有政府或者公司里的中国（或者对外）事务经理、双语水平比较高的中层经理、陪同领导的外办主任、负责培训的人力资源经理等。

"敌对者"是那些由于种种原因有意为难译员的人，有些是客户方的员工为了在上司面前显示自己的双语或者业务知识；有些是在场的其他译员，打压执行任务的译员是为了抬高自己；有些是对立方，比如在法庭或者听证会上，一方的律师会尽量争取译员的译法听上去对己方有利，否则就会打断译员提出自己的译法。

还有一种常见情况是听众并没有直接挑战译员，而是在下面交头接耳，很容易给译员留下可能错译或者听众不满的印象。

听众挑战会产生两个直接后果，首先会给译员带来巨大的心理压力。交传本来就是一种无法验证的工作，除非当场有录像，然后马上回顾，否则听众说你错了很难以证据反驳。其次，无论挑战是否合理，都会在一定程度上影响听众对译员的信心。所以，对于听众挑战必须认真地、系统地应对，不能当作意外情况，也不能不经过培训而临时应付。上述讲解是为了帮助译员理解听众挑战的类型和原因，以下讲解如何建立起应对系统，如何在出现挑战时冷静处理。

应对挑战的体系一共有五个组成部分：首次接触、保持镇静、分别处理、避免道歉、高度集中。

首次接触。预防是最好的应对方式。交传里往往越是新手越经常遇到挑战，虽然这在一定程度上是因为新手出错较多，但是出错不是最主要的原因。前面已经分析过了，恶性挑战的主要动机不是纠正错误。另外，第四课里讲解过，新手往往从执行任务开始的第一时间，即与客户联系人见面，进入会议室或者活动场所的第一时间就从声音、肢体语言以及言谈举止里缺少自信，等于是邀请听众挑战自己。如何纠正也已经在第四课（交传任务）里讲解过了，这里不重复。

保持镇静。译员需要做好两件事以保持镇静。首先，从思想上明确自己的重要角色。译员不是一般的服务人员，译员口译时是代表讲者说话。讲者的地位越高，译员开口时的地位也越高。所以，没有必要被别人指使去做其他事情。如果有人要求译员帮助发材料或者复印会议文件，除非时间非常充裕，一般都应该婉言谢绝，说明自己的身份，说明自己必须随时待命，不能轻易离开所处的地点。其次是培养会议或者活动开始前10分钟的镇静能力，这10分钟内往往气氛会突然热烈起来，工作人员人数突然增加，来往频率突然上升，译员的心跳也会随之加快。如果事先准备充分，就尽量排除脑子里的各种杂念，不去想今天的口译内容，不去想象可能会发生什么问题。相反，在选定的站立或者坐的地点集中精力做深呼吸，直至需要开始口译。

分别处理。如果听众提出挑战，译员必须马上确定挑战是否合理，即属于下述哪种情况：合理、不合理、不敢确定。如果合理或者不敢确定，就必须马上接受，纠正自己，然后接着往下译。如果挑战不合理，争取不予理睬，继续往下译便可。如果无法不予理睬，就极其简单地说明为什么不敢苟同，然后继续往下译。

- "我觉得这里不是那个意思"（不做更正，接着往下译）
- "我刚才的处理也是可以的"（不做更正，接着往下译）
- "好的，知道了"（不做更正，接着往下译）

出现挑战时要避免道歉，尽量在没有道歉的情况下，继续往下译。继续往下译是关键。

最后也是最难做到的就是在面临挑战的时候强迫自己更加高度集中精力听、记、译，强迫自己不要去评估自己，不要去反思挑战的内容或者想象听众对自己的看法。只要能够成功地集中精力本身就能避免挑战带来的心理压力，避免越慌越错，无法发挥应有的水平。当然，这是说起来容易，做起来难。所以需要从培训交传开始就注意训练，从"四别"（尤其是别露馅）的培训开始。

控制紧张

学员和新译员的一大障碍就是过度紧张并且因此发挥不出日常水平，由于任务当天发挥不好，下次任务就更加紧张，形成恶性循环。如何控制紧张是交传培训的重要内容之一，必须有系统地培训，不能留给学员或者译员自己去慢慢解决。

控制紧张可以分两步走：第一步是真正理解紧张的根源，第二步是建立起控制紧张的体系。

交传时的紧张主要有两个根源。首先是对于未知的担忧，既担忧"四没"（没听见、没听懂、没记下、没思路），又担忧发生"四没"时不知道怎么应对。紧张的第二个根源非常容易理解，太容易理解了反而很少受到注意，那就是大多数人都少有在大庭广众面前演讲的经历或者培训，而交传恰恰就是在大庭广众面前演讲。由于缺少经验又没有培训，不感到过分紧张反倒是不正常。这点在本课第一节里已经讲解过了。

知道了紧张的根源也就有了解决的办法。除了培训当众即席发表讲话的技能之外，就是要减少"四没"的几率。虽然语言和知识都需要长期积累，逐渐进步，但是如果交传任务之前准备充分，完成前次任务之后注意事后学习，如此循序渐进，就能大大减少"四没"发生的可能性，增强译员信心，从而比较顺利地完成任务。每次任务完成之后都能形成良性循环，增加下一次任务时的信心，减少紧张。如何做好充分准备在第四课里有详细的解释，这里不再重复。

本课小结

交传译员需要一组辅助技能。由于做简短即席演讲所需的能力与译员边看笔记、边组织思路、边口译的能力很相近，所以是必不可少的培训内容。译员必须善于处理人称、讲稿以及和讲者的关系。除此之外，译员还必须掌握应对听众挑战和控制紧张情绪的技能。

工作坊

全班采用大脑风暴的形式，群策群力地想出与"三"有关的事务或者概念，无论古今中外。同时，由一人写在书写板上。比如，西方有基督教里的三位一体，政体里的三权分立。中国有三足鼎立、三字经、三人行必有我师。

第八课　使用笔记

使用笔记是交传的四大核心技能之一，不是选项，对于译员持续保证交传质量至关重要。常用笔记记录有三大形式：写字、划符、划线。所写之字既可以是译出语，也可以是译入语。

持续保证质量的概念指译员可以每天交传 8 小时，连续一周；或者一天里工作 10 个小时而口译质量自始至终没有明显变化。虽然偶尔也有例外，但是绝大多数人都无法依靠自然记忆力胜任这样的马拉松式的任务。如果译员笔记熟练，就能大大减少对记忆的使用，减少对脑力的使用，大大延长持续高质量交传的时间。

使用笔记（英文为 the use of notes）与做笔记（英文为 note-taking）是不同概念，不能混淆。使用笔记的概念由四个内容组成：

- 建立笔记体系
- 做笔记（英文为 note-taking）
- 利用笔记、记忆和知识的互动做交传
- 演变、改善笔记体系

欧洲口译界在英文里常常使用 note-taking 这个词，显示出对笔记的角色认识不足。Note-taking 意思是做笔记，这只是笔记使用的一个组成部分。这个概念上的模糊常常导致交传培训时过度注意如何记笔记，而不是培训把笔记、记忆和知识结合起来的运用。而且由于孤立地看待做笔记这一个环节，影响了使用笔记能力的整体提高。

笔记的作用

很多人都以为笔记的作用是补充短期记忆，笔者在 2004 年出版的《实战口译》里也有类似的说法。但是，笔记的作用还有很多需要研究、了解之处。本课内容是笔者的最新认识。

译员使用笔记是为了通过笔记与短期记忆和已有知识的互动，达到完整的传译讲者原话，传达原话效果的目的。笔记能起到这样的作用原因在于：首先，比较理想的笔记能反映出原话的逻辑结构和部分细节内容，姓名、数字、单位都属于笔记里的细节内容。其次，如果笔记采用了译入语的文字或者符号，则已经是口译的半成品，直接有助于在译入语里的表达。再次，笔记有助于弥补知识的不足。比如：越是译员感到生疏的信息，就越是需要更多地记录原话的内容。最后，笔记越详尽，对于知识的依赖就越小，短期记忆的负担就越轻，从而有利于译员保证长时间交传时的质量。

笔记、记忆和知识的关系可以从以下三个极端情景来看。如果译员笔记神速，讲者所有的话都能记录下来，那就无需短期记忆和知识的补充。如果译员短期记忆近乎十全十美，那就无需笔记和知识的补充。年轻人做交传就时常出现接近于这种情景的情况。如果译员知识详尽，对讲者想说的每个词、每句话都了如指掌，那就无需笔记或者记忆的补充。这种情景往往是这样的：英国公司向中国公司代表团介绍一台先进机器，负责介绍的是英国公司的总经理，但是担任交传的是公司里的中国工程师。由于工程师对于机器的了解远远超过总经理，所以不是传译总经理的介绍，而是根据自己的知识在做介绍。

不过上述三种情景都是假设，绝大多数译员都是利用笔记、记忆和知识的互动做交传，只是三者的比例不同。总体来说，刚学交传时往往年轻，记忆力很好，但是笔记刚入门，很不成熟，而且知识有限。所以，交传时主要仰赖记忆，辅之以笔记和知识。随着实践的增加，笔记逐渐成熟，知识量有了很大的增加，但是随着年龄的增长，记忆力开始下降。所以，交传时越来越多地仰赖笔记和知识，辅之以有限的记忆力。请看下页示意图。

由于在笔记、记忆和知识之间有这种关系，所以只要有熟练的笔记、良好的记忆，再加上熟练的交传技能（包括如何在任务之前做好充分的准备），原来不熟悉某项专业内容的职业译员也可以胜任专业内容的交传任务，而且往往还能做得比虽然专业知识丰富，但是交传技能和记忆力都比较弱的专业人士。

示意图：笔记、记忆和知识的关系
（三者之间的比例是为了说明概念，不是准确地划分）

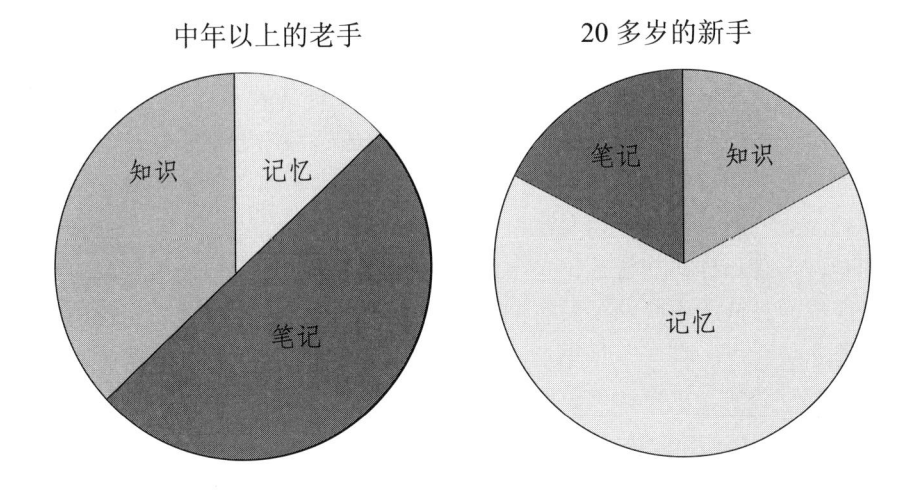

中年以上的老手　　　　　　20多岁的新手

知识　记忆　笔记　　　　　笔记　知识　记忆

笔记极限

  笔记极限指的是交传译员在标准环境里的最大记录量。所谓标准环境指的是讲者以标准速度说话而且译员全部都能听懂。所谓标准速度指的是平均每秒3个英文单词，或者是4–5个汉字。英国广播公司BBC的新闻主持人播音时采用的就是标准速度，所有新闻的编写也全部采用标准速度来确定所需编写的英文字数。

  虽然没有大量的科学实验作为证据，但是每秒3个英文单词似乎是一般人大脑处理英语信息的平均速度。而相应的汉语处理速度则为每秒4–5个汉字。在这个速度之下会让人感到语速较慢，而超过这个速度会让人感到语速快，听不清楚，即大脑处理的速度跟不上。

  由于无论在笔记时采用字、线还是符，都需要有个听到、听懂、反应、记录的过程。有时由于遇到了熟悉的内容并且采用熟悉的笔记方式，则所需时间较短。而当遇到了不太熟悉的内容或者笔记，则所需时间较长。平均起来基本上是每秒1个笔记（无论是一个字、一条线还是一个符号）。

  由此推理，对于绝大多数人来说，笔记的平均速度极限就是每秒1个笔记，即每3个英文单词，或者4–5个汉字1个笔记。笔记极限这个概念为交传笔记提供了一个可以量化的起点。当然，笔记极限的概念如果要在理论上做到有证可查，还需要有实证研究。

记什么？

无论是中国，还是在西欧口译界，在笔记记录什么这个问题上都存在着重大误区。其中最有代表性的概念就是"笔记必须记录讲话的重点"，这是个从西欧进口的概念。西欧双语的译员很多，即需要对译的两种语言都是译员的母语。对他们来说，听力和理解没有障碍。所以，听完之后判断哪些词或者概念是重点不成问题。

但是，尽管那样，交传笔记也不能以"记录讲话的重点"为指导，因为讲者的话是线性而且持续不断的，只有到一个句子结束时才能比较准确判断句中哪个词或者概念是重点，哪些不是重点。也就是说，判断重点必须回顾之前所言，才能进行比较。否则，讲者话里说的每个意群都会听上去像是重点。比如，如果讲者逐字说出这句话："We don't condole international terrorism whether it's dressed up as political ideology or religious belief"，译员会觉得几乎每个意群都很重要，不记不行。请看以下演示：

在听到这个词时	译员的直觉	很可能的反应
We…	"主语重要"	必须记
Don't…	"否定概念不能错，重要"	必须记
Condole…	"动作是关键内容，重要"	必须记
International Terrorism…	"宾语，重要"	必须记
Whether it's dressed up as…	"主语和谓语，重要"	必须记
Political ideology	"关键词和概念，重要"	必须记
Or religious belief.	"关键词和概念，重要"	必须记

另外从理念上看，记录讲话的重点也有悖笔记的初衷。使用笔记是为了减少对记忆力的使用。但是如果不得不随时判断听到的词是否重要，就不得不把刚听到的某个词与之前听到的其他词做比较，判定相对重要性。这不仅需要使用短期记忆，还不停地做出判断，增加了大脑的负担。

有人会说，译员掌握了方法之后，判断重点就成了习惯，无需多想。但这种看法忽略了前面提到的双语能力的问题。如果笔记仰赖于对于原话重点的判断,那么中国初学交传的人,或者在听英文时会遇到困难的人就无法正确使用笔记了,这等于说国内大多数学笔记的人都难以掌握笔记。所以,"记讲话的重点"这个从西欧进口的概念不适用于中国目前阶段的国情。

交传的笔记必须能够在记忆和知识的配合之下尽量全面地反映原话的内容,不是记下一些关键词或者重点内容,也不是用一系列符号取代某些词或者字的简单程序。要想全面地反映原话的内容光能记下一些字或者符号还不够,还必须在笔记里反映出这些字或者符号之间的关系以及整段话的逻辑结构。

所以首先,交传笔记必须是一个经过设计、演练的体系,而且必须不断演化。其次,在交传时,笔记与记忆和知识互动,而不是取代记忆和知识。再次,交传笔记是为了传译,不是阅读,所以必须一目了然。另外,只要译员本人能通过使用而完成交传任务便可,不必考虑他人是否看得懂,甚至自己是否事后能看懂。与一般概念里的速记不同,速记必须每个符号和标记都认真阅读,这反而有碍交传。

所以,交传笔记就是要在笔记极限的范围之内,尽量多记,在全面地反应原话内容的同时尽量减少给记忆带来的压力。在实战中,这相当于每3个英文单词(英译汉)或者4—5个汉字(汉译英)记一个笔记,这个笔记即可以是字,也可以是线或者符号。

至于这每3个英文单词中记哪个没有必要过分追究。首先,凭借对于英文的理解就能很自然地感觉到哪个单词相对重要。比如,看到 in front of, the importance of 这样的词组,凭感觉就知道需要记哪个词,无需思考。其次,无论记录下3个单词中的哪一个,剩下的都能够从记忆中或者在知识的配合下回忆出来。比如,在 turn off the light 这个词组中,无论记 turn 还是 light,在其他笔记的背景下,加上记忆和知识,都可以回忆出原话。

由于上述原因,在练习笔记时,必须养成一个意群里不超过一个笔记的习惯。即:在 turn off the light 这个意群里一定不要 turn off 和 light 都记。这是因为如果前一个意群多记一个笔记,势必占用了下一个笔记的时间,等于下一个笔记少记一个。笔记的总量由于笔记极限而没有,也无法增加。如果译员所处的不是标准环境,则笔记的速度就会下降,就需要更多地使用记忆和知识的支持。

英译汉和汉译英的笔记需要采用不同的策略,这是由于两种语言的性质不同而造成的。

不同策略

用于英汉两种语言本质的不同，英译汉和汉译英的笔记策略也不得不同。原话为英语里最常见的基本句子结构为：

主 + 谓 + 宾

在这种结构下，笔记一般采用：表示主语的字或者符号 + 表示动作的线条 + b 表示宾语的字或者符号。所以，英译汉的笔记可以基本不必以字，而是全部用线条代表动词。

原话为汉语时则不同。由于汉语句子里常常出现多个动词连续使用的情况，比如：继续坚持打击犯罪行为。如果都用线条，就容易出现连续几个线条的情况，给全面、准确地回忆原话带来困难。所以，汉译英时，如果以译出语做笔记，如果听到第二个动作仍然采用线条就会增加事后不解或者误解的可能性。

交传笔记里常听到的一个问题是用哪种语言做笔记更好，是译出语还是译入语。从理论上讲，采用译出语可以加快记录速度，采用译入语由于需要把译出语转换成译入语，所以记录速度会稍慢，而且这个稍慢是个相对概念。

如果是一个在双语里都很熟悉的概念，则无论用哪种语言做笔记都没有可以明显感觉到的差别。但如果是一个在译出语里不熟悉的概念，就需要一点时间稍作思考。或者是一个在译入语里不熟悉的概念，则需要稍作思考才能决定在译入语里如何做笔记。在这后两种情况下，为了不影响笔记速度，不影响继续听后续的话，最好以译出语记，把转换成译入语时所需的思考留到口译时完成。

这里讲解的是笔记策略的原则，即在标准环境下的策略。实战中情况会比课本上看到的复杂。比如，讲者的速度，声音的大小，口音的轻重，译员相对于讲者所处的位置，这些因素都会影响到译员的听，随即影响到笔记。所以，这里讲解的原则只是为学习提供目标，实战中所需的随机应变的技能还要通过培训掌握。

安德鲁·吉里斯体系

安德鲁·吉里斯于 2005 年出版了《交传笔记：短课》一书（St Jerome, Manchester, UK），成为过去 30 年来第一本详细论述交传笔记的英文教材，是了解西欧交传笔记使用的很好材料。但是，安德鲁在书中论述的理念和做法（以下简称安德鲁法）很明显地基本上完全以西欧的实践为基础。由于交传在西欧的使用无论是范围，还是深度都远远不如中国，西欧职业译员的语言水平和中国译员也无法直接相比，所以安德鲁法里的不少重要内容都不适用于中国。

首先是其基本理念。安德鲁法要求译员在听到讲话之后经过思考决定记什么，不记什么。他说："不要在没听完一段话之前就开始做笔记"（第 75 页："You should listen to a whole 'chunk' before noting anything"）由于绝大多数中国译员的英语都不如汉语，在英译汉时经常遇到没听懂，或者有生词的情况，安德鲁所要求的这种整体思考势必导致译员被卡住。

其次是笔记的形式。比如：安德鲁笔记法里使用了很多所有字母都拼写出来的单词，连人名都全部写出。绝大多数中国译员恐怕英文书写速度都达不到安德鲁的要求，而且除了常见的英文人名、地名以外，绝大多数中国译员都无法听到一个英文名字就能全部拼写出来（如何拼写撒切尔？萨科奇？蒙哥马利？麦克耐马拉？）。

最后是操作层面。安德鲁建议译员使用 A4 大笔记本。这仅适用于坐在会议桌前做交传，不适用于中国交传译员经常需要应对的场合。他们既可能坐在会议桌前，也可能需要站在没有讲台的主席台上，或者坐在摆满刀叉餐具的餐桌前，有时还不得不手持无线话筒做交传。在上述这些情况下，A4 大笔记本会给译员带来很大的困难。

笔记技能

笔记技能由笔记设计、记录形式、瞬间创作、随机应变四个部分组成。前两者更多的是技巧，后两者更多的是能力。

笔记设计既要考虑记什么、怎么记，也要考虑怎么用、怎么应变，不是一般概念里的听到某个词就用某个符号那种对号入座的概念。瞬间创作能力指译员在需要记录现有笔记体系里没有的内容时必须能够在瞬间决定采用什么形式做笔记以及记成什么样。随机应变指的是虽然译员需要记录的内容已经包括在现有的笔记体系中，但是由于种种原因，无法按照体系里的形式记录下来。比较常见的原因有：前一个概念比较生疏，译员采用瞬间创作法记录，耽误了时间，来不及把下一个已经熟悉的内容记录下来。

现在举一个实际例子，译员听到了这段话：

"Climate change concerns us all. Business as Usual is not an acceptable way forward. Not for WTO, or WHO or UNDP or any other international organizations."

译员现有笔记体系里有 WTO、WHO 和 UNDP 的记录形式，但是没有"Business as Usual"，不得不临时创作一个记录形式，因此耽误了时间。等到记完了"Business as Usual"，已经到了必须记录 UNDP 的时候，所以无法按照体系里的现成方案记录 WTO 和 WHO。

影响笔记的常见原因不仅有讲者的速度，还有词汇搭配。在英文里，WTO 可能与很多其他词汇搭配使用，比如：

- WTO led
- WTO driven
- WTO sponsored
- WTO engineered
- WTO approved
- Pre-WTO time
- Pro-WTO stance
- Anti-WTO demonstration

即使译员的现有体系里已经有了 WTO 的记录形式，但很可能没有上述所有搭配组合的记录形式，这就可能出现译员在听到 WTO 之后无法按照现有体系记录而不得不瞬间创作或者完全跳过 WTO 不记的情况。

缺少对笔记体系的总体认识，形成"听到什么、怎么记录"这种对号入座的认识和培训方式容易导致笔记培训了相当长的时间仍然用不上或者用不好。首先，笔记不是讲者原话的浓缩版，除了套话，不能简单地对号入座。

其次，只有把体系的三个组成部分同时培训，才能保证能边学边用、随学随用、学得越多用得越好。由于瞬间创作和随机应变基本上完全是一种能力，需要在实际操作中培训的技能，所以这里只讲解如何决定记录形式。不过必须强调的是交传笔记的培训一定要注重瞬间创作和随机应变的训练。

建立体系

交传笔记的建立有三个步骤：

- 设计:根据一组指导原则,设计记什么、如何记。
- 演练:把设计出来的笔记练习多遍,直至熟练。
- 演变:在使用过程中如果发现有更好的笔记方式就改善过去设计的笔记。

初学者往往是经过设计的笔记很少,经常需要瞬间创作笔记,随机应变。随着经过设计的笔记总量不断增加,瞬间创作的频率会不断下降,使译员感觉更加从容。

设计笔记时需要遵从 6 大原则:

1. 少写多划
2. 少字多意
3. 少线多指
4. 少横多竖
5. 快速书写
6. 明确结束

这 6 大原则由笔者在 2005 年由外研社出版的《实战口译》一书里首次提出,至今仍然适用。以下的讲解增加了对于这些原则如何理解、使用的最新内容。

少写多划:意思是少写字,多划线条以代之。首先,划线条比写文字快。比如:以带半箭头的上升斜线代表"发展""增加","改善"就比写这些词快。

同理,可以用带半箭头的下降斜线代表"减少""下降""恶化"等等。

其次,划线条可以把原话里词组所表达的关系用视觉的形式展示出来,便于译员一目了然。既加快了笔记速度,又由于笔记相当于半成品而减轻了从笔记里回忆出原话的难度。比如,采用带有箭头的横线表示先后关系,其中的箭头方向表示关系的方向（参见下页表格中的例子）。

```
主语              谓语           宾语
(动作发出者)  →   (动作)    →   (动作的对象)
```

少字多意：意思是以一个字代表多个字或者词，不要也不能每个字、词都去设计一个独特的笔记法。中文是你的母语、英语是你的第二语言，这两种语言你都不用，而是去设计一个自己完全陌生的第三语言用作笔记，有点像作茧自缚。

少字多意有两大用途。首先是同义词。比如，听到英文的 now、currently、at the moment、at present 可以通用一个笔记，口译到汉语里也往往是同一个词。另外，比如：international 和 world 也可以是一个笔记。由于 international 有时需要译成"世界"，而 world 有时也需要译成"国际"，所以采用同一笔记形式不仅减少需要记忆的笔记，加快笔记速度，而且不影响口译质量。

少字多意的第二个用途是以一个汉字代表一个词，甚至是一个词组。比如："改革开放"只要记一个"改"就能从知识里说出改革开放。写一个"社"字就能从知识里说出社会主义，再加上记忆的补充就能说出社会主义建设或者社会主义国家。

如果两个词比较相近但又需要有所区别，可以用同一个笔记方法但是增加一个很简单的符号以作区别。比如：无论是"我"还是"我们"都可以用一个笔记，然后在其右下角用闪电符号来表示复数的"我们"。这样的好处是如果来不及写闪电符合，就留给记忆去补充，而不必每次听到我或者我们都采用不同的笔记。

在有些情况下，可以充分利用上下文以及知识来补充笔记。比如，developed and developing countries 就可以记成：

Dev

Dev

口译时，很容易想起一个是发达国家，另外一个是发展中国家。

少线多指：意思是通用一小组线条来代表众多的意思，表示不同的关系。这与少字多意的道理一样。以下是最常用的一组线条：

线条	名称	表示
——	短横线	左右两边的内容相关
(	下划线	上下内容相关
∠	下折线	上述内容的继续 或者上下内容相关
—→	右行半箭头	向右发出的行动 或者先于右边内容
←—	左行半箭头	向左发出的行动 或者后于右边的内容
↓	下行半箭头	向下发出的行动 或者先于下面的内容
∫	小闪电符号	表示强调以及出于 其他原因需要做的提醒

少横多竖：指的是采取从上往下的结构做笔记，尽量少用通常书写时的横向记录。从上往下记能够从视觉上形象地体现出上下笔记内容之间的逻辑结构，有助于译员眼看笔记，口出译语。比如：如果需要连续用几个单字记录排列的内容时，横向记录的单字不容易断定他们是否属于同一意群，容易把自己搞糊涂。而排列内容如果竖着记，则每个字一行，每行为一个意群。译员看到一个字，就知道需要说出一个意群。比如：

"The programme was rolled out in all workshops, factories and offices"

如果"workshops, factories and offices"横着记，很容易形成"车工办"这种局面，导致口译时感到迟疑，不知道笔记所指是"车工""办"，还是"车""工"

办"。但是如果竖着记，显然每个字都代表一个意群：

车
工
办

快速书写：意思是书写速度必须符合交传的要求，大大超过日常书写的速度。提高书写速度有三大基本方法。首先是简少汉字笔划，其次是理顺汉字笔划的顺序，最后是英文字母不过三，即：如果笔记使用英文，则每个笔记所写的字母不要超过三个。而且最好不是顺序的前三个字母，短词往往首写和末尾字母便可，较长的词加中间一个辅音字母写起来也很快，很容易辨认。当然这些都需要设计、演练、演变。请看以下例子：

Ld — lead, leader or leadership

Ldn — London

plt — parliament

PR — public relations, political reform

以下是几个汉字减少、理顺笔划的例子，高、好、国、重、建可以设计写成：

很多汉字里的笔划都不起到关键作用，省略之后不影响识别。汉字的行书里就有很多这样的例子，草书更不用说。英文字母在记忆和知识的协助下也可以大大减少。

明确结束：意思是在每段笔记的尾部采用难以误解的形式来表明结束之处，以便笔记结束开始口译时能够迅速地找到笔记的开始之处，这在一页里记录多段话时尤其重要。比如，如果笔记是从本子的 1/3 处开始的，下一段话可能写了 2-3 页，翻回来口译时，眼光无法确定这页上面哪一条线，哪个符号是本段口译内容的开始点。

以下是三种不同的结束点记法：

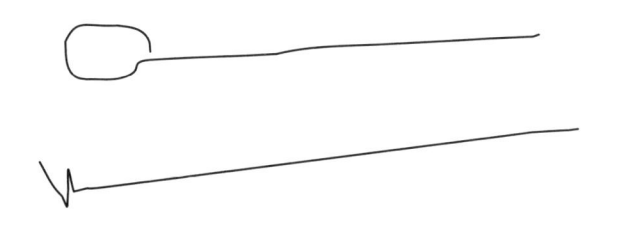

本课小结

使用笔记是交传的一个关键技能。记笔记只是使用笔记的一个组成部分,译员必须学会利用笔记、记忆和知识的互动来保证持续交传的质量。建立笔记体系的三大步骤是:设计、演练、演变。设计时需要遵从 6 大原则,这些原则依此是:少写多划、少字多意、少线多指、少横多竖、快速书写、明确结束。

工作坊

1. 录制一段英国或者美国主要媒体的新闻广播,将内容打字记录下来,然后用 Word 里的数字功能得出与每秒广播相对应的单词字数。

2. 如果有安德鲁·吉里斯的书,则把他的理念与本课的理念在以下方面做过比较:
- 对于讲者、译员和听众所作的基本假设
- 这三方的双语水平
- 译员所处的实际环境
- 译员需要或者可以使用的设备(比如麦克风)
- 笔记体系的建立方法
- 译员如何使用笔记做交传
- 译员在开始建立笔记体系之前需要掌握的知识
- 任何其他你注意到的安德鲁法与本课讲解内容的不同之处。

第九课　笔记演示

第八课讲解了如何设计笔记，本课以四段讲话来具体演示笔记如何记（包括已设计过的和瞬间创作的笔记），如何通过笔记、知识和记忆的互动做交传。

这段话的全文如下：

第一段

　　My Lords, Your Excellencies, Ladies and Gentleman, the Lord Mayor is head of the City of London Corporation which provides local government services for the Square Mile. It's an unusual place, with only 8,000 residents, but over 300,000 people coming to work here every day.

第二段

　　We provide all the usual local government services, but we also have an important role representing the needs of businesses located here. In elections for other local authorities the voters are all the local residents; here in the City the voters are a mixture of residents and voters from businesses located in each ward.

第三段

　　I imagine some of you here today are voters or might be in the future. This means that business has an electoral voice. The other difference in the City is that we all stand as independents and we are all unpaid.

第四段

　　As the business of the City is financial services, a key role of the Lord Mayor is representing the financial and related business community. But whilst the City is the historic centre of finance in UK, these days business is conducted all over London and throughout the UK.

这是伦敦金融城市长的一次讲话。根据交传任务的要求，译员必须事先做好以下准备：

- 掌握以下信息：伦敦金融城、现任市长、本次活动的主题以及主要嘉宾。
- 掌握本次活动的具体安排，如几点进行哪项内容
- 列出可能所需但尚不熟悉的词汇，在有限的时间内尽量记忆
- 采集有关伦敦金融城的材料练习视译
- 设计重点词汇的笔记，如：伦敦、金融城、金融城市长、平方英里（金融城的别称）、金融、金融服务，英国等

以下的笔记演示是以上述准备充分为前提的，演示内容分四栏讲解：

- 听到的话：是译员听到的讲者的话；
- 所用笔记：是译员经过大约30小时的培训可以达到的水平；
- 笔记讲解：描述的是如何利用知识（包括准备知识）与记忆的互动做出左边"所用笔记"一栏里看到的笔记；
- 交传版本：是交传译员根据知识、记忆和笔记的互动而说出的话。

这里必须强调两点。首先，笔记不是全面记录讲者的话，而是根据第八课的阐述，在每秒不超过一个笔记内容的限制之下所记录的原话的一部分内容。凡是笔记里没有的内容都必须靠译员的知识（包括准备知识）和记忆补齐。有时是无法记全，所以不得不把部分内容留给记忆。有时是可以从上下语里不难回忆出来，所以有意留给记忆。其次，所演示的笔记，即：记什么，没记什么，不是标准答案。每个译员的笔记，即使是听同一段讲话，都会不同。即使是同一位译员，分别两次听同一段话，也会两次的笔记不尽相同。交传笔记除了预先设计的笔记方式之外，都是瞬间创作的产物。哪些内容从笔记、哪些从知识、哪些从记忆回忆，根据第八课的原则培训就能够掌握。不要把以下演示的笔记当作公式背诵，不能对号入座，只能作为理解笔记设计的6大原则以及启发思路的参考。

听到的话	所用笔记	笔记讲解	交传版本
第一段			
My Lords, Your Excellencies, Ladies and Gentleman,	L͜ Ĺ Ĺ₅	每个称号只记一个笔记，而且竖着记。"女士们、先生们"是常用词组，应该预先设计。笔者有时采用右下角一般的小闪电符合以提醒自己这不是一般的 L。	勋爵们，诸位阁下，女士们，先生们，
the Lord Mayor is head of the City of London Corporation	L — Cit ↳ Loc	在准备时已经把 Lord Mayor 的笔记设计为一个 L。口译时根据知识和记忆说出 "金融城市长"。之后的 Cit 也是预先设计的笔记。用下折线加箭头表示 Cit 的动作，写 Loc 代表地方政府。	金融城市长是伦敦金融城政府的领导人。金融城政府为一平方英里的金融城提供地方政府的各项服务。
which provides local government services for the Square Mile.	↳ × pl⁻	此时听到 for the square mile，用一条上行箭头加箭头反指 Cit。	
It's an unusual place, with only 8,000 residents,	×pl⁻ — 8k	此时听到 it's...，知道还是指金融城。所以划一条下行折线表示关联。用 X 代表否定，此时听到 unusual，写 pl 代表 place。此时听到 with，划横线表示关联。此时听到 only 8000，写 8k。	金融城非同寻常，只有 8000 居民，
but over 300,000 people coming to work here every day.	>300k ↘	此时听到 over 300,000，写 300k。此时听到 coming to work here，知道与上述 place 相关。所以划一条反弓线条加箭头指向 place 表示关联。最后是结束符号。	但是有 3 万多人每天到这里上班。

第二段

听到的话	所用笔记	笔记讲解	交传版本
We provide all the usual local government services, but we also have an important role representing the needs of businesses located here.	ꝏ — loc ↙ R — Bᵤ	ꝏ 代表"我"或者"我们"，单复数由记忆补。听到 provide all，划左行线表示动作的方向。听到 usual local，"government services"留给记忆，主语同上，所以划线下来。also have，划右行线。听到 an important role，写 R 代表 role。此时听到 representing，知道是动作，加箭头表示动作方向。此时听到 the needs of business，写设计过的符号。Located here, 此时听到 loc。顺手划横线代表关联，另起一行写 Bᵤ。	我们提供地方政府提供的所有服务。但是我们扮演着代表当地商界的重要角色。
In elections for other local authorities, the voters are all the local residents;	El — loc V — Rₑₛ	听到 In elections，写 El；听到 for other，写 Loc；听到 voters，这是新内容，另起一行写 V。听到 local residents，写 Rₑₛ。	在地方选举中，投票人都是本地居民。
here in the City the voters are a mixture of residents and voters from businesses located in each ward.	Cit V — Rₑₛ ⟵ Bᵤ ᵂᵈ	听到 here in the City，新内容，另起一行写 Cit。听到 voters are，从前面的笔记下划线。听到 a mixture of 知道有两个内容，准备好竖写。听到 residents 和 Res。听到 voters，写 V。听到 from，写 V。听到 business，写设计过的 Bz。听到 located in each ward，写 wd。 最后是结束符号。	在金融城，投票人既有居民，也有每个选区的公司。

91

第三段

听到的话	所用笔记	笔记讲解	交传版本
I imagine some of you here today are voters or might be in the future.	8 — Sm — V。 mt — f	ዩ 表示"I"。听到 imagine，划横线表示动作的方向。听到 some of you，用设计过的 Sm 代表。听到 here today are voters，写 Vo 或者 V。听到 or，知道是另一层意思，所以坚着写。用 mt 代表 might。划横线表示关联。听到 future，写 F。	我想你们今天当中有些人就是或者将来可能成为投票人。
This means that business has an electoral voice.	∠B — EL voi	听到 this，知道与前述相关，划下折线。听到 business has，写 B。划横线表示关联。听到 electoral voice，写 El voi 或 voi。其余由记忆补。	这就是说商界在选举中有自己的声音。
The other difference in the City is that we all stand as independents and we are all unpaid.	oth — ℓ, — Ind G	听到 other difference，写设计过的 oth。听到 in the City，划横线表示关联，其余留给记忆。听到 is that we，写设计过的 I。听到 all stand，划横线表示关联，写 Ind。听到 as independents，知道主语相同，划下斜线。听到 unpaid，划又表示否定，写 P 代表 paid。最后是结束符号。	金融城与众不同的另外一点是我们都是独立候选人，都不拿工资。

第九课·笔记演示

第四段

听到的话	所用笔记	笔记讲解	交传版本
As the business of the City is financial services, a key role of the Lord Mayor is representing the financial and related business community.	B — Cit — Fs R — L — f + B	听到 As the business，写 B。听到 of the City，划横线表示关联，写 B。听到 is financial services，划横线然后写设计过的 Fs。听到 a key role，写 R，听到 of the Lord Mayor，划横线然后写 L。听到 is representing，划右指箭头表示动作方向。听到 the financial and，写 F+。听到 and related business，写 B。听到 community，留给笔记。	由于金融城的业务是金融服务，所以金融城市长的一个关键角色就是代表金融以及相关的社区。
But whilst the City is the historic centre of finance in UK, these days business is conducted all over London and throughout the UK.	M B — Lon [hu — Fuk G	听到 But whilst the City，知道主语相同，从上面拉下一条线，写 his。听到 of finance in UK，写设计过的 N 代表当今。听到 the historic centre，写 Fuk。听到 these days，写设计过的 N 代表当今。听到 business is conducted，写 B，划横线（也可划反向箭头）。听到 all over London，写 Lon。听到 throughout the UK，知道是重复前述的内容，所以划向上箭头指 uk。 最后是结束符号。	但是虽然金融城是英国传统上的金融中心，但是如今，金融业务遍布伦敦以及整个英国。

第十课　交传的培训

本课讲解交传的培训，其中既包括对于交传译员的培训，也包括对于交传技能的培训。首先需要区分什么叫学习，什么叫培训。两者有本质的区别，不可混淆。学习指的是学习有关交传的知识，培训指的是通过训练，掌握交传的技能（包括技巧）。前者更多的是靠阅读和思考，后者必须靠反复练习。前者培养的是能够研究、讲解交传的人，后者培养的是能够做交传的译员。

打个比方，学习有关武功的知识靠的是阅读和思考。但是如果想成为武功好手，就必须经过长期、艰苦的训练。学习有关高尔夫球的知识，研究高尔夫球要靠阅读和思考。但是要想成为优秀的高尔夫球手就必须经过长期、艰苦的训练。

在理想状况下，培训最好是量身定制，根据每个学员或者每组学员的具体情况设计、安排。但是由于写书的局限，本课只能提供原则和参考做法，需要由教师或者自学的学员决定适合自己需要的做法。

在此前的各课里有关交传的知识已经有了系统的介绍，可以根据培训课的时间表和培训生的情况安排课文的阅读和讨论，以达到掌握知识的目的。本课将集中精力介绍交传培训的以下四大方面：

1. 课程设计
2. 使用教材
3. 培训方法
4. 考核测试

课程设计

无论是为学位课程还是业余进修课程设计交传培训都必须清楚地区分有关译员的培训和有关交传技能的培训。这就要求大纲设计者从概念上清楚地区分什么是交传所需的知识，什么是交传所需的技能。比如，哪个表达法应该译成哪个表达法就属于语言知识，而如何把自己知道的知识表达出来才是技能。

举例：英语里的 climate change 在中文里是"气候变化"，这属于知识，不是技能。而如果译员听到 climate change 后能够按照应有的速度和语气说出"气候变化"属于技能。如果译员一时想不起来中文是"气候变化"时通过问、补、扔这三步法处理好这个词也属于技能。

要想成为一名优秀的交传译员至少需要有三组技能，缺少其中任何一组，或者一组当中的任何组成部分都将影响到交传译员能力和水平的提高。这三大组技能如下：

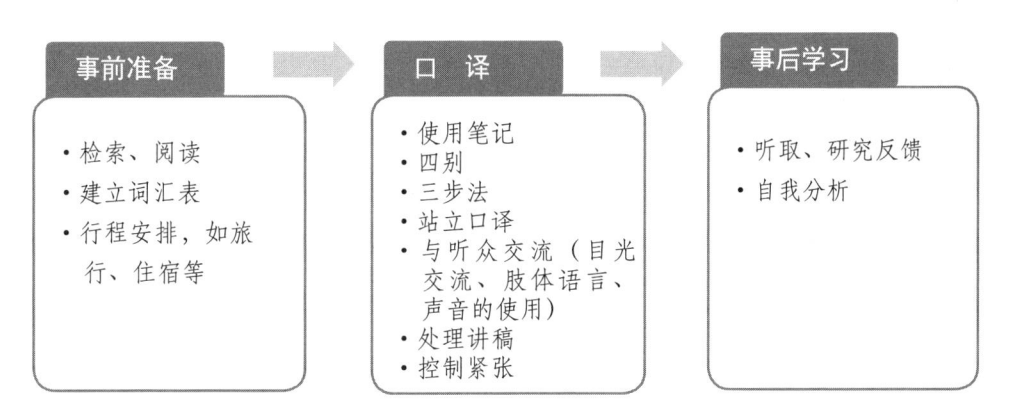

事前准备
- 检索、阅读
- 建立词汇表
- 行程安排，如旅行、住宿等

口译
- 使用笔记
- 四别
- 三步法
- 站立口译
- 与听众交流（目光交流、肢体语言、声音的使用）
- 处理讲稿
- 控制紧张

事后学习
- 听取、研究反馈
- 自我分析

以上示意图是从概念上说明技能培训的内容，是根据口译周期列出的，不包括其他与交传工作并行或者交叉的流程。比如，自由职业译员除了口译周期之外，还需要完成商业周期，即报价、确认、发付款通知、收款、做账、纳税等等。

有关事前准备和事后学习在第四课的口译周期里有详细介绍，建议在培训时把这两项放在交传模拟任务中培训。首先复习有关内容，然后让培训生在模拟中实施，最后由培训教师提供反馈。本课重点讲解口译中的技能（包括技巧）的培训。

由于交传需要以培训为主，学习知识为辅，交传培训大纲的设计首先必须考虑时间的保证。常规课程安排时间往往采用同样的模式：重要的课一次两节，每节 45–50 分钟不等，而且每周不超过两次。这种常规做法往往不适合于交传培训，由于课时太短，培训生刚刚练得有点感觉就下课了，一周以后再上课时几乎是重新开始。这样容易导致进三步退两步半的结局。

解决的办法有两个，一个是压缩，即：把可以安排的课时集中到几周内使用。比如，如果一个学期是 20 周，每周可以安排 2 小时，那就可以争取把这 40 小时压缩到 10 周内，每周一次，每次 4 小时，而不要每周 2 小时分散在 20 周里。采用压缩式可以为每次课堂的练习效果提供时间上的保证，再加上课堂练习时尽量为培训生多提供机会（稍后有介绍），就可以在很大程度上防止培训生在两次课之间感觉进三步，退两步半。

另外一个办法是加时，即增加分配给交传培训的课时。根据多年来的经验，如果课堂培训法使用得当，每周一次课，每次 4 小时便可以取得比较令人满意的效果。如果再加上适当的课下练习作业，也能够避免两次课期间退步的危险。

交传的培训过程建议分两大阶段：技能培训和实战模拟。具体内容于此后专门讲解。技能培训建议分成三个阶段：笔记的使用（约需 30 小时）、实际口译（约需 20 小时）、传达讲者的情感（约需 10 小时）。

由于交传是一个综合技能与知识的使用过程，在培训中虽然需要重点明确，循序渐进，但又无法避免各项技能的同时使用。所以，每个阶段的重点都是相对的。只要前一重点基本掌握就应该尽快引入下一阶段的重点。在两个重点的交接面上会出现两个重点兼有的时候，不过很快就会由于前一重点的掌握越来越好，培训时间越来越多地集中在后一重点上。笔记的使用、实际口译和传达讲者的情感这三个阶段将于之后详细解释。

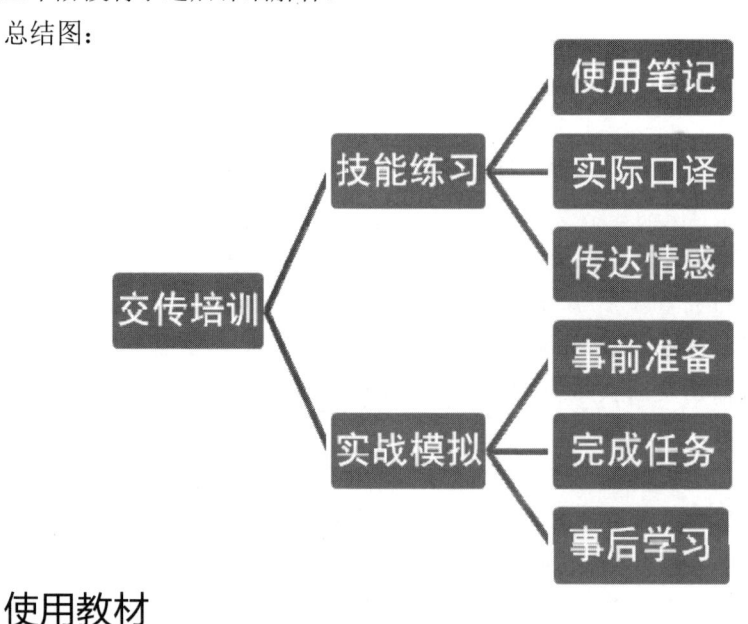

总结图：

```
                    ┌── 使用笔记
         ┌─ 技能练习 ─┼── 实际口译
         │          └── 传达情感
交传培训 ─┤
         │          ┌── 事前准备
         └─ 实战模拟 ─┼── 完成任务
                    └── 事后学习
```

使用教材

本教材内容由两大部分组成，明显区分知识学习和技能培训。

第一部分是按照理念阐述的逻辑为顺序，比较全面地讲解了交传各个方面的知识和技能。虽然有些课之后附有围绕该课主题的一些工作坊，提供练习的机会。但是这些练习并不是交传的实战练习，而是为了帮助学生加深对课文内容及其主要理念的理解和掌握，属于知识学习性质。交传技能培训的练习全部在本教材的第二部分。

第二部分由30个模拟实战的讲话组成，英译汉和汉译英各占一半。每个讲话分成8个自然段，每段的长度从开始时较短，到后来则较长，以增加难度。培训时可以根据课时安排和学生的进度决定每次上课的练习量。

与很多教材不同，本教材的注解部分内容相对较少。其目的是为了促使培训教师和培训生把每课都当作一次实战演练，大部分词汇都必须由培训生在课前准备里靠阅读解决，剩余生词必须采用第五课里的技能解决。培训教师应该争取避免提供标准答案，那样做无法帮助培训生掌握实战里的应对技能。具体操作方法在以下的"培训方法：任务周期"里还有介绍。

本教材的使用方法应该是知识学习部分由培训生自己课下阅读，上课以实际口译练习为主。培训教师可以根据培训生的表现或者出现的问题，使用知识部分里的概念作解释，提供答案，指导练习，解决问题。

如果是采用本教材自我培训也应该遵循这个原则，只不过需要自己承担培训教师的角色，仰赖自己的分析和判断能力。

一定要告诉培训生不要在课前看下次上课时将要用于培训的讲稿，也不要自己预先练习。交传培训是为了培训多种技能，如果预先自己练习，比如解决了所有语言问题，就会使课上有关口译时遇到难点的练习完全失去效果，导致培训生自己没有得到应有的收获。

参考译语

每个练习单元附带的参考译语都是根据交传实战的要求提供的，有四点需要说明。第一，由于交传里存在准确幅度（请看第二课）的情况，参考译语只是笔者认为属于准确幅度之内的诸多可能版本之一，不一定就是最佳版本。培训教师一定不可把参考译语作为标准答案，应该允许培训生采用任何在准确幅度之内的版本。第二，参考译语是根据笔者的理念而专门为交传提供的，不可用笔译的标准衡量。如果那样做不仅是对交传的误解，而且会严重影响交传的培训。第三，笔者对汉译英在交传里的处理有自己的见解，详细论述请参看笔者的《实战笔译》中翻英册。第四，为了体现实战里的准确幅度，参考译语不一定保持连贯。比如，同一个概念在一个讲话里的处理就可能不同于在另外一个讲话里的处理。交传不是笔译，其准确程度主要看当场口译的效果，而不能看之后写下的文字。

培训方法：任务周期

如果是每次上课至少使用一个练习单元的话，最好按照实战的要求，把每个单元都当作一次交传任务来对待。也就是说按照第四课交传任务的讲解，培训教师每次下课时交代任务，即：下次课上要练习的单元。培训生下次上课前按照第四课的相关要求做准备，而且最好是至少两人一组，以便互相学习、提醒、把关。

课前准备至少必须包括的内容是背景知识的阅读、词汇表、部分核心材料双语口头互译以熟悉两种语言对于同一话题的口头表达。不必担心头几课准备的质量不高，内容与课上讲话内容相差太远。培训教师可以在每次课的后半部留出专门时间，引导培训生自己讨论，总结经验，发现问题，努力在下次课前准备里提高准备的质量。这些都是交传职业发展不可缺少的技能，应该通过交传课来培养、提高。

课前准备没有覆盖到的词汇和概念，正好在课上练习问补扔（见第五课）。每次下课后都必须要求培训生回到小组里进行事后学习，主要内容之一就是回顾准备的过程和内容，看在哪些方面比较成功，哪些方面需要改进。然后把学习心得运用于为下次课所作的准备中。

如果这样使用本教材就不必担心上课练习时语言障碍太大。培训教师一定不要把交传培训课上成文字翻译课，把演练技能的时间用来讲解词义或者句子如何翻译。交传培训课应该是培养学生在当场现有的双语水平下口译的技能。双语水平的提高应该靠课前准备和课后学习，不应该在模拟实际口译的课上进行。

培训方法：使用笔记

三个步骤

使用笔记的培训基本上分三个步骤如下：

1. 模拟实战：放音频或者看讲稿。如果是音频，一定不要预听。如果是看讲稿，则必须每 3—4 个字写一个笔记，而且模拟听音频的速度和笔记频率。笔记结束后，模拟实战要求（4 别）看笔记口译一遍。一定要按照实战标准当真译，这遍是考核自己的实战能力。实战能力包括笔记使用的多个技能：边听边记（包括：瞬间创作、随机应变）以及依靠知识、记忆和笔记的互动完成口译。译完后走第二步；

2. 设计演练：根据 6 大原则衡量改善刚才的笔记。这个阶段不要着急，一定要逐个笔记改善，增加经过设计的笔记数量，而且设计必须遵循 6 大原则，尤其是前 4 大原则。每设计出一个比较满意的笔记，马上演练多遍直至熟练。这遍是培训自我提高，设计了就会用的能力。然后走第三步；

3. 测试进步：放同一音频或者看同一段讲稿。如果是后者则必须每 3—4 个字写一个笔记，模拟听音频的速度和笔记频率。笔记结束后，模拟实战要求（4 别）看笔记口译一遍。一定要按照实战标准当真译，这遍是测试自己是否达到了所需的水平。如果基本达到，则按照这三步法练习下一段讲话。如果明显不行，则必须重复第二和第三步。

为了增加全班的练习机会，第 2 步可以让全班分散站立在教室里的不同位置以减少相互干扰。录音暂停时，全部轻声做交传。然后根据情况，可以让全班转过身来，请一位或者两位培训生再译一遍。培训教师根据现阶段的重点给培训生提供反馈。采用这种方法可以显著增加上课的培训生人数。

常见问题

初练笔记的常见问题有：

1. 记干扰听：注意记笔记就影响到听
2. 缺少线条：笔记里只有字和符号，没有线条，尤其是没有表示字和符号相互之间关系的线条
3. 大而忙：字和符号太大，为了不影响记录速度而手指、手掌过分紧张

记干扰听的主要原因有两个，一个是没听懂而在想刚才听到了什么，另外一个是听懂了一时不知道怎么记。这两个原因导致的问题都可以用一个方法解决，那就是继续往下听，往下记，不管刚才没听懂或者不知道怎么记的内容。

听不懂的反正就是不懂，想了也不会懂，反而会影响接下来本来可以听懂，可以记下的内容。由于听不懂而没有记下的内容在口译时只好扔掉，没有其他办法。如果是听懂了一时不知道怎么记，那就留给记忆。口译时从记忆里补出需要传达的内容，不必担心会忘。

其实笔记最多也只是 3 个英文单词一个笔记，前面少记了，后面多记一点。只要笔记的总量不少，记忆所需承担的压力就没有增加，不会导致记忆压力过大而忘记的情况。总体来说，初学者笔记能力比较弱，势必更多地仰赖记忆。随着笔记能力的提高，笔记量自然就会增加到经常能够 3–4 个单词一记的水平。

站立笔记

虽然是培训笔记，但是不能忘记实战的要求。交传经常需要译员站立口译。由于站立口译操作起来比坐着口译复杂，所以应该着重培训站立口译的能力。如果掌握了站立口译的技能，坐下口译基本无需培训就能得心应手。所以，在培训笔记的使用时可以从坐下练习开始，但是一旦培训生开始上路，就应该马上过渡到站立记笔记，然后站立口译。

练笔记的使用不是练记笔记，而是掌握边听边记，然后边看边回忆，边口译的技能。所以，要注意避免光练记笔记。即使是刚开始时重点在笔记，也要尽快开始让培训生记完笔记之后马上轻声译一遍。培训教师在给培训生提供反馈时也要注意重点明确，反馈内容仅限于在当时阶段的重点练习内容上。比如，刚开始建立笔记系统的时候，重点必须是笔记本身，而不是口译的质量。虽然记完笔记之后必须口译，但是反馈时可以不谈口译质量，而是着重看笔记的质量。如果重点不明确，反馈内容超出现阶段的范围，就很容易导致培训生不知所措，顾此失彼，反而影响进步。

培训方法：口译四别

实际口译里的四别是：别停下、别露馅、别太快、别拖延。

四别的培训可以分成两个阶段。首先集中精力培训别停下和别露馅的能力。在这个阶段上，每次培训生试译之后，反馈的重点都在于是否停顿太久或者从表情或者其他肢体动作上暴露出译员遇到困难。每次都应该要求培训生无论如何不要停顿太久，每次停顿时间必须仅限于自然停顿的大约 2–3 秒。如果遇到困难，无论是笔记看不清，或者不知道如何译，都应该马上用问、补、扔这三步法来解决。每次发现培训生露馅，都必须再次强调要忍住了。可以让培训生在问题没有得到解决的情况下再译一次，努力不露馅。

培训四别的初期会出现有些培训生被卡住，长时间说不出话来的情况。而且往往会在这个时候抬头看培训教师，用目光询问"我该怎么办"。此时，培训教师一定不要过早为培训生解围，而是应该等待一段时间，看培训生能否自己顶过去，自己想起采用问、补、扔继续译下去。如果培训生自己顶过去了，继续往下译，结束后，培训教师一定要热情地肯定培训生的努力，鼓励下次继续这样做。采用这种方法，绝大多数培训生都能很快地养成别停下、别露馅的习惯。

如果培训生实在顶不过去，培训教师可以解围。但是解围的方法必须是说明培训生这样是不对的，本来应该顶过去。然后再次强调必须用问、补、扔的办法定过去。如果是露馅，则再次强调不要露馅。这样反复几次，培训生都能迈过这一关。

一旦别停下、别露馅不是太大问题了，就必须马上把注意力放在别太快和别拖延之上。别拖延比较容易纠正，只要在反馈时不断提醒一般都可以解决问题。但是别太快需要特别的训练。

别太快的培训也可以分两步走。首先是养成每个意群之后停顿的习惯。可以让培训生朗读讲稿，朗读时要求他们每个意群必须明显地停顿。这点听上去容易，但是绝大多数人都需要一定的练习才能有感觉。要经过一段时间的练习，才能养成习惯。

每个意群之后停顿的练习上路之后就可以开始练习控制自己的讲话速度，把速度控制在每秒 3 个英文单词（相当于 5–6 个汉字）。由于这是一般人大脑的信息处理速度，而人们的本能是一旦知道说什么，就会不停顿地说完。结果是，说完知道怎么说的内容之后，大脑的思维尚未跟上，马上出现大脑空白的现象，导致口误或者改口的发生。改口其实就是让大脑思维跟上口头速度的一种本能现象。所以一旦养成了每秒 3 个英文单词的习惯，加上每个意群明显停顿就能明显地减少口误、改口发生的频率，从而提高口译的流利程度。

培训方法：问补扔

问补扔指的是译员遇到困难时能问就问；不能问就用一些原则上没有错误的话补齐句子接着往下译；如果补也不解决问题就马上扔掉不会译的内容，接下去译会译的内容。练习时，培训教师可以向培训生交代清楚，接下去的练习中肯定会听到不懂或者遇到不会译的地方。一旦出现上述情况，马上问。如果问了还不懂，就补甚至扔。只要培训教师严格按照这个程序进行，培训生很快就会养成问补扔的习惯。

问、补、扔是译员在遇到困难时必须走的三步。实际口译的培训应该从四别里的别停下和别露馅开始，什么时候开始引入问补扔要根据培训生的进展以及能力而定。从原则上讲可以在别停下、别露馅练习大约 4–8 小时之后。培训教师可以考虑是否要培训在还不会问补扔的时候也能够做到别停下和别露馅，还是鼓励培训生采用问补扔的的三步法来帮助他们别停下、别露馅。不过，培训教师不能忘记一点，那就是如果同时培训的技能过多，反而可能导致培训生不知所措。所以，需要把握好平衡。

培训方法：即席演讲

培训即席演讲能力可以分成三个阶段。第一阶段，培训生练习说出三个词组的能力。这个阶段上，培训生可以坐在座位上，集中精力想内容。由培训教师提供主语，由培训生造句，在造句中使用"三"。第二阶段培训说三个要点或者三个方面内容的能力，由培训教师事先准备好话题清单，培训生听到话题后马上说出三句话。根据培训生的情况，第二阶段既可以坐着说，也可以开始站立。第三阶段加大难度，既可以要求培训生站立在小组或者全班面前演讲，也可以要求培训生延长演讲的内容。

逐渐增加难度的另外一个做法是从汉语开始练起，然后过渡到英语。其他可以考虑的变换方式是把全班分成几个小组，培训生在小组里演讲，然后每组选一个代表在全部演讲。从另外一个角度看，这也相当于先从面对 1–2 位同班同学开始，发展到面对全班。如果条件允许，还可以请其他教师或者外教坐在听众席前，与演讲者面对面。这些手法都可以增加对演讲者的心理压力，增加演讲难度。

培训即席演讲的初期最好选用培训生熟悉，并且往往是拥有强烈看法的话题。这样可以充分利用培训生现有的知识，减少当场创作的难度。随着培训生水平的提高，可以开始选用虽然培训生不熟，但是国际政界、商界、或者学界的热门话题。

演讲长度即使是第三阶段也需要控制在 2 分钟之内，超过了可能无法让全班同学都有机会，而且听 2 分钟不流利的演讲，尤其是要听很多个这样的演讲会影响练习的节奏和气氛。出于交传培训目的进行的即席演讲培训不是练口若悬河，而是练马上构思的能力，一般有 2 分钟的演讲能力就基本够用。

以下是部分初期话题的例子，都可以用在英语或者汉语的演讲练习：

- 女生就是比男生强
- 吸烟不是坏事
- 谈恋爱对学习没有负面的影响
- 军事化训练对子女成长很有好处
- 不会弹乐器不算受过教育
- 现有高考体制利大于弊

培训方法：实战模拟

注重实战的交传培训项目必须既要有一个学习、练习阶段，还要有一个模拟交传阶段。前一阶段的重点是通过培训教师的讲解，理解交传的理念，并且通过反复练习，初步掌握所需的技能。后一阶段的重点是把前一阶段的知识和技能运用在近乎实际交传的任务中。此外，模拟能产生第一阶段课堂练习时没有的，近乎实战情景中的心理压力。通过模拟能够让培训生在培训期间明显提高心里素质，做好迎接实战的心里准备。

如何设计模拟很有讲究。如果培训资源不够，还需要有创意，在有限的资源里让培训生在尽量接近于实战的情景下完成交传任务。以下的介绍以比较理想的资源为基本，说明交传培训的理想目标。读者可以根据实际情况，参照本课建议而实施。

模拟交传至少需要一个口译任务来源、一名译员和两位讲话人。口译任务来源可以由培训教师扮演，每周选择一名培训生担任主要联络对象。然后培训教师扮演客户，向培训生发出查询函件。培训生答复、报价、接收任务细节、确认。培训教师根据所需难度，先是提前几天，接着是仅提前一天，向培训生发第二天会谈的日程和相关材料。培训生收到材料之后马上转发全班，为口译任务做好准备。

为了给全班的培训生都提供足以生效的模拟练习，两位讲话人需要交谈足够长的时间。如果一个班有 20 名培训生，每人口译 15 分钟，讲话人就必须交谈 5 个小时。所以，讲者必须由健谈者，喜爱发表看法和意见的人来担任。尽管这样，也还必须稍加培训，说明口译模拟的目的和需要，鼓励讲话人在做了充分准备的基础上多多临场发挥，向对方提问，反驳对方的观点，延伸原先准备的谈话内容。比如：举自己生活里的例子以丰富对话等等。

讲话人的选择还有其他讲究。比如，既可以是都用母语的讲者，也可以使用带有明显口音的英语讲者。所选择的口译可以根据培训生的需要而定。在英汉口译里相对比较常见的口音有：英国人、美国人、德国人、法国人、西班牙和意大利人（二者口音相近）、日本人、韩国人、印巴人。

汉语的讲者可以请其他教师扮演，而由培训生轮流担任也很有好处。既可以深化培训生在特定话题上的知识，锻炼培训生的口才以及交谈时的应变能力，又有助于他们了解将为之翻译的讲者的思路和行为。

每次模拟都必须设计角色说明。角色说明必须包括的内容有：交谈的情景、交谈双方的姓名和身份、交谈的话题、双方的主要论点（必须相反）以及其他需要提醒讲者的事宜。本课最后附有一个交传模拟的角色说明。

为了尽量扩大效益，可以安排没有正在等待或以及担任过译员角色的其他培训生在教室的另外一边练习笔记，轻声口译。但必须与模拟会谈有一定距离，以免影响会谈。如果是在安装了同传设备的教室上课，则可以让其他培训生在同传箱里悄声练习（讲者必须使用话筒以便其他培训生可以在同传箱里通过耳机听到讲话）。如果光是练习笔记，建议时间为半天为宜，全天感觉很长。

要想最大限度地发挥模拟的作用就需要注意以下事项：首先，角色扮演人要避免脱离角色，自始至终都必须尽量按照角色的要求行事、说话。比如，把课间休息当作会谈休息，不与担任译员的培训生交谈。角色扮演人对担任口译的培训生越陌生，态度越正式，脸色越严肃，给培训生带来的心理压力就越大，模拟效果就越好。相反也成立。为了达到这个目的，除了预先向角色扮演人说明清楚之外，当天还必须再次提醒。

其次，最好能把模拟放在一个会议室，至少是另外一个房间做。模拟时的工作环境越陌生、越正式就越真实，给培训生带来的心理压力也越大。此外，培训生已经习惯于教室的环境，无知无觉中已经养成了心里依赖。即使是在教室里表现出色的培训生也会在改变环境之后表现失常，这些都是只有在模拟阶段才能解决的问题。从这个意义上讲，没有足够模拟培训的交传课是难以培训出能够在毕业时就能够担任实际交传任务的译员。

最后，交传模拟应该包括站立口译。最容易安排的就是模拟站立口译电脑幻灯演示，让角色扮演人做某个话题或者介绍某个公司或者组织机构的电脑幻灯演讲。讲者站立，译员也站立。如果担心讲者辛苦，也可以让讲者坐着，但是要求译员，即培训生站立口译。

考核测试

由于交传的培训是技能培训，必须保证培训生每周都取得应有的进展，所以必须建立起严谨的考核与考试制度。这个制度应该有两个组成部分，一个是定期小测用以保证前期的培训成果没有退化。另外一个是培训结束考试。

大凡考试一般有两种性质：一种是考掌握程度，即对于到目前为止所教的内容掌握了多少；另外一种是考实际能力，即培训生目前的交传达到了什么水平。培训教师应该根据自己课程的目的决定采用哪一种性质的考试。如果目的是培训出能够承担交传任务的译员，就必须在课程结束时考实际水平。如果培训的目的仅限于让培训生对于交传或其中某些技能有一定的了解，就可以考掌握程度。

如果是考掌握程度，就可以在考试时从所练习过的材料里任选一部分，考核培训生对所有材料的掌握程度。如果是考实际水平就必须选用培训生没有接触过的崭新材料，而且其难度必须符合课程培训的目标。这个目标，可以根据考核者是初级译员、中级译员还是高级译员而有所差异。但无论如何，考试所用材料都必须与所选级别的难度保持一致。

交传的考试是个缺少研究的领域，而且由于现实中的条件限制往往无法如愿以偿。比如，最客观的考试应该是考试时间长一些，内容多样化一些，全面考核培训生的能力。但是那样做需要大量的资源，一般的培训课程，甚至是大多数大学的学位课程也无法应付，面向全国的证书考试也是这样。所以，交传考试的设计往往是在客观程度和可及资源之间的妥协。

尽管这样，如果交传课程的目的是培养交传译员，则考试必须全面考核培训生对于交传技能和知识的掌握与运用。所以，考试应该考站立口译，应该总体衡量口译质量，既考虑语言转换的质量，也考虑传达情感以及与听众沟通的质量。本课最后附有一份交传课程结束考试的评分表作为参考，每位培训教师都需要根据自己课程的目标决定考试的评分重点和给分方法。

附录一　交传模拟角色说明

UK-China Joint Venture

Participants:

UK	Mr David Green (Procurement Manager) or Ms Jane Saunders (Procurement Manager), Gap, UK
China	Mr Cheng Li (Sales Manager) or Ms Zhang Hong (Sales Manager), Ningbo Yinshan Garments Co., Ltd, China

Background:

Gap (http://gap.eu/about/) is a leading clothing brand in the UK. Its target market is the age range from toddlers to late twenties. It is sourcing a supply partner in China. Ningbo Yinshan Garments Co., Ltd of China (http://www.chinayinshan.com/) is a leading clothes manufacturer in the southern province of Zhejiang. Managers from both companies meet in London to explore the possibility of Ningbo Yinshan manufacturing clothes for Gap. If the negotiation goes well, they may consider the possibility of setting up a joint venture company.

UK—speaking notes	China—speaking notes
General position: • Gap needs a partner in China to mass-produce clothes and other accessories at lower cost than in Europe • Wants to build a long-term, stable relationship	General position: • Very interested in the possibility of a joint venture company Ningbo Yinshan's strengths: • a leading clothes manufacturer in China

Gap's strengths: • leading brand • fast growing target market • fantastic track record Expecting from Ningbo Yinshan: • manufacturing quality • prompt delivery • very competitive prices • after-delivery service Want assurance from Ningbo Yinshan on the following: • Good corporate governance and a mechanism for corporate social responsibility • An investment of $15 million into upgrading production facilities and training • Acceptance of supervision at director level from Gap in London	• many years of experience in supplying to western companies • produces reliable quality products • cheap labor cost • prompt delivery • good customer service Seeking from Gap: • 20 million US dollars of investment into helping to upgrade production facilities • Some of that investment to be spent on training managers and key technical staff including secondments in London • Agreement of a trial period of 12 months • No interference in management or production from London, so free to run in the trial period • Transfer of technology from Gap • Transfer of design systems from Gap • A guarantee that Gap will not work with any other Chinese companies for a minimum of five years

附录二　交传考试评分卡（水平考试）

评分标准：

5 — 优秀：信息与情感把握准确、译语流畅、每段话都有目光交流。

4 — 良好：信息与情感把握基本准确、译语基本流畅、每段话都有目光交流。

3 — 可以接受（及格）：主要信息都在，但译语不够流畅或者不是每段话都有目光交流。

2 — 难以接受（不及格）：信息不准确、译语不流畅、缺少目光交流。

1 — 根本不会或者缺席或者作弊。

评分办法： 每发现一个明显不足之处就在相应的栏目下做个记号，结束时根据记号的多少以及加权计算得分。之所以需要加权是因为缺少一次目光交流的性质不如漏译一个重要信息，所以准确程度的分量大于目光交流。具体的加权比例由培训教师根据实际情况和需要而定。

培训生名字	准确程度	译语流畅	目光交流	分数
培训生1				
培训生2				
培训生3				
培训生4				
培训生5				
培训生6				
培训生7				
培训生8				
培训生9				
培训生10				

第二部分　交传练习

英译汉

1. 英中关系

1. In my speech today, I want to talk about how globalisation and the new G20 world order will reshape this century and how we are responding to these changes. I simply cannot understate the significance of this changing order. We have all been accustomed to a G8 world for many years. This largely symbolised how most of us in the West viewed the world. But it is no longer relevant.

2. In less than a decade, we have moved from a G8 to a G20 world. A world in which major powers such as China are catching up rapidly with the existing long-established economic powers. Recently, China's quartile GDP growth was 10.3% and the most recent quarterly total GDP put China ahead of Japan as the second largest economy after the US.

3. What makes this change in the world order even more significant than previous ones is that it is not just a shuffling of the seats at the top table, a new Group of 7 or Group of 8. It's not just that the characters have changed, but the architecture has too. The grouping at the top table, economically and

在我今天的演讲中，我想谈谈全球化和新的G20世界秩序将如何重塑这个世纪，以及我们如何应对这些挑战。我不能低估这次秩序变化的意义。我们都习惯了G8世界，多年如此。这大致象征了多数西方人眼中的世界。但是那个世界已经失去其相关性。

不到十年间，我们从G8发展到G20世界。这个世界里的大国，例如中国，迅速赶上现有的老牌经济大国。近期，中国的季度GDP增长达10.3%。从最近的季度GDP来看，中国已经超过日本，成为第二大经济体，仅次于美国。

这次世界秩序改变更加显著，甚于从前，原因是它不仅是重排贵宾席上的座次，不仅是新的7国集团或者8国集团。它不仅是人物的改变，也是架构的改变。贵宾席的分组，就经济和政治而言，更能

politically, is now much more representative of a globalised, 'networked' world.

4. These are not changes the UK should fear. It is in fact something we should wel- come as a great opportunity. First and foremost, there is an opportunity to expand financial and trading ties as the people of these emerging economies become wealthier. The World Bank estimates that by 2030 there is likely to be an increase in middle class consumers equal to the total population of the EU.

5. But it is also an opportunity politically and diplomatically to find new ways to harness international action to deliver the changes we will need to safeguard our collective security. The new world order will be a more multilateral one, politically as well as econo- mically. In one sense that will be a more complex world, which is why closer cooperation between governments, and understanding between peoples, will be more important.

6. It is increasingly the case that the prosperity of any one country today— whether big or small—is dependent on what happens in other countries. In a similar way, many of the problems faced by countries today are global rather than local—whether that's climate change, immigration, security, crime or any number of other issues that are blind to international boundaries.

代表一个全球化、'联网'的世界。

对于这些变化，英国不该畏惧。其实，我们应该欢迎这个很好的机遇。首先，我们有机会扩展金融和贸易联系，因为新兴经济体的人们将变得富有。世界银行估计，到2030，中产阶级消费者的增加人数很可能相当于欧洲总人口。

这也是一个政治和外交机遇，可以找到新方式借助国际行动，带来我们所需要的变化，以保卫我们的集体安全。新的世界秩序将更多边，政治和经济上都是如此。在某种意义上，这将是一个更加复杂的世界，因此政府直接加强合作以及人民之间的理解将更加重要。

现在的情况是：任何一个国家的繁荣，不论国家大小，都越来越多地取决于发生在其他国家的情况。类似地，国家面临的许多问题都是全球而不是本地性质的，不论是气候变化、移民、安全、犯罪还是许多其他问题都是无国界的。

1. 英中关系

7. There needs to be broader engagement between people. This engagement needs to be built upon foundations of mutual understanding and trust, and needs to be carried out by the many diverse organisations working to further international collaboration in fields such as education, science, culture and international relations. This engagement should aim at delivering deeper and broader ties between our two countries.

我们需要更广泛地开展人民之间的交流。这种交流需要建立在相互理解和信任的基础上，需要通过各种组织促进国际协作，所涉及的领域包括教育、科学、文化和国际关系。这些交流应该旨在提供更深、更广的联系，在两国之间建立这种联系。

8. We must deepen our understanding of each other as much as our dependence on each other grows. Strengthening relations with fast growing economies and powers is one of the key foreign policy objectives of the UK's new government. We recognise the importance to us of our close and historic relationships with Europe and North America — but also realise where the new opportunities increasingly lie, with countries like China.

我们必须加深相互理解，如同我们彼此仰赖程度的增加一样。加强与快速增长经济体和大国的关系是一个重要的外交政策目标，英国新政府很重视。我们认识到历史悠久、密切的欧洲和北美关系对我们很重要，但是我们也意识到在与中国这种国家的关系中新机遇将越来越多地出现在哪些地方。（来源：英国政府时任外交部次长的讲话节选。© 英国王室版权。）

注 释

Relevant
这个词在中文里缺少准确的对应，与之意思相近的词有，但是用法不同。由于这个词在当代英语里很常用，建议采用"外来化"，译作"相关"。

Harness
本来可以译为"把握"，但是在这个句子里由于其他词汇的搭配而不必译出，意思已经到位。

Engagement
这个词在中文里缺少准确的对应，既使有几个词分别表达其不同含义，但也用法不同。在这句话里可以看出是"交流"的意思。由此也可以反向学汉译英，汉语里听到"交流"就知道可以处理成 engage 或 engagement。

...close and historic relationships...
译语里照顾汉语习惯，颠倒了两个形容词的顺序。

2. 英中贸易

1. I would like to gather the threads together at the end of today's Business Summit. The UK Government is fully committed to building a closer trade and investment relationship with China. The scale and seniority of the UK business delegation on this visit is a strong signal of our intent. As today's Summit has demonstrated, there is immense potential for deepening and broadening areas of commercial co-operation to mutual benefit.

2. In addition, from my discussions with Chinese business and officials I am greatly encouraged by the possibilities for closer collaboration. We have the advantage of a long history of operating in competitive open markets and of having developed a competitive advantage in some sectors such as high value manufacturing, professional services and creative industries, which we are willing to share with China.

3. The UK ranks alongside Germany as the largest European investor in China, so we are fully committed to making a positive contribution to China's long-term economic development. The UK and Chinese economies have reached a complementary stage, and the sector-

我想在今天商业峰会结束时总结一下。英国政府完全致力于建立与中国更紧密的贸易投资关系。这次访问的英国商业代表团规模大，级别高，强有力地表明了我们的意图。今天的峰会显示，在深化和扩大商业互利合作的领域方面潜力巨大。

此外，从我与中国企业和官员的讨论来看，开展更紧密的协作的可能性很多，这让我深受鼓舞。我们的优势包括：在竞争激烈的开放市场运作已久，在某些领域已经发展出竞争优势，例如高价值制造、专业服务和创意产业，这些我们都愿意与中国分享。

英国和德国都是欧洲在华最大的投资方，所以我们非常致力于对中国的长期经济发展做出积极的贡献。英中经济已经进入互补阶段，今天下午您参加的会议按照行业

focused sessions you attended this afternoon will have helped to focus on areas of great potential for further collaboration to mutual benefit.

4. British expertise and experience in low carbon technologies can assist China's investment in clean energy, British engineering expertise is well placed to help Chinese partners continue the rapid expansion of China's infrastructure network in road, rail and logistics and to support the development of domestic consumption, providing supply chain opportunities in the automotive industry, mobile phone market, and luxury goods.

5. Britain is home to a strong creative media industry, world leading in terms of music, technology, film, fashion and publishing. And our services industry, with the City of London at its heart is well placed to assist Chinese companies succeed in the global market. Of course, there are ongoing issues which concern policy makers. In the last two days we have had a frank but amicable exchange on Chinese concerns.

6. China is concerned about what they see as the slow volume of UK technology exports and the slow progress to achieve market economy status. We have aired concerns about what our businessmen see as access barriers to trade and investment and about lack of effective protection for intellectual property. But we will not let the problems get in the way of the opportunities.

分主题，将有助于双方关注在进一步互利协作上有巨大潜力的领域。

英国在低碳技术上的专长和经验可以协助中国在清洁能源上的投资，英国在工程上的专长完全能够帮助中国伙伴继续在道路、铁路和物流这些基础设施网络方面快速扩展，支持国内消费的发展，在汽车业、手机市场和奢侈品业提供供应链方面的机遇。

英国拥有实力雄厚的创意媒体产业，在音乐、技术、电影、时尚和出版方面都领先世界。我们的服务业以伦敦金融城为中心，完全能够协助中国公司在全球市场取得成功。当然，尚存的一些议题让决策者们感到关切。过去两天，我们就中方的关切进行了坦诚、友好的交流。

中方关切的是，在他们看来，英国技术出口少，获得市场经济地位进展缓慢。我们关切的是英国商人所看到的贸易投资壁垒，知识产权缺少有效的保护。但是我们不会让这些问题影响机遇。

2. 英中贸易

7. I very much hope that today's Summit will lead to a surge of interest in Chinese investment in the UK, as more Chinese companies in the process of internationalising recognise the attractive business environment that exists in the UK. Ultimately, we both want the same thing. To do business, to create wealth for our citizens and encourage sustainable economic growth.

8. Key to Britain's growth is China. And I'd like to think that Britain can play a role in helping China grow too. I very much hope today has not only reaffirmed to those present the great potential for increasing UK China trade and investment links, but has also served to forge new business links between companies while cementing existing partnerships. I wish you all well in your endeavours.

我非常希望,随着更多正在国际化的中国公司认识到英国富有吸引力的商业环境,今天的峰会将使中国在英投资的兴趣大增。最终,我们都想要同样的东西:经商、为我们的公民创造财富、鼓励可持续的经济增长。

英国增长的关键在于中国。我想英国也能在帮助中国增长方面扮演角色。我非常希望今天的峰会不仅向在座的各位再次证实了英中贸易投资联系的极大潜力,而且还有利于在巩固现有伙伴关系的同时建立起公司之间新的商务联系。我祝大家事业成功。(来源:英国政府时任商务大臣的讲话。© 英国王室版权。)

注 释

Gather threads together

如果是第一次听到这个表达法,就顺着前话,按照字面直译为"把线条(或者线索)汇聚一下"。如果灵机一动,也可以处理成"把思路汇总一下"。

the scale and seniority of the UK business delegation

英译汉听上去生硬的几个常见原因之一就是没有处理好英语里的名词。有两种情况:在本句里,英语里的名词含义不仅限于名词本身,而是带有形容词在内。译成汉语时需要把相关形容词译出来才足够准确,而且保证汉语意思清楚。另外一种情况是英语里的名词带有原型动词的含义,需要在英译汉时把相关动词译出来。这后者将于其他课里出现例子时讲解。

cooperation and mutual benefit
为了照顾汉语习惯而颠倒了两个词的顺序，不颠倒也可以。

collaboration
英语里 collaboration 和 cooperation 无论是在定义上，还是在实际使用的所指上都有区分，但有时又可互换。如果一时掌握不了英语里的区别，不妨在汉译的版本里做区别。笔者建议除非有特别明显的原因，否则 cooperation 一概译合作，collaboration 一概译协作。

Expertise
该词有讲究，在政界、商界的使用里往往所指很广。不仅指知识和技能，而且还可能指人员、软件、做法、程序、系统等等。在没有更好的方案之前，笔者建议暂译为"专长"，其所指也可以比较广泛。

the City of London
正式译语应该是"伦敦金融城"，特指伦敦市内历史悠久的金融区，因面积大约一平方英里而号称"一平方英里"。伦敦金融城也是伦敦城诞生之处，今天的 Greater London 叫大伦敦，是后来发展起来的。所以，伦敦市内有个著名大学叫 The City University of London，借助伦敦金融城的优势而在金融课程方面有许多特长，但是却把自己称作"城市大学"。如果顺理成章命名为"金融城大学"即符合事实，又有利于宣传。

3. 英国油气业

1. I am delighted that this year's conference is the largest ever. And what better place to host it than Aberdeen? A city that is renowned for the skills and expertise it provides the industry. Aberdeen has much to be proud of. It is a recognised global hub for the oil & gas industry. It has the home grown skills, expertise and workforce that are exported all over the world.

2. This is where much of the technology used around the world was originally developed. Since we started exploring and producing in the UK's waters, we have been at the leading edge of a worldwide industry. And we still are. We have continually broken new ground—literally, on the geology, but equally on engineering, on safety, on the environment and even commercial disciplines—to explore and produce safely and efficiently.

3. Of course the tragic Gulf of Mexico incident was a shock to us all—a tragic human and environmental disaster. We in the UK have reviewed the various reports which have resulted from the US investigations, to learn as

我很高兴今年的会议规模是最大的。在阿伯丁举办可谓再好不过。这座城市为业界提供技能和专长，以此闻名。阿伯丁有许多令人感到自豪之处。它被公认为全球油气业的中心，拥有本土培养的技能、专长和劳动力，并且向全世界出口。

这里是世界上许多技术的发源地。自从我们开始在英国的水域勘探和生产以来，我们就一直站在一个全球产业的前沿。今天还是这样。我们不断地开辟新天地，在地质学意义上可谓名副其实。在工程、安全、环境、甚至是商业上，也同样开天辟地，以便安全、高效地勘探和生产。

当然，墨西哥湾的悲惨事故让大家都感到震惊，这是人类和环境方面的悲惨灾难。我们在英国回顾了美国调查所得出的各种报告，尽可能

much as we could of the causes of Macondo and on what lessons we can draw for our own regulatory system.

4. Now, we want to look at the nationally important Infrastructure we have in the North Sea Around 50% of the infrastructure we have is past its design life and a workgroup has been set up to consider how we reconcile this with the need to fully develop the current known reserves and the yet to find deposits, which will help us reach full productive potential.

5. The second area we want to look at is improving recovery. Currently the UK recovers only around 38% of the hydrocarbons in the reservoirs. Increasing this by even a small amount would be hugely beneficial — each additional percentage of recovery could be worth over $20billion. There is a limited time for us to achieve this and it is partially reliant on the lifespan of our current infrastructure.

6. This year seems to be shaping up to be our best year for new developments in at least a decade, on a par with some of the very early years of the industry. We are tracking a number of significant developments coming forward and I am keen to see some of the substantial value of these developments coming to the UK.

地多了解马孔多油井事故的起因，并且看看能从中吸取什么经验教训，以用于我们自身的监管系统。

现在，我们要关注位于北海、具有国家重要性的基础设施。我们现有基础设施的大约50%已经超过了设计寿命。我们设立了工作组，考虑如何把这一情况与充分开发当前已知的储备以及尚需寻找的储藏这一需要相协调，这将帮助我们充分实现生产潜力。

我们要关注的第二大领域是改善回收。目前，英国仅回收了储藏中碳氢化合物的大约38%。即使只提高回收率一点点也能带来巨大的益处。回收率每增加一个百分点都会带来200亿以上的价值。我们实现这一点的时间有限，其中有一部分要依赖于当前基础设施的寿命。

今年似乎正在成为至少十年以来进行新开发的最佳之年，与业界起步初期的情况不相上下。我们正在追踪几个具有相当分量的开发项目，而我也非常希望看到这些开发项目里的相当分量的价值来到英国。

3. 英国油气业

7. The UK has a proven ability to contribute in a major way to these developments, from our pre-eminent front end engineering and design through to our world-leading subsea technology and skills. Changes in the last Budget were not well received by the industry, but it has to be said that it has resulted in an important dialogue between the industry and the UK Treasury.

8. A parallel fiscal working group will be formed to allow an ongoing dialogue between Government and industry about the context in which oil and gas projects are proposed in the UK. This industry is unlike any other. I am in awe of its breathtaking ambition, the refusal to be daunted by overwhelming challenges, its long term ambition and the courage of its people.

英国的能力经过证实，能够对这些开发做出重大贡献，从我们卓越的前端工程和设计，到世界领先的海底技术和技能，应有尽有。英国政府上次预算中的变化并没有得到业界的欢迎，但必须要说的是这种变化促成了业界和英国财政部之间的重要对话。

我们知道要组建一个平行的财政工作组，以便政府和业界之间持续对话，讨论英国油气项目提议的背景。油气产业与众不同。我惊叹于业界惊人的雄心，他们拒绝被巨大的挑战吓倒，而是拥有长期的雄心，业内人士勇气十足。（来源：英国时任能源与气候变化部次长的讲话。© 英国王室版权。）

注 释

What better place to host it than Aberdeen

如果按照原话直译成"还有哪个地方比阿伯丁更好呢"也可以，但是建议的版本更加容易帮助译员表达出原话的口气。

the causes of Macondo

英语里常见这种指代方法，即前后使用不同的词汇或者称号指同一个人或者事情。英语可以这样关键是仰赖定冠词保证指代清楚。由于汉语里没有相应的定冠词，容易在英译汉之后出现指代不明的情况。所以，笔者建议在译 Macondo 时加几个字明确指代。需要说明的是这不是为了帮助听众加字，而是把原话 the causes of Macondo 里的定冠词所指译出来。

value of these developments coming to the UK
意思是希望看到开发项目能够使英国获得商业利益，比如英国公司获得承包或者分包合同、项目从英国采购设备、英国员工参加项目开发等等。

last Budge
大写的预算是特指的预算，大写起到定冠词的作用。同样，由于汉语里没有大写一说，所以需要把大写的特指译出来。在口译里做到这点不容易，因为译员靠听，但是大写是听不出来的。需要靠自己的判断决定这里是指英国政府的预算。

A parallel fiscal working group will be formed
交传时遇到被动语态，除非有特别的原因不能译出动作发出方，就可以自己把动作发出方译出来。

4. 英国宇航业

1. Aerospace has a proud history in the UK. The industry earns more than £20bn a year. Almost a fifth of the global market. There are 3,000 UK firms in the sector—the largest in Europe. It's not widely known that the UK builds the entire payload for a quarter of the world's communications satellites and is home to arguably the world's most successful small satellite manufacturer—Astrium.

2. Even through the recession, where a great many industries suffered, aerospace has supported a quarter of a million jobs. The sector is a huge regional employer and an engine of some of the regional economies. After a decade in which too much growth in the UK has slid inexorably into the South East, industry strengths at Derby, Filton and Broughton are valuable regional sources of growth.

3. For the future the aerospace industry matters for some important reasons. It's tackling a huge and inevitable technological transition to low carbon. The gains to the most successful movers in that

宇航业在英国有骄人的历史，每年的收入超过200亿英镑，占全球市场的几乎五分之一。业内有3000家英国公司，规模属欧洲之最。不太广为人知的是：世界通信卫星的四分之一都是由英国建造全套有效载荷，英国拥有可以说是世界上最成功的小型卫星制造商：阿斯特里姆。

即使在许多行业受到打击的衰退时期，宇航业也还支持着25万个就业机会。这一行业是区域层面的大雇主，是有些区域的经济引擎。十年以来，英国的太多增长都不断滑向东南部，但是德比、菲尔顿和布劳顿的行业实力成为区域增长的宝贵来源。

展望未来，宇航业因为几大原因关乎紧要。宇航业正在解决通往低碳这一巨大而又不可避免的技术过渡问题。在这一过渡中，最成功的行动者可以获得巨

123

transition can be huge and British firms have the potential to be part of that. The technological advances this sector is on the cusp of should make it one of the most exciting in advanced manufacturing.

大的收益，而英国公司有潜力参与其中。这一行业处在技术进步的尖端地位，应该能够成为在先进制造中最令人振奋的行业。

4. The aerospace industry is a big exporter. One of the key ways in which we can rebalance the UK economy after a decade of debt-fuelled growth is by rebuilding our export strengths. British aerospace is right at the centre of this. After pharmaceuticals this is the UK sector that spends the most on research and technology. It reinvests about 10% of turnover.

宇航业是很大的出口业。在经过十年以债务推动的增长后，我们能够重新平衡英国经济的一大方式就是重新增强我们的出口实力。英国的宇航业正处在这一方式的中心，是英国继制药业之后研发开支最多的一个行业，营业额中有10%都用于再投资。

5. The UK has a global supply chain economy. The supply chain niches are all linked to high levels of knowledge and technology. The aerospace industry is committed to knowledge and technology driven manufacturing and all the service industries that support it. The government is committed to making sure that the research base, and the skilled people that the industry needs to compete are in place.

英国拥有全球供应链式的经济。供应链方面的特长都连接着高水平的知识和技术。宇航业致力于以知识和技术驱动的制造，以及支持这一制造的各个服务业。政府致力于确保研究基地和行业竞争所需的高技能人才都能到位。

6. Big sectoral employers like Rolls-Royce have extensive and effective graduate and apprentice programmes. These are the foundations of tomorrow's success. Rolls-Royce are also about to train extra apprentices for their supply chains — enabling smaller companies to benefit from their excellent training programmes. I was delighted to see

业内的大雇主，例如罗尔斯·罗伊斯，拥有范围广泛、有效的毕业生和学徒项目。这些是将来成功的基础。罗尔斯·罗伊斯还即将为他们的供应链培养额外的学徒，让更小型的公司受益于他们出色的培训项目。我高兴地看到，去年空客公司宣

4. 英国宇航业

the announcement by Airbus last month that it will be investing £70m in a new Engineering & Technology Campus.

7. That's a real vote of confidence in the UK. Of course, this industry faces some challenging times. But the fundamentals of what it does and the demand for it should be cause for inspiration. The industry reckons passenger numbers will continue to grow at more than 4% a year for the next fifteen years. Right now, I'm on my way to take a look at an Airbus A380.

8. A380 is as good an example as any of the strength of Aerospace Industry in Britain and wider Europe. Wings designed by Airbus at Filton and made by Airbus at Filton and Broughton, Trent 900 engines made by Rolls-Royce and nose-landing gear made by Messier-Dowty. 400 UK companies supply equipment for A380 programme and I'm more than a little proud that 40% of it is UK-made.

布将投资7000万英镑新建一个工程和技术校区。

这是给对英国的信心投下了确确实实的一票。当然，宇航业也面临着富有挑战的时代。但是，宇航业的根本作为以及市场对业界的需求应该是令人憧憬的。业界认为，乘客数量在未来15年将继续以每年4%以上的速度增长。现在，我要去看看一架空客A380。

A380是一个很好的例子，证明了英国和整个欧洲宇航业的力量。空客在菲尔顿设计、在菲尔顿和布劳顿制造机翼、由罗尔斯·罗伊斯制造遄达900型引擎、由梅西埃·道蒂制造前起落架。400家英国公司为A380项目供应设备，我非常自豪的是空客有40%都是英国制造的。

（来源：英国时任商业大臣的讲话。© 英国王室版权。）

注　释

Derby, Ilton and Broughton

这些地名都是英国宇航业的重要城镇。如果课前准备到位，就应该能够预先准备好这些地名的音译。如果在交传时才听到陌生地名，则争取用汉语读音当场音译。如果由于不熟悉而吃不准英语发音，则尽力模仿英语发音说出。

Exporter

这个单词很容易根据习惯说成出口商。但是必须注意 er 或者 or 表达的只是动作的发出方,需要根据上文决定译什么。这里显然是出口国。但是如果无法确定,就译作"方"。即在这里译作"出口方"。

As good as any

意思就是 very good。

A little proud

这里是英式幽默。幽默的典型方式是走两个极端:夸大、缩小。汉语里也有"缩小"的用法,但是更多地是用来表示谦逊。

5. 英国汽车业

1. A very warm welcome to those of you who are convening in the UK for the first time. Automobiles are already established as the UK's number one manufactured export: last year, we exported over £27bn of vehicles and parts. Of the 1.39 million vehicles made here, 75% of the cars and 73% of the commercial vehicles were exported. Export levels are now nearly at an all-time high for the industry.

2. Britain is now one of the leading locations for engine production—2.4m units were made here last year, of which 72% were sold overseas. Many of the major auto companies recognise our strong track record in innovation, research and development and design—11 of the global volume manufacturers have bases here, backed by 19 of the world's top 20 suppliers.

3. In addition, a large number—over 110—of UK-based premium and niche manufacturers are driving developments in new materials, technologies and processes in the production of high performance cars, vans, taxis, buses and others. Without doubt, ours is a dynamic, innovative, cutting edge industry.

我热烈欢迎首次来到英国开会的各位。汽车确实已经成为英国第一大的制造出口品，去年，我们出口了价值270多亿英镑的车辆与部件。在英国生产的139万车辆中，75%的汽车和73%的商用车为出口。出口水平如今几乎达到了英国汽车业的最高水平。

英国现在是生产引擎的领先地之一，去年生产了240万单位，其中的72%销往海外。许多主要的汽车公司都很清楚我们在创新、研发与设计方面的强劲业绩。有11家全球批量制造商在这里设有基地，全球20强里有19家供应商为他们提供支持。

此外，有110多家英国高档与缝隙产品制造商正在驱动全新发展，发展包括对于新材料、技术与流程的研究，而这些成果将被用于生产高性能汽车、货车、出租车、公交车和其他车辆。毋庸置疑，我们的行业

Research and development investment in Britain's automotive sector is running at over £1.5bn a year.

4. The fact that this investment rose by 9% during the recession is a sign of the UK industry's commitment to sustained investment in innovation. Major investments are now coming through. Just today, Nissan announced that its all-new Nissan Qashqai is to be designed, engineered and built in Britain—with production based at its plant in Sunderland, and development at its technical centre in Cranfield.

5. This is on top of Nissan's investment of £420m—backed with a Government grant of £20.7m—in its new battery plant in Sunderland and the production of its Leaf electric car. Ford has committed to investing £1.5bn over the next five years in the UK, to research, develop and manufacture low-CO2 technologies for cars and commercial vehicles. These are exciting times.

6. GM has committed itself to the long-term future of Luton with the Vivaro van as well repatriating over £185m worth of supply chain contracts to date. And Jaguar Land Rover is predicting an investment of £5bn over the next five years, recruiting an extra 1,000 engineers to focus on developing engine technology and car body design, in response to the demand for lower emission and higher quality vehicles.

是动态多姿、充满创新和最先进的。英国汽车领域的研发投资每年超过15亿英镑。

汽车行业的投资在经济衰退期间还增长了9%，这显示出英国汽车行业对于不断投资、保持创新的决心。大型投资也正在英国落户。日产于今天就宣布了要在英国设计、机改和制造全新的日产逍客，其桑德兰的工厂将参与生产，克兰菲尔德的技术中心将负责开发。

除此之外，日产还有4.2亿英镑的投资，其中有2070万是英国政府拨款。这笔投资将用于日产桑德兰的电池新工厂和电动车聆风的生产。福特承诺在未来5年向英国投资15亿英镑，用于研发和制造用于轿车和商用车辆的低碳技术。如今是激动人心的时代。

通用汽车致力于长期发展设在卢顿的工厂，主推旗下的Vivaro工具车，到目前为止已经将价值1.85多亿英镑的供应链合同带回了英国。捷豹路虎的预测是在未来5年投资50亿英镑，额外招募1000位工程师，以聚焦开发引擎技术和车体设计，从而回应对于低排放、高质量车辆的需求。

7. The burgeoning global market in ultra low carbon vehicles is a key growth area for the UK. We are already established as Europe's leading producer of electric vehicles and UK work on hybrids is progressing well as I discussed at Toyota's launch of the Hybrid Auris. The shift to low carbon transport demands a profound technological transformation, and we are developing the infrastructure that's necessary.

超低碳车辆全球市场的兴盛对于英国而言是一个关键的增长领域。我们已经成为欧洲领先的电动车生产国，英国在混合车辆方面的工作也正在取得喜人的进展，这一点我在丰田推出混合动力的 Auris 型车时已经提及过。朝向低碳交通的转变需要深刻的技术转换，我们正在开发必要的基础设施。

8. We cannot reverse the structural factors that have led to deindustrialisation of output and employment in Western economies. There will not be a return of low skill, low productivity, metal bashing. But there is a role for a substantial and growing manufacturing sector. Britain still has the know—how to manufacture products that consumers at home and abroad want to buy.

我们无法逆转导致西方经济体里在产出和就业方面去工业化的结构性要素。我们无法回到低技能、低生产率和敲打金属的年代了。但是，有实力、不断增长的制造行业是能够起作用的。英国仍然拥有专有知识，能够制造出国内外消费者都想购买的产品。

（来源：英国政府时任商务大臣的讲话。© 英国王室版权。）

注　释

Commercial vehicle

指的是商业用途，即用这些车来赚钱。比如大巴、小巴、工具车、皮卡都属于这类。同样，英文里的 commercial properties 指的是办公楼或者用来开商店的房地产。而中文里的所谓"商品房"是指居民房，英语里称 residential properties。商务人士开的车叫 executive cars。

premium

在修饰产品或者服务时指的是高档。

niche

牛津在线词典的一个定义是：a small hollow place, especially in a wall to contain a statue, etc, or in the side of a hill，另外一个定义是：an opportunity to sell a particular product to a particular group of people。前者是该词的原意，后者是当今在商界里的常用法。笔者赞成译作"特别"，如特别市场、特别产品、特别服务。即符合原意，又符合现成的汉语习惯用法。但是现在常见的译法是"缝隙"或者"利基"，如果不随大流有可能被别人指责译错了。

hybrid

该词来源于 hybrid power，即混合动力，现在常被单独使用，泛指所有类型的混合动力车，甚至已经开始有了复数形式：hybrids。这种形容词当可数动词用的新例子还有：deliver, deliverable, deliverables；renew, renewable, renewables。

Deindustrialisation

指减少甚至完全失去工业化所带来的能力，比如制造业从发达国家大面积地转移到新兴市场的过程就是 deindustrialisation。

Know-how

这个词不容易处理，牛津在线词典的定义为：knowledge of how to do something and experience in doing it，也就是既包括知识，也包括经验。从含义上看，可以处理成知识经验。但是由于 know-how 的用法很多、很灵活，有时会出现"知识经验"无法胜任的情况。比如：technology know-how 处理成技术知识经验就有些别扭，因为技术与经验搭配不妥。由于当今用法里，know-how 往往带有本公司或者组织的特有含义，所以在本段里处理成"专有知识"，指英国在这方面的特长。

6. 英国制药业

1. Ladies and gentlemen, it's important to look at some of the critical issues we currently face as an industry, a government and as the NHS①. As an industry we are extremely diverse. We have global companies and those that operate only in the UK. We have small companies and we have large companies and everything in between. And we all share a passionate commitment② to improve health and healthcare.

2. But we have something else in common too. We're all living and operating in a period of unprecedented turbulence in the global biopharmaceutical sector. Companies are challenged by patent expiries and R&D productivity. We have higher regulatory hurdles and increasing demands from payers and pressure on prices. Across our industry, from the smallest to the largest company, we're changing our business models.

3. In this period of global sector instability the Government must be attuned to these choices so the UK can maintain, or even

女士们、先生们,我们很有必要考虑一下我们行业、政府以及国民卫生服务现在面临的关键议题。我们行业非常多样化,既有全球公司,也有仅限于英国国内业务的公司;既有小公司,也有大公司,什么规模都有。我们都有共同的热诚,那就是改善健康和卫生保健。

但是,我们还有其他共同点。我们都生活、运营在全球生物医药行业前所未有的波动时期。各公司面临的挑战有专利到期、研发产出率不高、监管障碍提高,支付方要求提高、减低价格的压力增加。

在这个全球行业不稳定时期里,政府必须熟悉这些选择,使英国能够保持全

---

① NHS—as well as the translation of UK government and agency names.
② passionate commitment—daowei bufan.

look to grow, its share of global investment. That's why we support and applaud Government's recent decisions: the protection of health and science spending, maintenance of R&D tax credits for large companies and an increase for small companies, and stimulating an improvement in the clinical trials environment.

4. These will create a strong environment where the UK can seek to grow its share of our global investment. However, it is equally important for us to have a strong domestic market and an NHS that supports access and diffusion of new and innovative medicines. For many years the UK had a strong domestic market, an early launch, stable market with good uptake of new innovation.

5. Today the UK is characterised by relatively low prices, compared to other European countries, a very efficient generics market and slow adoption of new medicines. An efficient generics market is good thing and it is right that savings are made to create headroom for investment in new and innovative medicines. But slow uptake should be a concern to all of us.

6. Of growing concern are the slow uptake and variable use of new medicines even when they are cost effective. There are more and more examples where cost effective

球投资的份额，甚至还有增长。所以，我们支持并且赞许政府最近的决定，保护卫生与科学方面的开支，保留大公司的研发税收信贷，增加小公司的税收信贷，刺激临场测试环境的改善。

这些都将创造一个有力的环境，使英国能够增加我们在全球投资里获得的份额。但是，拥有强劲的国内市场，由国民卫生服务支持新的、创新型药品的获得和广泛使用也同样重要。多年来，英国的国内市场很强劲，新药投放速度快，市场稳定，新药很容易被接受。

今天，英国的特点是价格比其他欧洲国家低，非专利药品市场效率高，新药的采用比较慢。高效率的非专利药品市场是好事，所节省的资金能够为投资新的、创新型药品提供空间。但是，新药品的采用速度不快值得我们大家关注。

人们越来越感到关注的是采用速度慢以及新药品的不同用法，即使成本效益好也是个问题。现在有越来越

---

① Tax credit—use this to off-set taxable income. 税收抵免，抵税款

medicines face further assessments, formulary committees and restrictions at local level ... introducing delay and inconsistency in availability for patients across the UK. This matters to all of us ... wherever you stand in the system.

7. We need an environment where research and development is encouraged and nurtured in partnership with the NHS and academia. We need energy and creativity to find and develop new medicines that deliver meaningful improvements to patient outcomes. We need medicines to be embraced as an investment rather than a cost. Getting this right will put the UK in a world-leading position to attract new investment.

8. It will enable the UK to grow the very substantial contribution that industry, from the smallest to the largest company, makes to the health and wealth of the UK. It's a win for patients ... a win for the UK economy ... and a win for the NHS. I truly believe that by working together we will save more lives, give more people comfort and make health care safer and more effective.

多的例子说明即使药品的成本效益很好，也还是面临地方层面的评估、配方委员会以及限制，导致药品使用被推迟，而且在英国各地，病人获得药品的做法不一致。这些都关系到大家，无论我们在系统里的哪个层次上都受到影响。

我们需要的环境是研究和发展在国民卫生服务部门以及学术界的伙伴关系里得到鼓励和培养。我们需要活力和创新力，发现、开发新药品，为病人的疗效带来有意义的改善。我们需要把药品当作投资来拥抱，而不是当作成本。把这件事做好能够帮助英国走在世界的前头，吸引新的投资。

这将使英国大大增加药品行业，无论公司大小，为英国的健康和财富所作的贡献。这对于病人，对英国经济，对国民卫生服务部门都是好事。我确信，只要我们合作，就能够挽救更多的生命，为更多人带来舒适，使卫生保健更加安全，更加有效。
(来源：英国药品行业协会时任主席的讲话。©ABPI 2011 www.abpi.org.uk)

注 释

Headroom
原意是头顶上的空间，这里指增长的余地。由于增长也是指上方，所以用这个词做比方。另外一个类似的词是 haircut（削发），指削减金额或者数量最高的部分。比如，业务部门报开支预算为 1000，上级只批准 900，削发额为 100。

Uptake
牛津在线词典的定义是 the use that is made of something that has become available，即对新出现东西的采用。

Win
不一定译"赢"或者"胜利"，还要考虑与其他词的搭配。在本句话里，用"赢"听上去别扭，用"胜利"不合适，因为没有提到战胜困难，所以处理成"好事"。

7. 英国创意业

1. I want to use my contribution today to touch on the progress of our Creative Industries but more importantly to identify the challenges and opportunities of the future. Firstly, the progress—over the last decade Britain's creative industries have been one of our great national success stories—between 1997 and 2006 the creative economy grew faster than any other sector.

2. By 2008 it accounted for more than two million jobs and £17.3 billion of exports. Arts and Culture are central to UK tourism which itself accounts for 3.7% of GDP and directly employs 1.4 million people. Last year, film in the UK turned over £6.8 billion. Direct contribution to UK GDP was £3.1 billion and film export was £1.3 billion.

3. Most strikingly of all an OECD study suggested that cultural industries accounted for 5.8% of GDP in the UK compared to 3.2% in the US and 2.8% in France. For some considerable time Britain's creative industries have been at the heart of our economic and social renewal. They have been

我想用今天发言的时间来谈一谈我们创意产业的进展，而且更重要的是，我要提出未来的挑战与机遇。首先，看进展。过去10年，英国的创意产业成为我们国家最成功的故事之一，1997—2006年间，创意经济的增长速度超过其它任何一个领域。

到2008年，创意经济已经提供了200多万就业机会、出口贡献达173亿英镑。艺术与文化是英国旅游业的中心，而英国旅游业自身又占到国内生产总值的3.7%，直接雇佣了140万人。去年，英国的电影业收入68亿英镑，给英国GDP的直接贡献是31亿英镑，电影出口达13亿英镑。

最突出的是：经合组织的一份调查显示文化产业占英国GDP的5.8%，而美国、法国分别仅占3.2%和2.8%。在相当长的时间内，英国的创意产业都处于我们经济和社会更新发展的心脏地位，是我们就业机会和

drivers of jobs and regeneration in many of our town and cities.

4. These industries have incubated the talent and creativity of so many of our fellow citizens, celebrating the best of our past with an eternal quest for the wondrous discoveries of the future. The creative industries are our global window—Britain's window to the world and the world's window to Britain's modernity and history. They are both a catalyst for our national renewal and an indicator of our national success.

5. The world has radically changed over the last five years. Not only the global financial crisis and consequent age of austerity but the rapid development of digital technology has led to the convergence of formats and globalisation of content. Creative companies need to think globally or risk losing out. So it is now urgent we act to maximise competitive advantage for British business.

6.Today I am calling for the creation of a cross Government group bringing together Treasury and Education ministers with leaders from our key creative industry sectors. The group's remit would be to produce an action plan by the summer, which will support Britain to be a world leader in creative industries over the next decade. I will outline briefly what the action plan should cover.

城镇再生项目的驱动因素。

这些产业孵化了许多民众的才能与创意，在庆祝我们过去成就的同时，又永不停歇地寻求未来瑰丽的探索。创意产业是我们的全球之窗，是英国向世界打开的窗户，是世界看到英国的现代发展与历史往昔的窗户，他们是我们举国更新的催化剂，是全民成功的指向标。

世界在过去五年已经大不相同了。不仅仅是全球金融危机和由其导致的紧缩时代，而且数码技术的迅猛发展还带来了格式趋同和内容全球化。创意公司需要有全球思维，否则就有可能败下阵来。所以，需要现在就立刻采取行动，在最大程度上增加英国公司的竞争优势。

今天，我在此号召创立一个跨政府的小组，集合财政部和教育部的部长级官员和关键创意行业的领军者。这一小组的任务就是在今年夏天之前拟定好行动计划，以此支持英国在下一个10年成为创意产业的世界领军者。我将简要地概括一下行动计划应当包括的内容。

7. 英国创意业

7. It should include: seeking a UK and EU regulatory framework which is fit for this new era of format convergence and content globalization; clear and robust intellectual property rights in the UK and EU; clarity about accountability and project management for broadband roll out, and the development of a demand led education and skills system. The group should also commit to overseeing the implementation of the action plan.

8. So my message today is simple. We are proud of Britain's great creative success stories like War Horse, Slumdog Millionaire and Harry Potter to name but a few. But if we fail to act now, politicians and industry working together, Britain will fall behind. Creative talent will be lost and our economy will suffer. It doesn't need to be like this.

内容应当有：寻求一个符合格式趋同和内容全球化这一新时代需要的英国和欧盟监管框架；英国和欧盟范围内清晰和强有力的知识产权；在推广宽带，以需求引领的教育与技能体系时明确问责制和项目管理。这一小组还应当致力于监督行动计划的执行情况。

所以，我今天的讯息很简单。英国在创意界的成功故事让我们自豪，比如《战马》《贫民窟的百万富翁》和《哈利波特》，这种例子不胜枚举。但是，如果我们现在不行动，如果政界与创意业界不一起协作，英国就会落于人后。创业人才会流失，我们的经济会受难。我们是能够避免这种情况发生的。（来源：英国政府时任文化、媒体与体育影子大臣的讲话。© 英国王室版权。）

注 释

OECD

首字母缩写词。全拼为：Organization of Econonmic Cooperation and Development，通译为经济合作与发展组织，简称经合组织。如果不知道，则直接用英语说。

War Horse, Slumdog Millionaire and Harry Potter

遇到这种情况，应该首先根据自己掌握的知识译出汉语。如果不知道，就争取用英语说出至少一个，然后说"等等"。

8. 英国专业服务业

1. Good morning. It's a real pleasure to be here and to have the chance to speak at this conference. Professional and business services are already the largest sector of the economy, generating nearly £170 billion annually after several years of strong growth. Today, this country is the largest net exporter of business services in the G7, outstripping the US, France and Germany.

2. UK lawyers, accountants and consultants set the standards for professionalism and integrity around the world. Our professional qualifications enjoy a strong reputation internationally and are highly regarded in the top echelons of business. The UK played a key role in setting up the International Accounting Standards Board, which has developed accounting standards now used by around 120 countries.

3. The vital role the services sector plays is seen across the wider economy, working with the public sector to improve performance, advising manufacturers on every aspect of the operations and buying and selling between each other, so the UK government

早上好。非常高兴来到此地并且有机会在本次大会上发言。专业和商业服务已经成为我国经济中规模最大的行业，在数年强劲的增长后，年收入近1700亿英镑。今天，我国超过了美国、法国和德国，成为7国集团中最大的商业服务净出口国。

英国的律师、会计和顾问在世界各地为专业水准和正直设立了标准。我们的专业资格证书享誉国际，在企业高层人员中备受推崇。英国在设立国际会计准则理事会方面扮演了关键角色，所制定的会计准则现在被大约120个国家采用。

服务业所扮演的关键角色在整个经济体中都看得见，服务业和公共领域一起合作来改善业绩、就运营以及互相之间买卖的方方面面向制造商提供咨询建议。因此英国政府重视服务业，

values the services sector as a crucial engine of economic growth. Professional and business services underpin competitiveness right across the UK economy.

4. In recent years business has been held back by barriers that stymie growth. That's why the Growth Review was launched, a root-and-branch analysis of the obstacles to growth, and the structural reforms needed to encourage a balanced, sustainable economy. It's a rolling programme, which will be the basis of the Government's agenda over the lifetime of the parliament. It'll inform our decision making.

5. The Review has been focusing on immediate priorities for business: improving the competition regime; increasing exports; reforming the planning system. We have also been examining different sectors of the economy to identify the specific barriers and challenges they face. Business and professional services is one of the first six key economic sectors the Review has been focusing on.

6. Many firms have identified regulation as a major issue, with arguing that the impact of general regulation needs to be reduced for the sector. For example, businesses have been telling us that the rules on money laundering are having an impact way beyond the original intentions of the regulations. We have also heard your concerns over the Bribery Act.

将其视为经济增长的关键引擎。专业和业务服务支撑着英国经济各个领域的竞争力。

最近几年，企业因为阻碍增长的壁垒而裹足不前。因此我们推出了《增长回顾》，这一文件彻底地分析了增长的阻碍，鼓励一个平衡、可持续的经济所需的结构改革。这是一个滚动的项目，将成为本届议会任期内政府议程的基础，为我们的决策提供信息。

《增长回顾》一直在关注商界近期的重点：改善竞争体制、增加出口、改革规划系统。我们还一直在剖析经济中的不同行业来找出它们所面临的具体壁垒和挑战。在《回顾》关注的六大关键经济行业中，商业与专业服务是其中之一。

许多公司已经将监管确定为一大主要议题，认为需要减少一般监管对商业和专业服务业的影响。例如，各家企业一直在告诉我们，反洗钱方面的规则所产生的影响远远超过了这一规则原有的意图。我们还听到了大家关于贿赂法案的关切。

7. Government plans are carefully designed to protect vital investments in Britain's economic fabric. Corporate taxes are being overhauled so they are lower and simpler. The headline rate of Corporation tax will fall to 24% in the next 5 years, one of the most competitive in the G20. And we are getting a grip on the unnecessary red tape and bureaucracy that weighs so heavily on business in this country.

政府的计划是经过精心设计的，旨在保护英国经济纤维中的关键投资。我们正在彻底改革公司税，让它变得更低、更简单。公司税的标题税率将在未来五年下降到24%，成为20国集团中最有竞争力的税率。同时，我们也在控制给我国商界带来沉重负担的、不必要的繁文缛节和官僚主义。

8. As I said at the beginning, the services sector will not lose out as we build a more diverse, resilient economy. Indeed, British professional and business services firms will benefit from increased international competitiveness. UK businesses have a deserved reputation for innovation and creativity, for quality and probity—so we want to see many more UK businesses sell their knowledge to the world.

正如我在开头所说的，在我们建立起一个更多元、更有韧性的经济的同时，服务业不会受损。确实，英国的专业和商业服务公司将受益于不断加强的国际竞争力。英国公司在创新、创意、质量和正直方面名不虚传，所以我们希望看到越来越多的英国公司向全世界出售他们的知识。（来源：英国政府时任商业部副部长的讲话。© 英国王室版权。）

注释

integrity

牛津在线词典的定义有两个，一个是the quality of being honest and having strong moral principles，另外一个是the state of being whole and not divided，本句话里用的是第一个定义。从第一个定义里可以看出，该词包含两个意思：诚实和正直，但是译入汉语两个词往往会出现前后词汇搭配或者句子结构难以处理的情况，最好还是译成一个词。正直含行为高标准之意，其中也可以包括诚实，所以译正直。第二个定义往往用于产品或者服务语境，比如：The packaging is to ensure the integrity of the product 包装是为了保证产品完好。

📌 underpin

也是支持的意思，只不过特指一种形式的支持。支持可以是各种形式，各个方面，而 underpin 特指在底部形成坚实的基础或者从下往上顶住。

📌 Growth Review

这种语言现象在笔译里不难处理，一看就知道是一份文件的名称。但是在口译里听不见大写，如果事先不知道这份文件，讲者提到时就有可能不知所云。届时就必须采用第六课里讲解的缺省译法，按照话面说出"增长回顾"。

9. 气候变化

1. Climate change is perhaps the twenty-first century's biggest foreign policy challenge along with such challenges as preventing the spread of nuclear weapons. A world which is failing to respond to climate change is one in which the values embodied in the UN will not be met. It is a world in which competition and conflict will win over collaboration.

2. An effective response to climate change underpins our security and prosperity. You cannot have food, water, or energy security without climate security. They are interconnected and inseparable. Plentiful, affordable food requires reliable and affordable access to water and energy. Increasing dependence on coal, oil, and gas threatens climate security, increasing the severity of floods and droughts, undermining energy security through the impact on water availability.

3. While no one weather event can ever be linked with certainty to climate change, the broad patterns of abnormality seen this year are consistent with climate change

气候变化可能是21世纪最大的外交政策挑战，其他挑战还有防止核武器扩散。一个未能应对气候变化的世界是一个不会实现联合国价值观的世界。在这个世界中，竞争和冲突将会战胜协作。

对气候变化的有效回应是我们安全和繁荣的基础。如果没有气候安全，食品、水或者能源安全无从谈起。所有这些安全都是互相联系而且不可分割的。充足、负担得起的食品需要可靠、负担得起的渠道来获得水和能源。对煤、石油、天然气越来越多的依赖威胁着气候安全、增加了洪水和干旱的严重程度，水有限就会削弱能源安全。

虽然无法确切地把某一天气事件与气候变化挂钩，但是今年所见到的异常现象的大致规律与气候变化模式是一致的，

9. 气候变化

models. They provide a vivid illustration of the events we will be encountering increasingly in the future. The clock is ticking. The time to act is now. We must take action. But we must also be clear-headed about the difficulties involved.

4. But we will not succeed if we act alone. We must aim for a framework that is global and binding. Only a response that allows everyone a voice will generate a sense of common purpose and legitimacy. Only a response that is binding will convince investors that we intend to keep the promises we make. Businesses need clear political signals. Let us show them an unequivocal green light.

5. A key challenge for Europe is to build an economic partnership with China that reinforces the steps China is taking towards a low carbon economy. These steps include its recent announcement of the five provinces and eight cities designated as China's Low Carbon Pilots. An ambitious approach to these schemes, tenaciously implemented, could provide a critical boost to global confidence in the concept of low carbon development.

6. Europe should place itself at the heart of these, working with China to maximise the ambition and the opportunities and to build the shared technology standards that will shape the global low-carbon market.

形象地显示出我们在未来将越来越多地面临的情况。时间正在流逝，现在是行动的时候了。我们必须采取行动。但是我们必须对涉及到的困难有清醒的认识。

但是如果我们单独行动的话，将不会取得成功。我们必须致力于形成一个具有约束力的全球性框架。只有让每个人都能发表意见的回应才能产生共同目的的感觉以及合法性。只有具有约束力的回应才能让投资者相信，我们计划兑现所做出的承诺。商界需要清晰的政治信号。让我们给他们展示一个明确的绿灯。

欧洲面临的一个关键挑战是怎样与中国建立起经济上的伙伴关系，加强中国在建立低碳经济时所采取的措施。这些措施有：中国最近宣布5个省份和8个城市被指定为低碳试点地区。对这些计划采取雄心勃勃的做法并且坚定地执行将有力地促进全球对低碳发展概念的信心。

欧洲应当把自身放在这一切的中心，与中国合作来最大程度地增加雄心和机遇，建立将会塑造全球低碳市场、大家共享的技术标准。就中国的情况

In China's case, low-carbon opportunity is matched by urgent low-carbon need. The pace of growth in China means average Chinese per capita emissions could soon eclipse those of the EU.

🎧 7. Climate change is one of the gravest threats to our security and prosperity. Unless we take robust and timely action to deal with it, no country will be immune to its effects. However difficult it might seem now, a global deal under the UN is the only response to this threat which will create the necessary confidence to drive a low carbon transition.

🎧 8. A successful response will not only stabilise the climate but open the way to a future in which we can meet our needs through cooperation, in accordance with the ideals of the UN. Failure will enhance competitive tendencies and make the world more dangerous. We have to get this right. If we do, we can shape our world. If we do not, our world will determine our destiny.

来看,与低碳方面的机遇相对应的是低碳方面紧急的需要。中国增长的步伐意味着中国的人均排放将很快超过欧盟。

🎤 气候变化是对我们安全和繁荣的最严重威胁之一。除非我们采取有力和及时的行动来应对,否则没有国家将独善其身。无论现在看起来有多么困难,以联合国为主导的全球协议是对这一威胁的唯一回应方式,将为驱动低碳过渡建立必要的信心。

🎤 一个成功的回应不仅将稳定气候,为未来开通道路,而且将在今后按照联合国的理想,通过合作来满足我们的需求。失败将加重竞争的倾向,让世界变得更加危险。我们必须把这件事做好。如果我们能做到的话,就能塑造我们的世界。如果做不到的话,我们的世界将会决定我们的命运。(来源:英国政府时任外交大臣的讲话。©英国王室版权。)

注 释

Affordable

这个词现在经常听到,意思虽然清楚,但是译到汉语里听上去有些别扭而且比较长,需要一段时间才会习惯。之所以不译低价或者廉价,是因为英语里没有说 cheap。Cheap 往往带有质量低下的含义，而 affordable 只是说购买者可以付得起。另外，affordable 还可以用在不适合于用 cheap 的地方。比如：This is an affordable solution（这是一个承受得起的解决方案）。

access to

在汉语里没有完全对应的表达法，需要根据上文决定如何处理。牛津在线词典的定义是 the opportunity or right to use something or to see somebody/something。由于是说获得水和食品，所以根据汉语里的词汇搭配处理成"渠道"。

The clock is ticking

把这句话处理成"时钟在嘀嗒地走"也很好。

10. 核不扩散

1. There is no more evocative image for any of us than the mushroom cloud. Anyone who grew up in the 1980s as I did will remember that. I'll use this occasion to speak about the nuclear debate. I think the debate is maturing very fast. It goes to the heart of our future, as a planet, and as people.

2. The International Atomic Energy Agency have shown that Iran has made progress in respect of its nuclear, uranium enrichment programme. This means that we're at a very critical moment. But the US administration creates an opportunity. The American President has said: 'America believes in its existing commitment under the Nuclear Non Proliferation Treaty to work ultimately to eliminate all nuclear arms'.

3. That is a very radical statement for a President of the United States to say. I believe there are three key steps that are necessary to begin to create the conditions for the goal of a world without nuclear weapons to be seriously engaged. I'll just run through them briefly and then we'll have a chance for wider

最能唤起所有人情感的图像莫过于蘑菇云了。所有成长于上世纪八十年代的人像我一样都不会忘记。我将借此机会谈谈有关核问题的辩论。我认为这场辩论成熟得很快。核问题是我们未来的中心，对地球和人都如此。

国际原子能机构表示伊朗在自己的核能和铀浓缩计划上取得进展。这意味着我们正处在非常关键的时刻。但是美国政府创造了一个机遇。美国总统已表示："美国相信自己在核不扩散条约下所做的现有承诺，即要不断努力最终消除所有核武器。"

美国总统说这样的话是很激进的。我相信有3个步骤不可缺少，可以凭借采取这些步骤开始创造条件，实现让世界不受真地动用核武器的影响这一目标。我就大致说说，然后我们将有机会广泛讨论。

discussions. The first is to prevent proliferation.

4. I think it is very welcome indeed that the United States should be seeking to enter the multilateral debate about the Iranian nuclear programme. This is a vital issue, not just for the Middle East, but also for the global integrity of the Non Proliferation Treaty. It's right that we put at the heart of our approach the need to counter proliferation.

5. The second area is the Comprehensive Test Ban Treaty (CTBT). I think that the reinvigoration of the CTBT through the commitment of the Obama administration is very significant. When the Chinese Premier and Foreign Minister were in London over the weekend, the meetings revealed that there's a lot of interest around the world in the fact that the United States wants to re-engage on the CTBT issue.

6. And then there is a third set of issues which are about the practicalities of moving to zero, of disarmament, of verification. We really do need a lot of expertise. It's fine for politicians to set goals, but we need very detailed work, and to put this work into practice. I think that the UK can claim to be at the leading edge of this debate.

7. But I want to just end on the relationship between disarmament and non proliferation. One obvious debating point

首先是防止扩散。

我认为美国寻求进入多边辩论讨论伊朗核计划是好事。这是个关键问题，不仅对中东如此，对不扩散条约的全球实施也是如此。我们应该把反扩散放在我们做法的中心位置上。

第二个领域是《全面禁止核试验条约》。我认为通过奥巴马政府所作的承诺而恢复《全面禁止核试验条约》很重要。中国总理和外交部长于周末在伦敦参加会议，会议显示很多国家都对美国想重新参与讨论《全面禁止核试验条约》很感兴趣。

然后是第三个方面的问题，即：逐渐到零、裁军和核查的具体细节。我们确实需要许多专长。政界人士可以设定目标，但是我们需要做非常具体的工作并且把工作付诸实践。我认为英国可以说是在这场辩论中处于领先地位。

但是我想结束时谈谈裁军与不扩散的关系。一个明显的争论点是：在有些国家

is: how can you urge other countries not to proliferate when there are nuclear weapon states. But, when countries like Britain achieve a 75% reduction in warheads, which has happened in this country over the last fifteen years, we are fulfilling an important part of our responsibilities.

8. We're also showing that we're serious, and forty or so years after the signatures of the Non Proliferation Treaty it is time that we are serious. One way we show this is by bold commitments, the other way is by serious thought, serious debate and serious dialogue. And that is what this meeting is intended to develop. So thank you all for coming.

拥有核武器的同时，怎么能够敦促其他国家别扩散。但是一旦像英国这样国家把弹头减少了75%，而英国在过去十五年中已经实现了这个目标，我们就是在兑现我们责任的重要部分。

我们也表明我们是认真的，大约四十年前，我们签署了不扩散条约，现在是严肃对待的时候了。一方面我们是通过大胆承诺显示认真，另一方面是通过认真的思考、辩论和对话。而这正是此次会议有意发展的内容。所以感谢大家的参与。

（来源：英国政府时任外交大臣的讲话。© 英国王室版权。）

注　释

'America believes in its existing commitment under the Nuclear Non Proliferation Treaty to work ultimately to eliminate all nuclear arms'.

这句话需要注意的是 ultimately 是修饰后面的 to eliminate，而不是前面的 work。

Welcome

听到这个单词就可能想译成"欢迎"。牛津在线词典有个定义是 to be pleased to receive or accept something，即：很高兴地接受。在本句里由于词汇搭配的原因处理成"是好事"。

Re-engage on the CTBT issue

"重新参与讨论《全面禁止核试验条约》"是采用了同传里介词译成动词

的技巧，把 on 处理成"讨论"。这样可以按照原话顺序译，不必按照笔译的常规做法，把整个《全面禁止核试验条约》调到前面来。同传顺序译的技巧在交传里用好了，可以提高译语质量，减少对译员大脑的压力，推迟疲劳的感觉。

which has happened in this country over the last fifteen years

这句话是插入语，应该争取用口气来体现，让听众明显听出插入语。做法是在译到插入语时口气一沉，音调降低。在插入语之后再把口气和音调一提，两者的反差可以比较清楚地体现插入语的作用。

11. 反恐怖主义

1. It is a pleasure to be here this morning to speak at this important event. I have personally seen much that has impressed me in the way that the UK does counter-terrorism: the hard working men and women who do so much, unnoticed, to protect our security—from law enforcement, the armed forces, the emergency services and the wider community. I wish to thank them for their hard work.

2. A successful counter-terrorism policy must involve law-makers, business and industry, academia, law enforcement and our international partners. This is why, it is important that we use the opportunity we have today to consider the issues at the very heart of our strategy. I would like to reflect briefly on the changing shape, and complexity, of the terrorist threat we face.

3. A number of incidents over the course of the last year demonstrate how the threat from terrorism continues to diversify. In December, a Swedish citizen who had spent sometime living in this country partially detonated two bombs in Stockholm city centre. In May a young women attempted to murder

非常高兴今天早上在这个重要活动中讲话。我亲眼看到了很多情况，英国反恐的方式令我印象深刻：努力工作的人们取得了很多成就，默默无闻地保护我们的安全：执法人员、武装力量、紧急服务部门乃至整个社区。感谢他们的努力。

成功的反恐政策必须涉及法律制定者、商业和工业、学术界、执法部门和我们的国际伙伴。因此，我们要利用现在的机会，考虑我们战略的中心问题，这点很重要。我简要地反思一下我们面临的恐怖分子威胁的形式变化和复杂性。

去年发生的几个事件显示出恐怖主义的威胁持续多样化。十二月，一个曾经在英国居住过的瑞典公民在斯德哥尔摩市中心几乎引爆了两个炸弹。五月，一个年轻女性试图在东伦敦谋杀一位在选区办公室工作的议

a Member of Parliament at his constituency surgery in East London. These events show that the threat we face is changing.

4. The UK government wants to balance the vital measures taken to ensure safety and security with the other rights we value. We must strike a balance between the requirement for government intervention in the interests of security and the need to guard our civil liberties and restore public confidence in our counter terrorism powers. The key to delivering this approach is the rigorous assessment of both proportionality and necessity.

5. No strategy, however perfectly crafted and well implemented can entirely mitigate the threat we face — but how should we ensure that our efforts and resources for tackling terrorism are properly focused amid a constantly evolving threat environment? If we want a more integrated and cohesive society we must be much more assertive in promoting common values and challenging the views which undermine them.

6. To prevent terrorism we will focus upon countering terrorist ideology by empowering communities with the theological and technological expertise necessary to challenge terrorist ideology. Where individuals are at risk of becoming terrorists we will intervene to prevent this happening and crack down on those who radicalise others. In doing all of this we will

员。这些事件显示出我们面临的威胁正在改变。

英国政府想要平衡为确保安全和治安而采取的重要措施以及其他我们珍视的权利。我们必须掌握好平衡，既要让政府能够为保证安全而进行干涉，又要保护公民自由、恢复公众信心。实施这一方法的关键是严格评估比例和必要性。

无论战略制定得多么完美，实施得多么好，都不能完全减缓我们面临的威胁。但是我们如何才能确保我们应对恐怖主义的努力和资源在一个威胁不断演变的环境中能够做到焦点足够明确呢？如果我们想要社会更加包容，更加团结，我们必须更加坚定地提倡共同价值观，并且挑战破坏这些价值观的观点。

为了防止恐怖主义，我们将通过用技术和专长赋予社区挑战恐怖分子意识形态所必须的力量，重点反对恐怖主义的意识形态。当某人有成为恐怖分子的危险时，我们将干预以阻止其发生，并打击把别人变成激进分子的人。为了做到这些，我们

provide support to those institutions where radicalisation is most prevalent, including, universities, schools and prisons.

7. To protect the UK from terrorism we have reviewed aviation security and are now bringing forward measures to stop terrorists attacking the international air freight system including the suspension of air freight from Yemen and unaccompanied freight from Somalia. We are also committed to providing updated guidance to airport security personnel to assist them to identify future potential threats.

8. Effective counter-terrorism work relies not only on government but on the continued efforts and cooperation of many individuals working across a range of sectors. To deal with these challenges we all need to listen to the views of all those who can help improve our understanding of how best reduce the risk that terrorism poses—and I hope that we can do that here today. Thank you.

将为激进化情况最为突出的机构提供支持，例如大学、学校和监狱。

为保护英国免于恐怖主义威胁，我们已经审议了航空安全问题，采取措施阻止恐怖分子袭击国际航空系统，包括暂停了也门航空货运和索马里无人货运。我们也致力于为机场保安人员提供最新的指导，协助他们识别未来的潜在威胁。

有效的反恐工作不仅要靠政府，还要靠在各个领域工作的所有人不断努力与合作。要应对这些挑战，我们要听取多方意见，他们能够帮助我们更好地理解如何减少恐怖主义风险。谢谢。（来源：英国政府时任内政部副部长的讲话。©英国王室版权。）

注 释

Partially detonated
既然是 partially 就是没有完全引爆，所以处理成"几乎"。

Surgery
大多数人学这个词的时候都是与医生或者手术相关，但是牛津在线词典里还有一个定义是 a time when people can meet their Member of Parliament to ask questions and get help，即：议员与选民会见的时间。

12. 汇丰银行讲话

1. Ladies and Gentlemen, good morning. HSBC's economic forecasts for 2050 project a very different world. So-called emerging markets will collectively be bigger than the developed markets. In fact, 19 of the top 30 economies by 2050 will be from what we call today the emerging world. By 2050, China will long since have overtaken the US as the world's largest economy. HSBC was founded in Hong Kong and Shanghai in 1865 with an unbroken presence since then, and has expanded now to 87 markets.

2. So we are easily convinced that financial market development will continue to contribute to China's future success, just as it has during the remarkable transformation of the past thirty years. Over the next five minutes, I will try to outline three key ways in which financial market development can contribute to sustainable growth. First, a broader and deeper personal financial services sector can help to distribute the benefits of growth equitably between the people.

女士们，先生们，早上好。汇丰银行对2050年的预测推算出一个非常不同的世界。所谓的新兴市场加起来将超过发达市场。2050年，最大的30个经济体中有19个将来自于我们今天所称的新兴世界。中国将早已超过美国，成为世界最大的经济体。汇丰银行于1865年成立于香港和上海并且自那以来，业务从未间断过，而且如今已经扩展到87个市场。

所以，我们不用多说就相信金融市场的发展将继续为中国未来的成功做出贡献，就像在过去三十年里中国的变化令人刮目相看一样。在此后的5分钟里，我将概述金融市场的发展能够怎样有助于可持续的增长。首先，更加广泛，深化的个人金融服务行业能够有助于在人民中公平地分配增长所带来的益处。

3. McKinsey forecasts that the number of middleclass households in China could quadruple over the next 15 years, to reach nearly 280 million. As they grow wealthier and older, people will increasingly demand longer-term wealth solutions to fund healthcare, schooling for their children and retirement, including pensions, insurance and asset management products. For example, China's life insurance market is expected to grow at a compound annual growth rate of nearly 25 per cent in the next 5 years.

4. Also, allowing citizens to invest in foreign assets would be an important step in diversifying investment alternatives. These alternatives would also be enhanced by the stock exchange listing of foreign companies, as contemplated by China with the international board. This would provide diversified investments and therefore reduce risk and improve returns. Currently, Chinese households put over 65% of their savings into bank deposits, which generated an annual real return of only 30 bps over the past 10 years.

5. Second, a reliable and more diverse supply of affordable finance will be essential for investment and innovation in China's seven emerging strategic industries. China has emerged as a leader, not only as a manufacturer, but as an innovator and developer of new technology in a number of areas, including wind and solar power. However, progress from conception

麦肯锡的预测说中国的中产阶级家庭有可能在今后15年里增长4倍，达到2亿8000万人。随着财富和年龄的增加，人们将越来越需要长期的财富解决方案，为保健、子女教育和退休提供资金，其中包括退休金、保险和资产管理产品。比如，中国的人寿保险市场预计在今后5年将以每年25%的复合率增长。

而且，允许公民投资外国资产是使投资形式多样化的重要步骤。这些形式还可以通过外国公司在中国正在考虑的国际板上市得到提升。这样做将提供多样化的投资，以此减少风险、改善回报。目前，中国家庭储蓄的65%是银行存款，年回报率在过去10年里只有30个百分点。

第二，可靠、更加多样化地提供负担得起的金融对于中国7大新兴产业的投资和创新很有必要。中国正在成长为领军者，不仅在制造，而且在几个领域的创新和新技术开发方面，比如风和太阳能发电领域就是这样。但是，从

to execution requires a range of funding sources and the efficient allocation of capital.

6. This means moving beyond traditional bank lending into more diverse sources of finance. We are encouraged by China's commitment to developing its capital markets further. And we believe that, as the economy enters a new phase, China's corporate bond market would benefit from increased participation from international firms — helping to speed up the development of financing products and securities services as well as continuing direct lending domestically. Similarly, overseas institutional investors could help create market competition and liquidity.

7. Third, as we enter the next phase of globalisation, China's success will be dependent upon its ability to finance its growing trade and investment flows. We forecast that China's trade with the rest of the world will be worth 6 trillion US dollars in 5 years time, implying a compound annual growth rate of 18 per cent. At the same time, China is investing more of its surplus overseas, with over 80 per cent directed to the rest of Asia, Latin America, Africa and other emerging markets.

8. Our experience elsewhere has shown that relaxing capital controls can help broaden access to the credit and capital that companies need to expand and grow. To close

概念发展到执行需要一系列资金来源，需要资本的有效分配。

这意味着需要超出传统银行贷款的模式，获得更加多样化的资金来源。我们感到鼓舞的是中国致力于进一步发展资本市场。我们相信随着中国经济进入新的阶段，中国的公司债券市场将得益于国际公司的更多参与，帮助加快金融产品和证券产品的开发，同时继续在国内直接放贷。类似地，海外机构投资者可以帮助建立市场竞争和流动性。

第三，随着我们进入全球化的下一个阶段，中国的成功将取决于是否有能力为不断发展的贸易和投资提供资金。我们预计，中国与世界其他国家的贸易将在5年之后达到6万亿美元，相当于年复合增长率为18%。同时，中国正在把更多的海外盈余用于投资，其中80%多投在亚洲地区、拉美、非洲和其他新兴市场。

我们在其他地方的经验显示，现有的资本控制有助于扩大公司扩展和增长所需信贷和资本的来源。在结束

my remarks, I would like to quote the Chinese Vice Premier who during his visit to the UK in January said: "China's development will not be possible without the world — and world development needs China." I believe financial services are a key part of this interdependency. Thank you.

讲话前，我想引用中国副总理在一月访问英国时说的话："中国的发展不能没有世界，世界的发展不能没有中国"。我相信，金融服务是这种相互依赖的关键组成部分。谢谢大家！
（来源：汇丰银行时任集团总裁的讲话。）

注 释

Presence

英国商业用法里 presence 所指非常广泛：成立了公司、仅有个办公室、仅有个代理、仅时不时派人去走走、仅有一个产品被转卖到当地、甚至上述全无但有个户外广告牌，都可以称 presence。所以往往有两种用意：一是把自己说得好听一些。二是事情比较复杂，用 presence 一言以概之。如果要十分准确地保留 presence 的含糊，就不得不用外来化，处理作"存在"。如果要避免外来化的生硬感，则需要根据对客户情况的了解处理。比如：We are expanding our presence in China 可以考虑的选择至少有：我们正在扩大在中国的业务（或：团队、业务活动、阵容）。

13. 西门子讲话

1. When I first introduced myself at Wittelsbacher Platz here in Munich nearly four years ago, I said, "I'm looking forward to join the community of more than 400,000 Siemens people worldwide." Today we are once again an esteemed and respected corporation. Siemens is again a world-class company. We're proud of our strength and of our achievements: of our innovation power, of our responsible way of doing business, of the recognition we receive, and of the trust and expectations placed in us as a pioneer in sustainable technologies.

我第一次在这里自我介绍是四年前,我当时说:"我期待着加入一个由全球40万西门子人组成的社区"。今天,我们再次成为受人敬仰、尊重的公司。西门子恢复了世界级公司的地位。我们为自己的力量和成就感到自豪,为我们的创新力、开展业务的负责方式、我们所受到的承认、人们对我们作为可持续技术的开创者的信任和期待感到自豪。

2. Our company's success includes the performance of Siemens stock, whose value rose 44 percent last year. Our stock also performed very well last year in comparison with our competitors. Siemens stock is one of the best on the DAX. And globally, with a market capitalization of 81 billion euros, Siemens has moved up significantly in the ranks of the most valuable companies in the world. With these accomplishments, we gratefully and respectfully carry on the baton with which Werner von Siemens founded the company in 1847.

我们公司的成功包括西门子股票的业绩,去年,我们股票上升了44%。我们的股票去年与我们的竞争对手相比也表现得很好。西门子股票是德国股市的最佳之一。从全球角度看,我们的市值为810亿欧元。西门子明显地提高了在全球价值最高的公司中的排位。在取得这些成就之后,我们满怀感激,充满敬意地继续跑我们的接力赛,这场由西门子先生1847年创办公司时开始的接力赛。

3. We uphold the tradition that he began, of value-based business management, pioneering technical achievements, and integration in countries and cultures around the globe. In addition, our company's culture has always been marked by a perspective that extends beyond the short term: in other words, durability, stability and sustainability. Siemens is more innovative than ever. During this fiscal year, Siemens employees came up with some 40 inventions per business day—8,800 inventions for the entire fiscal year. The number of registrations per inventor has doubled over the past ten years.

4. That is a fantastic achievement! Siemens has never been so innovative! We hold nearly 58,000 active patents—more than 18,000 of them in "green" technologies. More than 30,000 employees work in our research departments in 30 countries—13,000 of them in Germany alone. Innovations are not successful until they are also market successes. There are outstanding examples of that. This year, we will be handing over the "Irsching 4" power plant to one of our customers—a facility with the most efficient, most powerful gas turbine in the world.

5. Above and beyond our innovative strength, we're also proud of our financial strength. Orders from our customers picked up substantially over the year. By year's end, our order backlog was 87 billion euros. We posted a record profit for the second time in a row. The

我们坚持西门子先生树立的传统，我们的传统是以价值为基础的业务管理，具有开创性质的技术成就，在全球范围内，融入东道国的社会与文化。此外，我们公司的文化的特点一向是超越短期的视野。也就是说，耐久、稳定、可持续。西门子日益注重创新。在本财政年度，我们的员工每个工作日都产生出40项发明，全年总共8800项。每个发明人的发明登记比过去十年增加了一倍。

这是非凡的成就！西门子从来没有像今天这样富有创新！我们拥有的有效专利将近58000项，其中18000项是绿色技术。我们有3万员工在30个国家的研究部门工作，仅在德国就有13000人。创新只有在市场上获得成功之后才算成功。这方面也有出类拔萃的例子。今年，我们将把厄新4号电厂移交给我们的顾客。这个电厂拥有世界上最有效率、马力最大的涡轮机。

除了我们的创新能力，我们还为我们的财务能力感到自豪。顾客的订单过去一年大幅上升，年底时我们尚需交付的订单达870亿欧元。我们连续第二次创利润记录。几大领域的利

total profit from the Sectors soared to 7.8 billion euros. Net income after taxes likewise grew significantly. The largest contribution among our three Sectors once again came from Energy. In particular, the Fossil Power Generation and Renewable Energy Divisions landed numerous major contracts.

6. We also worked constantly on sharpening our positioning. Today, like no other company, Siemens stands for integrity and sustainability. Siemens employees have a clear understanding of the values that go all the way back to our company's founder: responsible, excellent, innovative. Our guiding principle here is: Clean business only! In November I spoke with the World Bank President about these values. We have joined the World Bank in launching 30 projects worldwide in which Siemens will support nonprofit organizations in their commitment to integrity and fair competition.

7. We once again achieved a top score in the Dow Jones Sustainability Index. This shows that throughout the world Siemens is considered a role model in compliance, in corporate governance, and in the comprehensive practice of sustainability. Today, Siemens is the green infrastructure pioneer. We are pleased and honored shareholders, customers and partners, people in politics, and the general public see us that way. The old battle line between economy and ecology is no longer relevant. Our aim is

润飙升至78亿欧元。税后净收入也同样明显上升。我们三大领域利润的最大来源再次是能源。尤其是化石发电和可再生能源分部获得了无数大合同。

我们还不断地明确我们的定位。今天，与其他公司不同，西门子代表的是正直、可持续性。西门子的员工清楚地知道我们公司创始人树立的价值观：负责、卓越、创新。我们的指导原则是：清白商业，非此不为！11月，我和世界银行行长谈起这些价值。我们加入到世界银行的行列，共同在世界各地启动30个项目。西门子将在这些项目里支持非盈利组织对于正直和公平竞争的承诺。

我们再次在道琼斯可持续性指数里获得最高分。这表明，无论在世界哪个地方，人们都把西门子看做是在合规、公司治理、可持续性的全面实践方面的榜样。今天，西门子是绿色基础设施的开创者。我们很高兴而且很荣幸，我们的股东、顾客、合作伙伴、政界人士以及公众这样看我们。过去那种经济与生态之间的战线已经失去了相关

to apply our innovative power to develop resource-saving technologies.

8. "A giant awakens"—that was the headline of an article about Siemens in Britain's Economist last year. The giant is awake, and strong, and determined. Shaping the future—that's what we've been doing for more than 160 years. And that remains our commitment as we set out for new horizons. Today, people have the vision of a green planet. 400,000 Siemens employees are working on making that vision a reality, day in and day out. That is our passion. That is what makes Siemens unique.

性。我们的目的是利用我们的创新能力，开发节省资源的技术。

"巨人苏醒了"，英国杂志经济学人去年一篇有关西门子的文章就是以此命题的。巨人苏醒了，很强壮，决心坚定。塑造未来，这就是我们在过去160多年来的所作所为，而且仍然是我们前往探索新的地平线的决心。今天，人们的愿景是绿色的地球。40万西门子员工正在努力工作，日以继夜，以实现这个愿景。这就是我们的激情所在。这就是西门子的独特之处。（来源：西门子时任总裁兼首席执行官 Peter Löscher 的讲话。）

注 释

at Wittelsbacher Platz here in Munich

如之前所述，课前如同实战里的任务前准备非常重要。如果是为西门子总裁担任译员必须对西门子有相当的了解，其中包括西门子的总部所在地。译员必须事先决定如何音译总部地名。

DAX

德国股市的简称。英国股市简称 FTSE（读音为"footsie"）。

Fiscal year

财政年往往是各公司和组织机构自己确定，有的与日历年相同，有的完全不同。英国政府的财政年是每年4月6日至下年4月5日，所有政府税收也按照财政年安排。如此确定财政年是历史遗留下来的。

"Irsching 4" power plant

产品或者项目的名称时不时无法在任务前的准备中掌握，这就需要能够当场应对。方法仍然是采用第六课里的缺省译法，按照话面意思直译。无法按照意思直译，就音译；无法音译，就争取按照英语发音重复。如果属于必须准确说出的内容就需要根据情况决定是请讲者再说一遍，还是请讲者说明他（她）讲了什么。

launch

这个词经常被译作"发布"，其实很值得商榷。牛津在线词典的定义是 to make a product available to the public for the first time, to start an activity, especially an organized one，即：推出、或者投放（产品），开始活动或者启动项目、计划。所以，汉语里常听到的"启动""开始""公布"都有可能是 launch。

14. 英国招商

1. Well, thank you very much. It's a pleasure to be here today. I've got in front of me 100 of our leading foreign investors. We have 57,000 foreign investors in the UK from different countries and industries. There is an enormous stock of overseas investment and you are—I would say. You are very welcome. I would like to stress the point that the Prime Minister made; that you as foreign investors are enormously important to our economic strategy.

2. As inward investors, you create jobs and you stimulate growth, as well as the more subtle things like bringing technology and good management practice. All of these things we want, and you bring. The figures that we have in front of us for the last financial year—which was a very difficult environment—are actually quite encouraging. If you look at the global picture, flows of global investment actually fell by 40 per cent last year. It was a catastrophic year for the global economy.

3. Overall foreign investment flows fell by 40%, and in the M&A sector it fell by two thirds. In the UK, total volume of cash turns

非常感谢！我很高兴今天来到这里。我面前有一百位领军的外国投资商。在英国的外国投资商数量达到五万七千，他们来自不同国家、不同行业。我们吸引到的海外投资数额巨大，可以说这个数额就是各位。欢迎你们的到来。我想重申一下首相的观点，那就是，外国投资商对于我们的经济战略至关重要。

作为外来投资者，你们创造就业，刺激增长，并带来一些更为微妙的东西，比如技术和良好的管理方法。这些都是我们想要的，你们恰恰能带来。我们面前有一些上一财年的数据，去年的大环境很艰难，但这些数据却鼓舞人心。在全球来看，全球投资的流动下降了百分之四十，这对于全球经济来说是灾难性的一年。

整体外商投资下降了百分之四十，并购领域下降了三分之二。在英国，现金流的

fell about 7%. So relative to the rest of the world, we did extraordinarily well last year in what was undoubtedly a very difficult international financial environment. Even more encouraging is that aggregate figure masked the fact that we had over 1,600 foreign direct investment projects involving investment from 54 different countries.

4. We're no longer talking about a handful of developed countries; we're looking at a much wider spectrum. And that's the context in which the coalition government is positioning itself. We think we start from a position of strength in terms of our approach to foreign investment and we want this to grow. I think there is one thing we were able to build on, that this country has been, for a very long time, open and liberal in our approach to trade and foreign investment.

5. Let me just set out a few facts by way of background. The total UK stock of inward investment is currently about $1 trillion. And it's the second largest in the world after the USA, roughly on a par with France. So in terms of the accumulated stock, we start from a very strong position. It's worth noting that outward investment is worth $1.5 trillion. But that's fine, in a globalising economy, you invest overseas and you attract investment—it's like trade. Imports are good and exports are good.

总量下降了约百分之七。所以相对世界其他地区而言,在去年这样一个无疑是非常艰难的国际金融环境中,我们已经做得非常好了。更令人鼓舞的是,总计数据掩盖了一个事实,那就是,我们有一千六百多个外商直接投资项目,带来了五十四个国家的投资。

我们说的已不再是几个发达国家了,而是更加广泛的来源。这也是本联合政府定位的大背景。我们认为,我们在外商投资方面的做法使我们的起点很有力,我们希望外商投资能继续增长。我认为我们有一个良好的基础,那就是,长期以来英国在贸易和外商投资方面一直是开放、自由的。

下面我提几个事实作为背景。目前,英国的外来投资总额为十万亿美元,位居世界第二,仅次于美国,和法国差不多。就累积总量来看,我们的起点很有力。值得注意的是,我们的对外投资达十五万亿美元。但没关系,在全球化的经济中,向海外投资,吸引外来投资,就像贸易一样。进口和出口都是好事。

6. In addition to the aggregate numbers, Britain is home to more European headquarters than all the other European economies combined. I've only just discovered this, but it's a striking reflection of the extent to which we have become a hub for foreign investment. Just running through the countries where we attract inward investment. The US is, as expected, the number one source. A lot of very high profile investment. Japan is the top destination from Asia. India is now the fourth largest in terms of projects in the UK.

除了这些总计数据以外，英国所拥有的欧洲总部超过了其他欧洲经济体的总和。我也是刚刚知道这一点，但这是个引人注目的迹象，反映出我们在很大程度上已经成为外商投资的枢纽。我们来看看英国外来投资的来源国吧。如同意料之中，美国是第一大来源，有很多重大的投资。日本是亚洲的首要目的地。印度目前就在英国落户的项目来看位居第四。

7. Nestor, for example, the Delhi-based pharmaceuticals company, has just expanded very rapidly with its UK HQ in Suffolk. And China, too, has become a major inward investor. One of their big manufacturing companies has established a large R&D sector, based around Nottingham. Not just that, but when we look down the list of significant investors in the UK, we have countries like Turkey and Mexico. So it is not just traditional sources of capital from the Euro-zone. There was substantial investment from France and Germany respectively creating 4,000 jobs directly.

比如说，位于德里的制药公司奈斯特公司，将英国总部设在萨福克郡，扩展非常迅速。中国也一样，已经成为一个重要的外来投资源。一个大型中国制造业公司在诺丁汉附近成立了大规模的研发部门。不仅如此，顺着关键投资者的名单往下看，我们还有土耳其和墨西哥这些国家，所以，我们并不是只有来自欧元区的传统资本来源。法国和德国也分别进行了大量的投资，直接创造了四千个就业机会。

8. But we can't put ourselves forward as a major centre of investment unless the government has got its own accounts in order. The Coalition budget was a tough one, but we think it's fair. There is clear unequivocal

但是，如果我们政府不把自己的帐户管理好，就不能说英国是一个重要的投资中心。本届政府的预算比较严厉，但我们觉得这是公平的，显示出

14. 英国招商

determination to get on top of problems in the public finances. You as foreign investor are at the heart of what we are trying to achieve. Moving out of fiscal consolidation, at the heart of that is business investment, and the heart of that is inward investment by companies like yourselves.

处理公共财政领域问题的明确决心。你们外国投资者是我们目前为之努力的目标的核心组成部分。且不说财政整顿，核心在于商业投资，而商业投资的核心在于来自你们这些公司的外来投资。

（来源：英国政府时任商业大臣的讲话。© 英国王室版权。）

注 释

Inward investors

从话语的表面看像是"向内投资者"，但是如果熟悉英国的用法就知道，他们常说 inward 和 outward，把两者作为一对来使用。所以，inward investors 是外来投资者，inward investment 是外来投资，或简称外资。Outward investment 是向外投资，即前往海外投资。

The Coalition

不仅有定冠词，而且首写字母大写，这表明是特指英国的联合政府。所以，应该加词把指代表达清楚。由于讲者是时任英国政府大臣，所以处理成"本届政府"。

15. 伦敦招商

1. Throughout history the UK has been a hub for global business, trade and investment. From the 18th century, as the first nation in the world to industrialise, we cemented our position as one of the leading economies of the world. With a trade network that extended from North America and the West Indies, to South Asia and Africa, we became the engine that helped drive future globalisation. In those days our merchant fleet traded goods such as bullion, textiles and tea—a staple of every British household.

2. And since this time, international business has evolved at an incredible pace. Now the world is truly a global market-place; and the UK needs to set out its stall. I strongly believe that the UK will remain an excellent place to do business. I strongly believe that the City of London will always be an international centre for financial services. Not because I take London's strengths for granted but because we in this Government will do as much as we can to strengthen not weaken London.

3. The UK has always been at the heart of international finance, and our openness

纵观历史，英国一直是全球商业、贸易和投资的枢纽。18世纪以来，作为第一个实现工业化的国家，我们确立了自己的地位，成为世界领先的经济体。我们的贸易网络从北美和西印度群岛延伸至南亚和非洲。我们推动了后来出现的全球化并且助了其一臂之力。当时，我们的商船交易黄金、纺织品和茶叶，而茶叶是每户英国家庭的日常必需品。

自那以来，国际商务飞速发展。现在世界已经成为名副其实的全球市场，而英国需要摆好摊位。我坚信英国将依然是个做生意的好地方，伦敦金融城将总是国际金融服务中心。我这么说不是因为我觉得伦敦的实力毋庸置疑，而是因为我们英国政府将会竭尽全力巩固伦敦的实力，而不是削弱它。

英国一直都是全球金融中心，其开放性是英国

is a real asset to our economy—and one we're keen maintain. As the Prime Minister said at a recent Business Summit: "it is absolutely vital for our economy that we attract the maximum amount of inward investment, and that we do everything we can to demonstrate that the British economy is open for business, trade and investment."

4. I'm sure you all recognise the many factors that make the UK an excellent place to do business. Our time zone acts as a bridge between the US and Asia. Our native language is global in its reach. We have developed strengths over the many hundreds of years that the UK has been a global centre for commerce: the flexibility of our labour market; our highly skilled workforce, and world-class educational institutions; and our position as the gateway to Europe—the largest single market in the world.

5. It is these factors that have helped make the UK one of the most open and internationally successful locations for trade and investment in the world: More companies choose to locate their European headquarters in the UK than anywhere else. One in four jobs in the UK is linked to business abroad. And our global financial service centre attracts more overseas business to the UK than any other nation. A strong financial sector is vital to the well-being of our economy as a whole.

经济的极大财富，也是我们非常希望保持的特征。正如首相在最近的商业峰会上所说："对于我国经济至关重要的是，我们要在最大程度上吸引外来投资，竭尽所能展示出英国经济很开放，为商业、贸易和投资敞开大门。"

我相信大家都意识到有很多因素促使英国成为做生意的好地方。我们的时区连接美国和亚洲。我们的母语在全球范围内使用。我们不断增长实力，在过去数百年间，英国一直是全球商业中心：劳动力市场灵活，劳动力技能高，教育机构世界一流，我们还是通往欧洲的门户，欧洲是世界上最大的单一市场。

正是这些因素使得英国成为最开放，也是国际上最成功的贸易和投资地。选择将欧洲总部设在英国而不是其他地方的公司总数最多。英国有四分之一的工作岗位与海外业务相关。我们的全球金融服务中心吸引到海外企业到英国来的数量超过了任何其他国家。强大的金融领域十分重要，关系到我们整个经济的发展。

6. Through business lending, investment, trade finance and insurance—our financial sector is the glue that holds UK business together. Not just in London, but also across the whole country, as many areas outside of the capital have developed their own financial specialties, such as Edinburgh's internationally recognised expertise in asset management. Leeds combined strength in professional services and finance. And many other regional centres—such as Bournemouth and Birming-ham. These local clusters are supporting growth and investment across the UK.

7. Our strengthsencourage investment in London, and make us an attractive place for firms to locate. But when taken in isolation, these factors mean nothing without:an efficient and stable legal framework; high standards of transparency and corporate governance; a deep and highly skilled pool of talent; and a cluster of professional and associated businesses.The very things that set the UK apart as a global centre for business, and world leader in the field of international finance.

8. The Coalition Government's policies shall build on this platform. We will work with—rather than against—those who wish to contribute to our economy. We welcome the fact that companies from across the globe are increasingly interested in the UK, and see us as an ideal base from which to achieve their international ambitions. The UK has a long history

通过商业信贷、投资、贸易融资和保险，我们的金融领域将英国商业紧密连接。不仅在伦敦，而且在整个英国，许多其他地区也都发展出自己的金融专长，例如爱丁堡具有国际公认的资产管理方面的能力，利兹兼有专业服务和融资方面的实力。还有许多其他的区域中心，比如伯恩茅斯和伯明翰也是如此。这些地方集群支撑了经济的增长和投资。

我们的实力促进了在伦敦的投资，吸引了众多公司落户。但是单独来看，这些因素毫无意义。他们之所以举足轻重是因为我们拥有高效稳定的法律框架，高水平的透明度和企业治理，雄厚的高技能人才大军以及专业水平高、相互关联的企业集群。正是这些因素使英国成为全球商业中心和国际金融领域的领军者。

本联合政府的政策将以这一平台为基础。我们将与那些愿意为我国经济贡献力量的人合作而不是排斥他们。我们乐于看到全球的公司对英国越来越感兴趣，将我们视为一个理想的基地，能帮助它们实现全球发展的雄心。英

of international trade and investment; and this Government is committed to its future.	国拥有国际贸易和投资的悠久历史，而本届政府致力于促进其未来发展。（来源：英国政府时任财政部金融秘书的讲话。© 英国王室版权。）

注 释

Governance

这个词在英国是 90 年代中期开始时兴的。当时，公众和媒体纷纷指责一些大公司的总裁在公司业绩下降的时候照样拿奖金，提出需要改善公司高层的行为。由于管理往往指上级对于下级的作用，公司最高层就不适合于用管理一词。所以，开始采用 governance。不久，这个词流入中国，根据当时的国情翻译成"治理"，沿用至今。其实，翻作"治理"很值得商榷。"治理"明显带有"问题很大，需要大力解决"的含义，但是 governance 的定义并没有这种含义。如今 governance 在各种场合广泛使用，都使用"治理"会出现不合适的情况。比如：cultural governance 指的是文化领域的机制和管理，译作文化治理好像是说文化里有问题。再如：We want good governance 指的是希望建立良好机制，以高水平的道德水准要求管理层，用"治理"难以表明原意。有关新词翻译时需要考虑的因素，请参见笔者由外研社出版的《实战笔译》。

work with—rather than against

英语里这种表达法是两谓一宾，即：两个谓语动词，同一个宾语。汉语里也有类似表达法，但是英语里两谓一宾的使用频率高很多，尤其是在法律文件里。口译时的挑战在于必须马上决定在汉语里的词汇搭配是否合适，如果不合适就必须处理成两谓两宾。

汉译英

16. 中英关系

1. 今天，我应邀访问久负盛名的英国皇家学会，深感荣幸。刚才，英国皇家学会授予我"查理二世国王奖"。这不仅是我个人的荣誉，也是对中国科技进步的肯定。对此，我向你们表示衷心的感谢！

2. 担任中国总理以来，这是我第四次访问贵国。这一次和上一次时隔两年，感觉大不相同。2009年初，贵国经历着国际金融危机的煎熬。如今仲夏的伦敦，人们又恢复了往日的从容和自信。

3. 我对贵国应对危机所作的努力和可喜进展，表示由衷的钦佩！上世纪80年代初，中国改革开放的总设计师邓小平，曾提出我国现代化进程分"三步走"的战略构想。第一步，基本解决温饱问题。

Today I feel deeply honoured to be able to accept an invitation to visit Britain's prestigious Royal Society. Just a moment ago, the Royal Society awarded me the King Charles II medal. It is not only a great personal honour but also an affirmation of China's progress in science and technology. I thank you for this honour.

This is my fourth visit to your country since I became Premier of China. Two years have passed since my last visit, and this time my visit feels very different. At the beginning of 2009, Britain was suffering from an international financial crisis. However, London is now in the height of summer. People have recovered their former calm and confidence.

I admire the effort and the encouraging progress that Britain has made in responding to the crisis. During the early 1980s, the architect of China's reform and opening up movement, Deng Xiaoping, put forward the strategic notion that China's modernisation should be accomplished in three steps. The first step is to be able to feed and clothe the nation.

4. 第二步，全面建设小康社会；第三步，基本实现现代化。2010年到2020年，是中国全面建设小康社会的关键阶段。沿着这条社会主义现代化道路前进，中国必将会有一个更加光明的未来。

5. 未来的中国，将是一个经济发达、人民富裕的国家。集中精力发展经济，不断改善人民生活，始终是中国政府的第一要务。我们将坚持科学发展，走绿色、低碳、可持续的发展道路。

6. 我们将更加注重改善民生，努力扩大就业，优先发展教育、卫生等公共事业，深化收入分配制度改革，增加城乡居民收入，加快建立覆盖城乡居民的社会保障体系，让各族人民共享发展成果。

7. 21世纪应是合作的世纪，而不是冲突和争霸的世纪。中国是世界和平的坚定维护者。我们一贯主张和平解决国际争端，反对使用武力。中国将同国际社会一道，

The second step is to build a moderately prosperous society. The third step is to achieve initial modernisation. The period from 2010 to 2020 will be key for China in building a moderately prosperous society. Following this road of socialist modernisation, China will have an even brighter future.

The China of the future will be an economically developed country with a well-off population. Focusing on the economy and improving the lives of the people has always been the top priority for the Chinese government. We shall uphold scientific development. We shall continue the path of green, low-carbon and sustainable development.

We shall place greater emphasis on improving the livelihoods of the people and on increasing employment. We shall give priority to public services such as education and healthcare. We will deepen our reform of the income distribution system, boost both urban and rural incomes, and speed up the establishment of a social welfare system covering the whole population. We want people of all ethnic groups to enjoy the results of our development.

The 21st century should be a century of cooperation, and not one of conflict and fighting for supremacy. China is a firm defender of world peace. We have always been in favour of peaceful solutions to international disputes and against the use of military force. China will

共担责任、共迎挑战。

8. 英国伟大思想家培根说过,"智者创造机会,而不是等待机会"。富有思想和智慧的中英两国人民,一定能创造更多的机会,推动两国合作迈上新的台阶!我对中英关系的明天充满信心,更充满期待!

work with the international community to fulfil responsibility and meet future challenges.

The great British thinker Sir Frances Bacon once said, 'A wise man does not wait for opportunities, but makes them.' The thoughtful and wise peoples of China and Britain can certainly create more opportunities, and push cooperation between our two countries up a step! I am full of confidence and anticipation for the Sino-British relations of tomorrow!(来源:中华人民共和国国务院总理温家宝的演讲。)

注 释

深感荣幸

英语演讲开始部分往往是惯用法,有关荣幸的说法最常见的有:It's an honour、I feel honoured、I'm privileged。如果需要加重语气,可以加上 greatly、deeply 或者 particularly。

英国皇家学会

英文里的正式名称是 The Royal Society,英国是包含在定冠词里的。所以,汉语里说"英国皇家学会",英语里只要加上定冠词就行,不要译成:the Royal Society of the UK。如果是非正式讲话,或者同传里来不及说时,还可以简称为 the Society。

改革开放

中国目前的政府版本是 the Reform and Opening Up,这是为了更加准确地反映原文的意思而部分牺牲英文的质量,因为英文里并没有一个与在"改革开放"里的这个"开放"完全对应的单词,而且 opening up 不是名词。所以,汉译英时有三种处理方法,一是完全按照政府版本;二是加 movement 后英语里听上去比较工整;三是借助定冠词的作用只译 the Reform,让"开放"也包括其中。口译时采用哪个版本需要根据第六课讲解哪种版本时提出的原则(为谁译、给谁听、为何效果)而判定。

小康社会

这是一个邓小平提出的全新概念,英语里没有对应词,连相近的词也没有,只能用几个词来表达。在英文里有多种版本,各有长短。本段里采用的版本不一定是最佳选择。笔者认为,这种中国特有的概念应该用音译的方式介绍到英语里,小康社会应该处理成 Xiaokang Society。然后笔译时加注解,口译时留给听众提问。如果无法提问,则由其事后去了解。翻译时常用的那个"必须让听众听得懂"的指导原则是很值得商榷的,更不应该用作口译的最高原则。第三课里还有更多的探讨。由于当年没有足够的信心把 Xiaokang 的概念输入英语,现在只好每次都用不完全准确的英语来表达。

科学发展观

这个词在英文里如何表达也是非常有挑战的问题。中国领导人对科学发展观的阐述为"科学发展观,第一要义是发展,核心是以人为本,基本要求是全面协调可持续,根本方法是统筹兼顾。"目前看到的官方版本似乎是 The scientific Outlook of Development。这种处理遵循的原则类似于"改革开放",即部分牺牲英文的质量来表达一个中国特有的概念。如果是英文质量比较好的版本就有可能没有完全准确地表达中文概念里的含义。其中一个原因就是"科学"这个词。在英文里 science 特指经过实证而得到的知识。比如:热胀冷缩就是科学,因为可以通过提高或者降低温度而看到物体的胀缩。这种概念与科学发展观里的科学有一定的距离。最后一个需要考虑的问题是汉译英时有时不必,有时不能每个汉字都译。所以,科学发展观在特定话语里完全有可能只译作科学发展。

……注重改善民生,努力扩大就业……

汉语的特点是可以一个主语之后连续并列使用多个谓语,而英语的特点是一个主语之后一般最多两个谓语。所以汉译英时需要把一个汉语长句分成多个英语句子处理。

民族

这个词很长时间里都被误译为 nationality,给人留下国籍的印象。需要尽快纠正成 ethnic groups。所以少数民族应该是 ethnic minorities。

17. 中英贸易

1. 两个月前在北京召开的中英工商峰会上,我同在座的许多朋友见过面,今天又结识不少新朋友。这使我感受到中英经贸合作不断加强的活力。在此,我向长期致力于中英友好的英中贸协朋友们表示感谢!

2. 在继续应对国际金融危机中,英国政府大幅削减财政赤字,加强金融监管,扶持中小企业发展,更加重视同新兴经济体发展经贸关系。这些富有勇气的决策,展示了英国促进经济增长的决心和行动。

3. 当前,全球经济正在恢复增长,调整变革的步伐也在加快,但国际金融危机的深层次影响依然存在,复苏的基础仍不牢固。适应全球经济的深刻变化,只有勇于创新与变革,才能为世界再繁荣提供不竭动力。

Two months ago at the UK & China Business Summit in Beijing, I met many of you. Today, I'm making many new friends. This has given me a sense of the increased vitality of economic and trade cooperation between China and the UK. I would like to thank all my friends at the China Britain Business Council for their continued efforts in promoting China-UK friendship.

In its continued response to the international financial crisis, the UK government has dramatically reduced its deficit and strengthened financial regulation. It is supporting the development of SMEs, and is placing greater emphasis on developing trade relations with emerging economies. These are courageous decisions demonstrating the UK's resolve and action to promote economic growth.

The world economy is returning to growth. Restructuring and reform are accelerating. But the deep-seated influence of the international economic crisis is still present. Recovery is still fragile. The global economy is undergoing profound changes. We need to innovate and change to provide world prosperity the perpetual drive it requires.

17. 中英贸易

4. 我愿借此机会，介绍一下中国的发展现状和发展思路。第一，扩大国内需求。我们决心把经济增长更多地建立在开拓国内市场的基础上。我们将让经济增长的成果惠及所有人群，增强内需对经济增长的拉动力。

5. 第二，突出创新转型。目前，中国科技进步对经济增长的贡献率比发达国家低25至30个百分点。这既是差距所在，也是潜力所在。我们将更多地依靠科技进步和管理创新来推动经济发展。

6. 第三，注重绿色发展。今后，我们将继续朝着绿色、低碳的方向努力，大力发展清洁能源、可再生能源和循环经济，强化污染治理，增加森林碳汇，使单位国内生产总值能耗和二氧化碳排放继续较大幅度降低。

7. 几十年来，中英关系历经风雨。现在，双边关系正步入成熟、健康、稳定发展的新阶段，经贸合作十分活跃、富有成果。今天，两国企业家又举行了中英经贸论坛。这充分体现了双方深化经贸合作的愿望。

I'd like to take this opportunity to talk about China's development and our thinking. Firstly, we want to expand domestic demand. We are committed to growing our economy by expanding our domestic market. We want to extend the benefits of our economic growth to all people, and increase the pull of domestic demand.

Secondly, we will focus on innovative transformation. In China, science and technology contributes 25-30% less to economic growth than in developed countries. That's where the gap as well as potential lies. We will rely more on science and technology, management and innovation to drive our economic development.

Thirdly, we will stress green development. We will continue in the direction of a green and low carbon economy. We will drive the development of clean and renewable energy and a circular economy. We will strengthen waste treatment and increase forest carbon sinks. We will continue to reduce significantly energy consumption and CO_2 emissions per unit of GDP.

Over the past few decades, China-UK relations have been stormy at times. Now, our bilateral relations have entered a mature, healthy and stable stage. Our economic cooperation is very active and fruitful. Today, business people from both our countries are once again holding a China-UK trade forum. This is manifestation of the desire of both sides for further trade cooperation.

8. 创新永无止境，繁荣需要合作。在世界经济复苏和中英两国发展的重要时刻，只要我们双方以开拓创新、互利共赢的精神携手合作，必将迎来两国更加繁荣发展、中英关系更加美好的未来。

There are no boundaries to innovation; prosperity requires cooperation. At this important moment in the world economic recovery and in the development of both China and the UK, if we join hands in the spirit of innovation and mutual benefit, we will see even more prosperous development for both our countries and a better future for China-UK relations. （来源：中华人民共和国国务院副总理李克强的讲话。）

注　释

中小企业

英语是 small and media sized enterprises，简称 SME。

减字

这段处理时要注意减字，凡是修饰动词的副词都需要考虑是否译入英语。只要谓语动词意思到位，就必须减去副词不译。这是因为在英语里如果动词谓语已经清楚了，加上副词反而会削弱动词谓语的力度。这牵涉到英汉两语之间文化上的不同。汉语里加词是加强语气，英语里是简明为加强语气。所以，减去"勇于"，只译"创新与变革"。

决心

英语里有两个表达法都有"决心"的意思，一个是 to be determined to do something，另外一个是 to be committed to doing something。前者更适合于尚未开始做之事，后者更适合于已经开始但是决心继续下去的事情。

拉动

来源于英文里的"拉动经济"，所以必须译回英语 pull。

科技

又是一个挑战。在英语里，科学和技术是两个不同的概念。科学特指对于经过实证而获得的对于世界的认识和知识，技术特指科学知识在实际里的运用。中文里使用科技的地方在英文里常常仅限于技术。所以,译员面临着倾向哪一个语言用法的抉择:倾向汉语,容易在英语里产生误解;倾向英语又怕被别人指责传译不准确。如何抉择需要根据第六课里为谁译、给谁听、为何效果的原则来判定。

企业家

汉语里的企业家和英语里的 enterpreneur 有很大的不同。在汉语里,凡是经商的都是企业,经商者都可以称作企业家,企业是与事业相区分的概念。而英语里 enterpreneur 特指自己承担商业风险、开创公司的人。所以,应该译作创业家比较合适。例如,中国代表在英国向英国公司代表发表讲话,经常在说"各位企业家"时被译成 you enterpreneurs。其实在座的英国老总们都是职业经理人,都不是 enterpreneur。本教材里的参考译语完全是根据讲者原话里"企业"或者"企业家"的具体所指决定是处理成"公司""企业"还是"创业家"。

18. 中国电讯业

1. 大家上午好！非常高兴能参加今天这个会议。今年我们工业和信息化部通信发展司的工作将继续深入贯彻落实科学发展观，坚持促进行业健康发展，服务社会，服务经济，服务民生这一管理理念。

2. 在通信建设领域方面，工作主要有以下几项：第一个方面是，要继续加大推进电信基础设施共建共享的力度。保护资源和环境，防止重复建设。及时解决出现的一些新问题，新困难。

3. 第二个方面，就是要继续做好通信工程建设标准制定和修订工作。加大强制性标准宣贯力度。首先我们想完成通信工程建设，标准体系的研究和编制。制定工程建设标准发展规划，以及前瞻性的标准项目。

Good morning everybody! I am delighted to be able to attend today's meeting. This year, the work of the Department of Telecommunication Development of the Ministry for Industry and Information Technology will continue to pursue scientific and healthy development of the industries. Our management philosophy is to serve the society, the economy and the people.

In terms of telecoms development, our work is principally in the following areas: firstly, we must continue our efforts in expanding joint construction and sharing of telecoms infrastructure. We must protect resources and the environment, and prevent duplicate construction. We must resolve new issues and difficulties in a timely manner.

Secondly, we must continue to carry out the work of setting and revising standards in telecoms engineering. We must strengthen the publicity and implementation of mandatory standards. We first want to complete telecoms engineering development and research and establish a standards system. We must establish an engineering constructions standard development plan and standards which show foresight.

18. 中国电讯业

4. 第三个方面，是要进一步规范通信建设项目招投标行为，建立良好的市场秩序，规范招投标工作。今年，我们要首先完善相关招投标管理制度，加大推进招标范本在通信建设项目招标活动中的应用。

5. 第四个方面，是要依法做好通信建设市场监督管理工作，严格行政许可的审批。对管理人员包括各个省通信管理局负责行政许可人员，都要进行培训指导。严格把住审批关，真正做到行政许可公正、公平、公开。

6. 第五个方面，是要加强通信网络抗震防灾监督管理工作，提高通信网络的安全性、可靠性。完善通信网络抗震防灾管理体系，做好电信建筑抗震设防分类标准，以及通信设备安装图集修订本颁布工作。

7. 今后我们通信发展司也会一如继往地支持企协、专业委员会的工作。我们会尽最大努力，来做好这个事情。政府机关更是要为大家服务。我们

Thirdly, we must take further steps to standardise the tendering process in telecoms projects, establish a sound market order and standardise the tendering process. This year we must first improve related bidding management systems and promote the application of bidding models in telecoms construction project bidding activities.

Fourthly, we must ensure that the telecoms construction market is properly supervised in accordance with the law. There must be strict control of the licence approval process. We must train and provide guidance to administrative staff including those responsible for approving licenses. There must be strict control of approval. We need to ensure that the approval process is just, fair and open.

Fifthly, we must improve supervision and management to make telecom networks earthquake and fire resistant. We must increase the safety and reliability of telecom networks. We must ensure that the earthquake and fire resistance management systems are fit for purpose. We must establish standards for telecom buildings in the form of classes of resistance. We need to revise and publish the illustrations for telecom equipment installations.

In future, we will, as always, support the work of enterprise associations and professional committees. We will do our best. Government departments must serve everybody. We hope that if you encounter problems, you

希望大家遇到一些问题，不要有什么顾虑，直接向我们反映。

🎧 8. 我们也希望了解更多的信息来帮助我们把工作做好。最后再次感谢张会长，孙主任，对我们通信发展司工作的支持。今后希望大家对我们工作有什么意见，建议，多批评指正。我们会尽全力地为大家服务好。

won't hesitate to tell us directly.

🎤 We also hope to find out more to help us do our job better. Finally, I want to thank you for your support for our work. I hope that if you have any ideas or suggestions about our work, you will make them known to us. We will do our best to serve you all. （来源：中国工业和信息化部通信发展司副司长祝军的讲话）

注　释

📌 工业和信息化部通信发展司
笔者在网站上没有查到该司的官方英文翻译，所以根据原话处理。

📌 通信工程建设
一般来说，建设有两个常用的英语处理方式。一个是 development 另外一个是 construction。后者特指具体的建筑方面的建设，前者泛指所有相关工作。所以，需要根据原话判断所指的是哪一个。

📌 审批
这个词在汉语里包含了两个方面，一个是审，另外一个是批。英语里 approval 虽然从字面意思上看仅限于"批"，但在实际使用里所指也包含审。没有仅仅负责"批"，完全不"审"的做法。所以，汉译英只需要译"批"，意思就基本到位了。

📌 向我们反映
这也是一个汉译英时需要译所指而非所言的很好例子。不能看到"反映"就想这个单词英语是什么，而是应该考虑"反映"在这里指什么。因为是指"告诉我们"，所以处理成 tell us directly。

19. 中国汽车业

1. 尊敬的大会主席，尊敬的各位嘉宾，大家下午好。过去描述中国汽车工业十年前情况的时候，概括为生产规模小、劳动生产力低、产品开发能力弱、整车几乎没有出口。大家对过去十年犹然在心。

2. 当时同世贸组织谈的时候，中国汽车工业定位为幼稚的企业，是为了取得在有效期限里面得到有效保护，让我们有喘息的机会。过去十年，在短短的十年里面，中国的汽车工业成为最令人振奋的产业。

3. 广阔的市场空间使汽车世界的重心向中国转移，中国企业家有更广阔的视野，中国汽车水平与国际水平差距大大缩小。在未来汽车产业的发展中国将扮演举足轻重的角色，我们要起到更加明确的催化剂的作用。

Conference Chairman, distinguished guests, good afternoon. In the past, when we were describing China's automotive industry over the previous ten years, we would say production was small, productivity was low, product development was weak. There was practically no export of finished automobiles. We all remember the past decade.

When we were in negotiation with the WTO, China's automobile industry was in its infancy, and our talk was to achieve effective protection within a validity period and to give us some breathing space. Over the last ten years, in just ten short years, China's automotive industry has become the most exciting industry.

The size of the market has meant that the automotive world has shifted its emphasis onto China. China's businessmen have a broader field of vision than before. Chinese cars are catching up with the international standard quickly. In the future of the automotive industry, China will play a decisive role. We want to have an even clearer catalytic effect.

4. 总体来讲，在过去的十年之间，我们汽车产量、产值和汽车产品的出口额大体上增长了10倍。我们成为了支撑世界汽车工业发展的重要力量，我们今天可以讲我们占有全球汽车市场四分之一的规模。

5. 十年前，我们自主品牌的轿车产量大概不到2%，我们在这样一个过程中，我们大企业集团的市场地位已经基本确立，也就是说他们已经开始或者正在成为具有国际竞争能力的大集团。

6. 我们与世界同类水平的产品相比，有的还差一个台阶，但这样的距离正在缩小。我们开始实行的国一排放标准的时候，我们跟国际上那个时候算差了二十年的差距，而短短十年过去了我们大大缩小了差距。

7. 如果讲过去十年之前，我们国际化还是处在比较被动的环境，那么今天一部分国际化的合作都有了大大的改观。新的产学研合作机制正在建立，政府与企业携手解决零部件落后的问题。

Generally speaking, during the last decade our output of automobiles, output value and total export have increased roughly more than ten times. We have become a major pillar of the world automobile industry. We are able to state today that we account for a quarter of the global automobile market.

Ten years ago, the total output of our own saloon car brands was probably less than 2%. We're in this process. Our large companies have established their position in the market. In other words, they have started to become, or are already becoming, groups that are internationally competitive.

In comparison with the international standard of similar products, we're still a step behind. But the gap is getting smaller. When we started to implement a national emissions standard, there was about a twenty year gap between us and the rest of the world. But within ten years, the gap has substantially narrowed.

If we talk about ten years ago, our internationalisation was still relatively passive. Today, part of our international cooperation has improved substantially. We're establishing new mechanisms for cooperation between industries, universities and research institutions. The government is working with industries to solve the problem of backward components and parts.

8. 我想在这里简单回顾一下两年前总书记在他的报告中谈到的，为中国人民的幸福生活而做出汽车产业越来越大的贡献。幸福生活的创造，就是汽车产业发展的最好的媒介，和最好的推动力，谢谢大家。

I want to reflect on something the General Secretary talked about in a report he made two years ago. He said the automotive industry should make a greater contribution to making the lives of Chinese people happier. Building happy lives is the best medium and driving force for the development of the automotive industry. Thank you.

注　释

尊敬的……

这是中方发言人常用的尊称，英语里面没有相对应的说法。所以，有两种处理方式。一种是倾向于汉语原话，说 respected 某某。另外一种是倾向于英语的习惯，直接说 conference chairman。

悠然在心

口译中，在处理成语或者类似成语时，如果事先不熟悉，则有两种处理方式。一种是按照原话字面直接译成英语。这种方式仅适合于话面意思字字清楚的情况。在本句里"悠然"两字可能会一下子不敢断定准确意思是什么。那就采用第二种方式，译所指而非所言。"悠然在心"指"记得"，所以处理成 We all remember the past decade。此后的"举足轻重"也采用了同样方式。

中国汽车工业定位为幼稚的企业

汉译英经常会遇到这种情况，即汉语句子里的准确意思是什么不清楚。比如，这句话里"定位"指的是什么？谁给中国汽车行业定位了？是"定位"还是"给中国汽车行业所处地位的评价"？遇到这种情况译员必须做出判断，到底是内容关键必须了解清楚之后再译？还是属于可以减字不译之例，剩余的话已经到位？在本句里，笔者的判断是不必译。

我们占有全球汽车市场四分之一的规模

这是第六课里讲解的汉译英里需要减字的典型例子之一，这句里的"规模"属于"总结词",即:需要表达的内容已经讲完了,再增加一个词总结前述。"我们占有全球汽车市场四分之一"意思已经完全,"的规模"属于不必译者。

自主

就像"吃饭"不要译成 eat rice 一样,"自主"不要处理成 self-determining。还是一个原则,译所指而非所言。"自主品牌的轿车"指的是中国自己品牌的轿车,所以处理成 our own。

企业

之前讲过"企业"和"企业家"的英译。这里的"企业"是相对于"政府"而言,所以按照英语里的习惯说,这叫做 government is working with industries to solve the problem。之后的单元里还有"企业"被处理成 businesses 的做法。总之,看"企业"所指是什么。译所指而非所言。

20. 中国建筑业

1. 大家上午好！首先，我代表中国建筑业协会对参加会议的各位领导、专家和来自全国各地的代表表示热烈欢迎！这次会议的主要目的就是进一步学习贯彻住房城乡建设部有关加强建筑业信息化建设的文件精神。

2. 随着我国建筑市场规模的持续扩大，人民群众对建筑产品的高端需求日益增长，建筑业的支柱产业地位不断增强，企业资质制度在调控规模、优化结构、规范市场等方面仍将发挥更大的作用。

3. 要充分认识信息化建设对加快促进建筑业发展方式转变的重要性。党的最近全会提出以科学发展为主题，以转变经济发展方式为主线，来促进我国经济平稳快速发展，要完成这一任务，其要义在于转变发展的驱动力量。

Good morning everybody! Firstly, on behalf of the China Construction Industry Association, I want to welcome all the leaders, experts and delegates from all over the country! The main objective for this meeting is to study and implement the policies of the documents from the Ministry of Housing and Urban-Rural Development on strengthening information development in the construction industry.

As the construction market in China expands, the general public's demand in high end construction products increases. Construction is increasingly becoming a pillar industry. The Enterprise Credentials system will play a greater role in controlling the scale and optimizing the structure of the market as well as regulating it.

We must fully understand the importance of information development in speeding up the transformation of the development mode of the construction industry. The party's recent plenary meeting advocated scientific development. It means we need to transform the mode of economic development and promote fast but stable development of China's economy. If we are to accomplish this task, the key focus must be on transforming the driving force for development.

4. 要由主要依靠资源驱动特别是投资驱动的发展方式,转变为依靠技术进步和提高效率来驱动发展。以信息技术的应用提升国家、行业和企业综合实力是当前转变发展方式和实现企业转型升级的核心问题。

5. 要全面提高信息化水平,推动信息化和工业化深度融合。对于建筑业这一劳动密集、依靠投资驱动、市场竞争激烈的传统产业,更要通过高新技术的应用,切实转变发展方式,提升综合实力和产业素质。

6. 当前,我国正处于工业化、城镇化和信息化加速推进的发展阶段,建筑业在改善城乡面貌和人民居住环境、加快城镇化进程、增加就业机会、带动相关产业发展、建设和谐社会等方面做出了重要贡献。

7. 我们国家正处于全面建设小康社会的重要战略机遇期。城镇化建设要加快推

From depending principally on a resources-driven, and in particular an investment driven development mode, we must shift to relying on technological progress and increasing efficiency. We must use information technology to increase the overall strength of the nation, industry and enterprises. This is the key to the transformation of the mode of development and of enterprises.

We must comprehensively raise our level of informatisation, and promote deeper integration of informatisation and industrialisation. The construction industry is labour intensive, driven by investment. It is a traditional industry and a very competitive market. We must increase overall strength and industry quality through the application of high and new technology and by realistically transforming our mode of development.

China is in the process of accelerated industrialisation, urbanisation and informatisation. The construction industry is helping to improve cities and the countryside as well as the living environment. It is speeding up the process of urbanisation, increasing employment, spurring the development of related industries, and contributing to the development of a harmonious society.

Our country is in an important strategic phase in its development of a moderately prosperous society. We should speed up

20. 中国建筑业

进，建筑业又将迎来一个改革发展的春天。我们所处的时代是一个承上启下的时代，建筑行业任重道远，广大企业责任重大。

8. 让我们团结携手，走科技进步与管理创新之路，走节能减排与绿色施工之路，走产业结构优化与科学发展之路，为我国建筑业转变发展方式与企业转型升级做出新的贡献。预祝本次会议取得圆满成功！

urbanisation. The construction industry will welcome a new spring of reform and development. We are living in an age where we build on previous successes. The construction industry shoulders a heavy responsibility on the way ahead. Businesses in this industry have a major role to play.

Let's join hands on. Let's continue on the path of scientific and technological progress, of innovation in management, follow the path of energy saving, reducing emissions and green construction, follow the path of industry structure optimisation and scientific development, and make a new contribution to transforming the development mode of China's construction industry and upgrading enterprises. I hope that this meeting will be a complete success.

（来源：吴涛秘书长在施工总承包企业特级资质信息化评审标准解读与信息化推进会上的讲话。）

注　释

中国建筑业协会、住房城乡建设部

这些都属于任务前的准备内容，必须在上课前解决。如果猛然听到不熟悉者，则按照字面直译。

学习贯彻……的文件精神

这有点像是汉语里的两谓一宾，两个谓语同一个宾语。由于汉英词汇搭配的差异，在英语里既不能说 implement a document，也不能说 study the spirit。所以，处理方式有两种。一种是加入两个谓语都可以带的词取代"精神"作为宾语：to study and implement the policies of the documents。另外一种方式是处理成两谓两宾：to study the documents and implement the policies。

资质

在英语里的常用选择至少有两个：qualification和credentials。前者特指经过学习或者培训获得了证书，后者泛指整体的水平适合于做某事，即可以是学历、阅历，也可以是业绩或者第三方的推荐或者证明信。

转变、转型、转型升级

只要在英语里用了transformation，一般情况下就没有必要再译其他汉字了，因为transformation已经是彻底地改变，而且都是向更好、更高层次变，如果译成transformation and upgrading反而会在英语里听上去觉得好像transformation不够彻底，否则为什么还要单独再说升级呢？

无主句

汉语里经常出现无主句的情况，有时甚至是在一个句子的中间出现这种情况。译员需要在英语里及时把主语补上，以免英语成为病句。本讲话中，第三段、第四段和第五段都有比较明显的无主句。

承上启下

成语的处理两种方法，一种是按照字面直译，还有一种是译所指而非所言。承上启下在本段里显然指的是在过去的基础上发扬光大，所以处理成：we build on previous successes。

21. 中国家电业

1. 随着中国工业化、城镇化的速度加快，国内家电市场将迎来新一轮消费结构升级和产品的更新，特别是农村市场将进入快速普及期，成为一个重要的市场，未来五年，我国城市市场、农村市场、出口市场将均衡发展。

2. 在行业发展方面，中国家电业正在向先进的制造业发展。技术改造速度加快，装备的自动化水平将大幅提高，企业从传统劳动密集型为主的组装业向先进的制造业发展。高端家电产品将快速发展，高档产品比重提高。

3. 未来五年，大容量多门多温区冰箱将得到重点发展，风冷冰箱、变频冰箱将得到进一步普及；洗衣机方面，大容量、变频

With the increasing speed of China's industrialisation and urbanisation, the domestic household appliances market will welcome a new round of consumption structure upgrades and updated products. In particular, the rural market will enter a faster phase of expansion and become an important market. Over the next five years, China's urban, rural and export markets will all develop in sync.

In terms of sector development, China's household appliances industry is developing into an advanced manufacturing industry. The speed of technological reform is increasing, the level of equipment automation will increase significantly. Companies will develop from being mainly traditional labour-intensive processing and assembling businesses to advanced manufacturers. High-end household electrical products will develop at a fast pace, and the proportion of high-end products will increase.

In the next five years, high-capacity, multi door, multi temperature zone refrigerators will be a focus. Frost-free and inverter refrigerators will be even more popular. In terms of washing machines, high capacity inverter machines will lead.

将成为其发展方向；空调器则重点在高效节能产品，其中变频空调、新冷媒空调更受市场欢迎。

4. 家电行业重点研发的技术有：变频技术、热泵技术、太阳能利用技术、新材料和材料替代技术、智能化和网络化技术、空调器新冷媒替代等重点技术在家电产业将得到更广泛的应用，同时，核心技术将有突破。

5. 家电行业将通过技术进步，不断提高家电产品的能效水平来达到节能减排的目的。同时，随着废弃电器电子产品回收处理基金的实施，废弃电器电子产品资源的回收和再利用体系将逐步建立。

6. 品牌建设将得到长足发展。家电产业国家规划提出要培育三到五个国际性家电品牌，在这一品牌建设的任务下，对家电产业整体品牌建设的工作也将不断加强，逐步引导一些国内知名品牌向全球品牌转变。

In the case of air conditioners, the focus will be on high efficiency energy saving products, among which inverter and new coolant air conditioners will be even more popular in the market.

Key technologies under development in the household appliances industry include: inverter, heat pump, solar energy utilisation, new materials and material substitution, intelligent and network technologies and new coolants. These and other such key technologies are being adopted widely in the household appliances industry. At the same time, there will be breakthroughs in core technologies.

The industry will continue to improve energy efficiency of household appliances through the progress of technology and to reduce emissions. With the launch of the product recovery fund, discarded electrical and electronic products will gradually be recovered and re-used through the system as it is established.

There will be significant progress in brand development. The National Plan for the Household Appliance Industry wants to see the emergency of three to five international brands. Given that, we need to work harder on brand development in the entire industry and to provide guidance to leading domestic brands to help them go global.

7. 未来五年，中国家电产业将从国内制造为主向全球布局转变，加快境外收购和境外建厂的步伐。而在国内市场的产业布局中，家电生产基地正在从东部地区向中西部转移，出现了新兴家电生产基地。

8. 随着参与竞争的程度深入，我国家电企业的发展理念和价值观将发生重大转变。企业正在从单纯追求规模和利益最大化，转变为主动承担企业社会责任、环境责任、成为受人尊敬的企业。

In the next five years, the household appliances industry of China will move towards international operations from their domestic focus. It will increase the speed of M&A and development of facilities overseas. Domestically, manufacturing bases of the industry are moving from eastern to mid and western regions. There are now new household appliance manufacturing bases emerging.

With increasing levels of competition, development philosophies and values of China's household appliances industry will transform significantly. Businesses are transforming from pursuing scale and maximum profit to proactively assuming social business responsibility and responsibility towards the environment, in order to become respected businesses.

（来源：中国家用电器协会理事长姜风在首届中国家电产业高峰论坛上的讲话。）

注　释

国内家电市场将迎来新一轮消费结构升级和产品的更新

现有参考译语只是诸多可能版本之一，而且是比较偏向于原话的版本。如果是比较偏向于英语习惯的话就有可能处理成：the domestic household appliances market will continue to move up the value chain with new product launches。

均衡发展

按照话面意思可以处理成develop evenly。按照所指，尤其是采用比较英式的表达法就可以说develop in sync,即几个方面协调发展的意思。从这里可以看出，"协调"不一定都是coordinated，也可以是in sync。前者强调通过干预来保证，后者强调已形成的状态。

大容量多门多温区冰箱

技术词汇、产品名称都属于任务前的准备内容，必须在上课前解决这些问题。临场遇到陌生词就按照话面意思直接译入英语，能译多少译多少。缺漏之处根据情况补：与技术有关的说 special technology（如：special technology fridge）；原话里的列举如果译不出来，就说一两个，之后加"等等"。关键在于补的时候要果断、平稳、自信。

随着废弃电器……体系将逐步建立

汉译英经常遇到这种很长的句子。由于汉语里很少句法，基本上是依靠不断地增加汉字表达意思，必须在英语里把汉语的长句处理成多个短句。这样就会导致出现很多版本的情况。不必担心，这不是说其他版本不准确。根据第二课的原则，这些版本可能都属于交传准确幅度之内的。关键是要译得果断、平稳、自信。一定不要自我纠正，反复重新开始（汉译英常见弊病之一）。

提出要培育……

"提出"的含义很广泛，即可以是探讨、建议、提议，也可以是宣布、公布、颁布。英语里没有一个完全对应的词。虽然 put forward 是最接近的，但是也还是有与其他词汇搭配的问题。所以，汉译英需要采用笔者反复强调的方法：译所指而非所言。即不要使劲想"提出"怎么译，而是想"提出要培育"指的是什么？这里指的是国家希望在 3—5 年后看到中国拥有国际家电品牌，所以处理成 want to see。

22. 中国风电业

1. 近年来中国风电发展很快，突出表现是我们的风电装机规模快速地增加，现在已经超过了4500万千瓦，应该是全球第一了。第二是风电设备的制造能力这几年也增长很快。中国的并网风电得到迅速发展。

2. 中国风电累计装机容量已经达到260万千瓦，成为继欧洲、美国和印度之后发展风力发电的主要市场之一。去年我国风电产业规模延续暴发式增长态势，截至去年底全国累计装机约600万千瓦。

3. 中国风电装机总量已经达到700万千瓦，占中国发电总装机容量的1%，位居世界第五，这也意味着中国已进入可再生能源大国行列。到明年底，风电规模就可能达到1000万千瓦，两年之后累计装机容量可达2000万千瓦。

Over the last few years, wind power in China has been developing very fast. Wind power installations have been developing particularly fast. With more than 4,500 million KW installed, we're probably number one in the world. Secondly, our ability to manufacture wind power equipment has increased very quickly in the last few years. China's grid-connected wind power has developed very quickly.

China's accumulated wind power installed capacity has already reached 2.6 million KW. Following Europe, America and India, China has become one of the major wind power producers. Last year, the wind power industry in China grew at an explosive rate. By the end of last year the total installed capacity was approximately 6 million KW.

China's total wind power installed capacity has reached 7 million KW, which is 1% of the total installed power generation capacity. It ranks China in 5th position globally. This means that China is now one of the renewable energy superpowers. By the end of next year, wind power may reach 10 million KW, and after two years, total installed capacity could reach 20 million KW.

4. 去年以来，国内风电建设的热潮达到了白热化的程度。中国风力等新能源发电行业的发展前景十分广阔，预计未来很长一段时间都将保持高速发展，同时盈利能力也将随着技术的逐渐成熟稳步提升。

5. 但是，中国风电的发展也遇到了更大的难题，就是风电并网运行和电力系统的融合。当然，中国风电的发展，还面临一些其他的矛盾，比如说设备的质量，也包括风电的一些安全问题。

6. 最近在风电的安装、调试检修过程中也连续发生了一些事故。但是，我们相信这些都是发展中的问题，通过不断地改进、努力，是可以逐步地走向好转的。

7. 目前，制约风电规模化发展的最主要因素还是入网后的电网运行、电力市场。产生这个问题的原因是风能资源具有随机和间歇等特性，这是天然的，至少目前还难以改变。同时我们知道用电的负荷是有规律的。

Since last year, the domestic upsurge in wind power development has reached fever pitch levels. The prospects for the new power generation sectors such as wind power in China are very broad. It is expected that there will be fast growth for a long time into the future. At the same time, profitability will also rise in line with the gradual maturation of technologies.

However, the development of wind power in China has also encountered bigger difficulties in terms of power grid connection and integration with electric power systems. Of course, there are other problems. For example the quality of equipment, including safety issues associated with wind power.

Recently there have been accidents during the process of wind power installation, testing, maintenance and repair. However, we trust that these accidents were all problems in development. Through continuous improvement, things will become better.

The main constraint on scale of wind power development is the operation of the power grid after connection. The reason for these problems is that wind power is by nature random and subject to intermissions. This is natural. For now, there is no solution. At the same time, we know that power load is regular.

8. 有的负荷不能调整，需要稳定，有些负荷时间也不能改变，比如照明就不能白天照明。风能资源和电力负荷的各自特性，导致了在发展中的一些矛盾。我们研究风电并网问题，就是要解决风能资源和电力负荷的不匹配问题。

Some loads cannot be adjusted and require stabilization. Some load times cannot be changed either. For example, lighting won't be needed during the daytime. Wind energy resources and power loads are different in nature. That has caused problems in development. Our research into wind power grid connection is in order to solve the problem of the mismatch between wind power resources and power loads.（来源：中国国家能源局新能源和可再生能源司副司长史立山的讲话。）

注　释

风电装机规模快速地增加
汉译英必须减字。所以，一定不要把上述每个汉字全部译入英语。需要决定的是这句话说的是什么的快速增加，是风电装机还是其规模？两者译一个。

4500万千瓦
电力有两种处理方法，一种是把千瓦直译为 kilowatt，简称 KW。还有一种是把万千瓦译成 megawatt，简称 MW。笔者倾向于比较简单的前者，4500 万就是 45 million。千瓦是 KW，所以是 45 million KW。此后的电力数字也都同法处理。

去年我国风电产业规模延续暴发式增长态势
这里的"态势"显然是"总结词"，完全应该不译。把"增长"译完就已经意思清楚、到位了。

电力系统的融合
从原话里可以听出电力系统不会是融合（融合好像有融化再结合的含义吧？），所以译所指而非所言，处理成 integration。

具有随机和间歇等特性

如果不知道"随机"和"间歇"英语如何表达，则译所指而非所言。"随机"指的是可以是任何时候，那就处理成：can be at any time。"间歇"指的是风有时有，有时无，那就处理成：sometimes it comes, other times it goes, there is no pattern。

23. 中国纺织业

1. 中国纺织工业实际上已经进入了强国建设的关键时期,大家知道刚刚结束的中央经济工作会议,对我们今后经济工作提出了四个重要的方面,包括了要牢牢的把握扩大内需,要牢牢地坚持实体经济这样一个坚实的基础。

2. 在这个背景下,中国纺织行业如何来加快我们的强国建设,尤其是如何以创新来推动我们强国建设当中的科技、品牌、可持续和人才这样四个方面,是我们非常重要,而且也是非常紧迫的任务。

3. 今年我们纺织行业的经济形势表现应该讲使我们的创新工作趋于更加紧迫,虽然反映我们行业经济增长的主要指标,包括工业总产值,大类产品的产量,内销的产值,出口额,基本上还都处于正常的增长水平。

China's textile industry has already entered a key phase in the development of a powerful nation. We all know that the Central Economic Work Conference that has just concluded raised four important aspects in our future economic work, including the need to manage domestic demand and stick to the real economy.

Given that, how can China's textile industry accelerate the pace of national development? In particular, how can we employ innovation in driving science and technology, brands, sustainability and talent in our development of a powerful nation? These are very important and very urgent tasks for us.

This year, the performance of the textile industry, I would say, has made us more aware of the urgent need for innovation. Although key indicators of economic growth in our industry, including total industrial output, main products, domestic sales and exports are all increasing at a normal rate.

4. 根据我们国家统计局和海关的数字来看，全行业基本上还都保持两位数以上的增长。但是受到国际市场需求低迷，国内原料价格波动的影响，目前我们处于出口数量下滑的明显趋势。

5. 这些使我们行业的自身调整和创新工作面临着新的挑战。目前，我们不能完全左右得了外部形势的改善，而确实需要竭尽全力的把自身的力所能及的事情做好，把创新工作持续的作出成效。

6. 说到创新，我想它不需要用各种词汇进行渲染和点缀。概括的讲，创新应该是我们推动纺织强国事业的灵魂和动力，围绕这个核心，结合我们自身实际，这个创新应该涵盖到并且扩张到科技的创新。

7. 目前在行业中也包括我们社会上的提法，比较多的讲了一种科技创新和产品创新，这并不错，但是脱离管理创新、体制创新、观念创新、模式创新去讲科技和产品创新，往往容易徒劳无功或者事倍功半。

According to figures from the National Bureau of Statistics of China and China Customs, the industry as a whole has maintained double digit growth. However, with the depression in the international market and fluctuations in domestic raw material prices, there is still a clear downward tendency in quantity of exports.

That presents a new challenge to self adjustment and innovation in our industry. We cannot improve the external environment as that's beyond our control. What we can do is to do everything within our ability well, and continue innovating until it produces results.

Talking of innovation, I don't think it needs to be played up or decorated. Essentially, innovation should be the soul and driving force behind promoting textiles as a way of developing a powerful nation. That's the core. We then look at the reality we're in. Innovation should extend to science and technology.

In our industry, as well as in society, there is often talk of innovation in science and technology and innovation in products. This is not wrong. But innovation in science, technology and products without innovation in management, in systems, ideas and models, would mean achieving much less than is due, or nothing at all.

8. 我们这60家企业由于创新能力不断提高，开发先进实用技术的应用，品质的管理、盈利能力和社会责任意识等方面都有长足的进步，他们是我们行业创新的榜样，要重点学习和推广他们的经验。

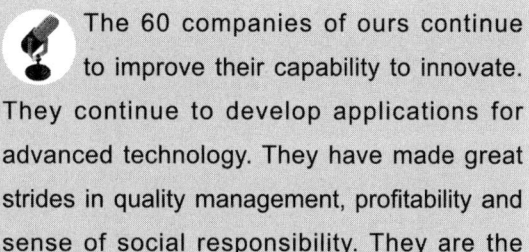

The 60 companies of ours continue to improve their capability to innovate. They continue to develop applications for advanced technology. They have made great strides in quality management, profitability and sense of social responsibility. They are the models for innovation in our industry. We should study them and make their expertise available throughout our industry. （来源：中国产业用纺织品行业协会会长王天凯的讲话。）

注　释

中国纺织工业实际上已经进入了强国建设的关键时期

如何处理"强国建设"很重要，这里需要复习一下第六课里跳词组句的理念。采用跳词组句的理念也就是说汉译英时不必，有时还不能，单独地考虑某个汉语表达法如何译成英语，而是要把之前的话（以及在可能的情况下，之后可能说的话）通盘考虑之后，决定如何处理。既有可能按照汉语词组的原意处理，也有可能减去该词组里的部分汉字，甚至整个词组都减去不译。如果单独看"强国建设"，不译成 development to strengthen the nation 就有不准确的感觉。但是在这句话里就可以说成 in the development of a powerful nation。如果是同传，出于顺序译的需要，还可以处理成 China's textile industry is helping to build a strong nation. We're at a critical juncture。

工业总产值，大类产品的产量，内销的产值，出口额

从汉语话面上看，似乎产值、产量、额这些词都必须译，否则不准确。但是在英语句子里不译的话，意思也很清楚，而且英语质量由于避免了重复而有所提高。

不能完全左右

英汉对译里的一个技巧就是正话反说，反话正说。即：如果原话是肯定

句,但是由于词汇搭配的缘故在译入语里有问题的话,就可以马上考虑把原话的肯定句译成译入语里的否定句。相反也成立。这句就是一个例子,原话里的"不能完全左右"是婉转口吻,实际上是说"我们无法左右外部形势"。但是按照原话译成英语就会产生歧义:we can't completely control external environment,好像是说"我们可以在相当大的程度上控制外部形势,只是不能完全控制而已"。这个时候反话正说,就能避免歧义:beyond our control。

渲染

遇到一个不熟悉或者不好处理的词,首先通盘考虑是否需要译,能否作为减字部分处理?如果决定译,那就采用译所指的技巧。渲染指的是夸张、夸大,英语里可以说 play up 或者 exaggerate。

24. 气候变化

1. 各位同事：今天，各国领导人汇聚联合国，共商应对气候变化大计，这对推动国际社会有力应对气候变化具有十分重要的意义。全球气候变化深刻影响着人类生存和发展，是各国共同面临的重大挑战。

2. 40年来，我们为保护全球环境、应对气候变化共同努力，取得显著成就。共同但有区别的责任原则已成为各方加强合作的基础，走可持续发展道路、实现人与自然相和谐已成为各方共同追求的目标。

3. 气候变化是人类发展进程中出现的问题，既受自然因素影响，也受人类活动影响，既是环境问题，更是发展问题，同各国发展阶段、生活方式、人口规模、资源禀赋以及国际产业分工等因素密切相关。

Colleagues, today, the leaders of each country are gathering at the United Nations to discuss collectively a plan to respond to climate change. This is a deeply significant move in the response by the international community to climate change. Global climate change has a profound impact on the survival and development of mankind. It is a major challenge that every country faces.

Over the past 40 years, our collective effort to protect the environment globally and to tackle climate change has achieved clear results. The principle of 'common but differentiated responsibility' has become the basis for all sides in strengthening cooperation. Sustainable development and harmony between man and nature have become the objective sought by all parties.

Climate change is an issue that has arisen in the development of mankind. It is not only affected by natural factors, but also by man's activities. It is more of a development issue than an environmental one. It is closely connected with factors such as the stage of development, way of life, population size, natural resources and international division of labour of each country.

4. 归根到底，应对气候变化问题应该只能在发展过程中推进，应该只能靠共同发展来解决。应对气候变化，涉及全球共同利益。在应对气候变化过程中，必须充分考虑发展中国家的发展阶段和基本需求。

5. 当前，发展中国家的首要任务仍是发展经济、消除贫困、改善民生。国际社会应该重视发展中国家的困难处境，尊重发展中国家诉求，把应对气候变化和促进发展中国家发展紧密结合起来。

6. 中国从对本国人民和世界人民负责任的高度，充分认识到应对气候变化的重要性和紧迫性，已经并将继续坚定不移为应对气候变化作出切实努力，并向其他发展中国家提供力所能及的帮助。

7. 中国高度重视和积极推动以人为本、全面协调可持续的科学发展，明确提出了建设生态文明的重大战略任务，强调要坚持节约资源和保护环境的基本国策，坚持走可持续发展道路。

Ultimately, climate change can probably only be tackled through development—collective development. Responding to climate change is in the common interest of the whole world. In tackling climate change, we need to fully take into account the stage of development of the developing countries and their basic needs.

The current priority for developing countries is still developing their economy, eradicating poverty and improving the lives of the people. The international community should take the difficulty faced by developing countries seriously. It should respect their appeals. It should combine response to climate change with promoting development in developing countries.

China is highly aware of its responsibility to its own people and the people of the world. We fully recognise the importance and urgency of responding to climate change. We have already made, and will continue to make, persistent effort to respond to climate change. China will also provide help to other developing countries to the extent that its ability allows.

China attaches great importance to, and is actively promoting, scientific development that focuses on the people, that is comprehensive, coordinated and sustainable. China has set itself a clear strategic task of developing ecological civilisation. China will stick to its fundamental national policy of energy conservation and environmental protection. China will stay firmly on

24. 气候变化

8. 世界期待着我们就事关人类生存和发展的气候变化问题作出抉择。在加快建设资源节约型社会和建设创新型国家的进程中，中国将不断为应对气候变化作出贡献。中国愿同各国携手努力，共同为子孙后代创造更加美好的未来。

The world awaits our decision on the issue of climate change. It's critical to the survival and development of mankind. In the process of speeding up the development of an energy saving model for society and of building an innovative nation, China will continue to contribute to the fight against climate change. China would like to join hands with other countries and bring about a better future for our children, grand-children and generations to come. （来源：中国国家主席胡锦涛在联合国气候变化峰会开幕式上的讲话）

注 释

各位同事

英语里的复数形势应该充分利用，是一个无需增加词汇量就能使英语更加地道的捷径。每当听到汉语里"各位""众多""各级"这类代表复数的词时，首先用复数，而不要先译"各位""众多""各级"。用完复数之后往往会发现已经准确口译完毕，无需译"各位""众多""各级"。但是，有时为了强调，还是需要把"各国"译成 every country 或者 all countries。

共同但有区别的责任

这是当今气候变化议题里的一个重要概念，必须在任务之前的准备里解决，在课前掌握。否则，仍然可以按照话面直译。

以人为本

一定不要看到这样的词组就想英语里的对应表达法！之前的注解里解释过，汉译英要跳词组句，需要把目前为止说过的话通盘考虑，先决定是否需要译，如果是，哪些字可以减去。如果单独看以人为本，则有多种处理方法：putting people first，people first，people-orientated，focus on people，focusing on people，需要根据之前的话决定用哪个。

25. 能源安全

1. 目前，中国能源安全主要面临结构性危机和制度性困境两大挑战。中国政府可考虑实施以多边合作为依托重点加入国际能源机构，以国际能源新秩序为目标积极参与国际能源贸易价格定价机制等战略。

2. 近年来，中国能源结构正在进行重大调整，能源安全的形态正在发生质变。这给中国的政治、外交、军事、科技和产业结构等提出了一个全新的课题——如何保障中国能源安全。目前中国能源安全，主要面临以下挑战。

3. 第一能源结构不合理，依然是以煤为主。中国是世界上唯一以煤为主的能源消费大国。第二，能源人均占有量低，能源资源分布不均匀。虽然中国能源总量生产居世界第三位，但人均拥有量远低于世界平均水平。

China faces two major challenges in energy security: a structural crisis and institutional difficulties. It is worth the Chinese government considering the strategy of multilateral cooperation as a way of joining international energy organisations, aiming for an international energy new order and taking an active part in price setting for international energy trade.

In the last few years, China's energy structure has been undergoing a major readjustment. There has been qualitative change in the nature of its energy security. This change has raised a brand new topic in areas such as politics, foreign relations, defence, science and technology and industrial structure. It is how to safeguard China's energy security. China's energy security is facing the following challenges:

Firstly, the energy structure is not appropriate. China still relies on coal. It is the only large energy consuming country that relies on coal as its major energy source. Secondly, China's resources per capita figure is low, and the distribution of energy sources is uneven. Although China's total energy production ranks third in the world, per capita consumption is far below the world average.

25. 能源安全

4. 第三能源供需矛盾日益突出。20世纪90年代以来，随着中国经济的快速增长，能源供应不足成为制约中国国民经济发展的瓶颈。从1992年开始，中国能源生产的增长幅度小于能源消费的增长幅度。

5. 为了解决能源安全所面临的重大挑战，中国政府正在采取一系列对策措施，正在积极参与能源安全的国际合作，实现能源供应多元化。中国与美国、英国、俄罗斯、欧佩克等建立了双边或多边的能源对话机制。

6. 中国政府坚持能源生产、消费和环境保护并重的方针，把清洁能源技术的开发应用作为一项重要战略任务，采取多种有效措施，降低能源开发利用对环境的负面影响，减轻能源消费增长对环境保护带来的巨大压力。

7. 总之，中国能源安全主要面临结构性危机和制度性困境等两大挑战。为此，中国政府采取了一系列应

Thirdly, energy demand and supply is seriously out of balance and getting worse. During the 1990s, with China's rapid economic growth, insufficient energy supply became a bottleneck of the national economy. Since 1992, China's increase in energy production has been less than the increase in energy consumption.

To tackle the challenge of energy security, the Chinese government is putting in place a series of measures to actively participate in international cooperation on energy security, and to diversify energy sources. China has established bilateral or multilateral energy dialogues with the U.S, U.K, Russia and OPEC.

The Chinese government upholds the principle of equal emphasis on energy production, consumption and environmental protection. It has set the development and application of clean energy as an important strategic task. The government has adopted many effective measures to reduce the negative impact on the environment of exploitation and use of energy and to reduce the pressure on environmental protection from increased energy consumption.

To summarise, China's energy security is facing two main challenges: a structural crisis and institutional difficulties. For this reason, the Chinese government has responded with a

对措施。从微观上讲，中国政府从供需入手，充分利用国内外两种资源、两个市场，应对结构性危机。

series of measures. At micro level, the Chinese government is starting with supply and demand, to make full use of both domestic and international resources and both markets in order to tackle the structural crisis.

8. 就宏观战略而言，中国政府应克服困难，实施以多边合作为依托重点加入国际能源机构、以区域合作为基础推动建立"东北亚能源共同体"、以国际能源新秩序为目标积极参与国际能源贸易价格定价机制等战略。

At macro level, the Chinese government should overcome obstacles and implement the strategy of multilateral cooperation as a way of joining international energy organisations, promoting regional cooperation in order to establish a 'North East Asian Energy Community', aiming for an international energy new order and taking an active part in price setting for international energy trade.（来源：人民网）

注 释

结构性危机和制度性困境

听到这种说法的时候可以考虑把"危机"和"困境"处理成一个词。从话面上听，好像"结构性危机"和"制度性困境"不是同类问题，仔细一想这很有可能是讲者为了修辞而做的区别，不一定就是断言目前机构上的问题已经属于危机性质，而制度上的问题仅仅属于困境，还不到危机程度。所以，可以考虑处理成：a structural and an institutional challenge。

拥有量

看似清楚，其实不然。从话面上听，"拥有量"似乎是指每个人拥有多少。但是这里讲的是中国能源总量生产，似乎没有听说过世界各国之间有个人均能源生产量的比较，一般都是比较人均消费量。所以，本句按照消费量译成英语，不一定准确。

采取一系列对策措施

"采取措施"一般都译成 adopt measures，没有错。但是在英国，更多听到的是 put in place policies。Put in place 听上去似乎更加确定一些。本书练习单元里两个处理法都用了。

26. 知识产权

1. 这次全国知识产权保护与执法工作电视电话会议的主要任务是，总结近年来知识产权保护工作，动员和部署打击侵犯知识产权和制售假冒伪劣商品专项行动，全面提高知识产权保护工作的水平。

2. 知识产权制度是尊重创造性劳动和激励创新的一项基本制度，是建设法治国家和诚信社会的重要内容。建设创新型国家，完善社会主义市场经济体制，必须坚定不移地保护知识产权。

3. 伴随着改革开放的不断推进，我国知识产权制度逐步建立和完善。进入新世纪以来，我们制定实施《国家知识产权战略纲要》，保护知识产权的力度不断加大，取得明显成效。

4. 一是不断完善知识产权法律制度。目前，我

The main tasks for this audio and video national intellectual property protection and enforcement conference are to review the intellectual property protection work of the last few years, to put into motion a focused campaign to combat violations of intellectual property and the manufacture and sale of counterfeit or inferior products, and to increase the standard of intellectual property protection work.

The intellectual property system is fundamental to respect for creative work and to innovation. It is an important element in developing a country ruled by law and a society based on credibility and trust. To develop an innovative nation and a socialist market economy system requires resolute protection of intellectual property.

As reform continues, China's intellectual property system is improving too. With the turn of the century, we have established and implemented the 'Outline of the National Intellectual Property Strategy'. We're doing more than ever before to protect intellectual property. We've achieved clear results.

Firstly, we continue to improve the legal system for intellectual property. In intellectual

国在知识产权领域已制定 4 部专门法律，颁布 19 部行政法规，完成专利法第三次修订，商标法、著作权法修订工作正在推进，全面履行与贸易有关的知识产权协定。

5. 二是大力加强知识产权宣传教育工作。连续 7 年开展全国范围内的知识产权宣传周活动，重点加强对青少年、科技人员、企事业管理人员的教育，知识产权培训从省部级领导干部到一线执法人员全面展开。

6. 我国知识产权保护工作仅用 30 多年时间走过了发达国家几百年的历程，成绩来之不易。但必须看到，知识产权保护状况还不适应建设创新型国家的要求。一方面，一些地区和领域侵权盗版、制售假冒产品的现象比较严重。

7. 另一方面，我国企业运用知识产权参与竞争和维权意识不强、缺乏经验，不少商标、版权等在海外被侵权。我国知识产权保护的法律体系和管理体制有待完善，全

property, China has 4 specialised laws and 19 sets of administrative rules. We have completed a 3rd revision of the patent law. The revision of trademark law and copyright law is progressing. We are implementing intellectual property agreements relating to trade.

Secondly, we have significantly strengthened education on intellectual property. For seven successive years, we have run national Intellectual Property Publicity Week, focusing on strengthening education among the youth, scientific and technological personnel and managers and administrators. Training on intellectual property has been delivered at multi levels from provincial leaders to front line law enforcement personnel.

China's intellectual property protection has in only 30 years come as far as developed countries have done in several hundred years. The results have not come easily. However, we have to be clear that intellectual property protection in China is still not what is required of an innovative nation. On the one hand, in some regions and spheres, piracy and the manufacture and sale of counterfeit products is quite serious.

On the other hand, Chinese companies lack awareness and experience in leveraging intellectual property in competition and in protecting IPR. Many trademarks and copyrights have been infringed upon overseas. China's intellectual property protection system and

26. 知识产权

社会知识产权保护的意识仍然需要进一步提高。

administrative system are in need of improvement. Awareness of intellectual property protection in the whole of society still needs to be raised further.

8. 知识产权保护工作涵盖范围广、涉及部门多，各有关部门要各司其职、密切协作，有条件的可以开展联合执法，建立健全重大案件沟通协调机制。要注重从政策、制度和机制上解决新出现的问题。

Intellectual property protection covers a wide range of work. It involves many government departments. They should fulfill their own functions and work closely together. Those that are in a position to do so should enforce law together. They should establish a communication and coordination mechanism for major cases. Focus must be on resolving newly emerging problems through better policies, systems and mechanisms.（来源：中国总理温家宝的讲话。）

注 释

总结
看到总结就会想译 summarize。但是要小心，译所指而非所言。汉语里的总结含义很广泛，而英语里的 summarize 以及 summary 含义相对窄很多。牛津在线词典给 summary 下的定义是 a short statement that gives only the main points of something, not the details，即：没有细节的简短陈述。汉语里用作动词的总结指的是把过去的工作全部回顾一遍，所以是 review。

伴随着改革开放的不断推进
由于这句的中心内容不是改革开放，所以可以简化处理成 reform。

保护知识产权的力度不断加大
这种带有"总结词"的句子都可以减去"总结词"而译剩余部分：保护知识产权不断加强（需要调整词汇搭配）。

企事业管理人员
汉语里管理人员的概念比较松散，比如机关管理人员就可能包括普通行政人员。而英语里的 managers 特指经理人员，所以处理成 managers and administrators。

27. 中航讲话

1. 这次会议是集团公司成立以来推进国际化开拓的首次会议,也是航空工业成立近60年来第一次关于国际化工作的大会。这个会议将吹响集团公司向国际跨国公司进军的号角,所以具有十分重要的意义。借此机会,我代表集团公司党组,向为国际化开拓做出贡献的同志们表示衷心的感谢和诚挚的问候!

This is the first meeting to promote our internationalisation since the establishment of our group company. It is also the first large-scale meeting on internationalization since the establishment of the aviation industry almost 60 years ago. This meeting will be the bugle call of our march on the road to becoming a multinational corporation. It is therefore of great significance. I would like to take this opportunity, on behalf of our party committee, to say a big thank you to all the comrades who have made a contribution to our international expansion.

2. 今天我发言的题目是"树立全球眼光,开拓国际市场,努力打造世界一流的跨国航空工业集团"。国际化开拓是集团公司深刻把握世界潮流、服务于国家改革开放事业、加快航空工业改革发展的重大举措。各单位、各级领导干部必须要有深刻的认识,成为国际化开拓的忠实拥护者和模范执行者。

Today, I'm talking about how to 'establish a global vision, expand in the international market and build a world class multinational aviation industrial group'. International expansion means we must have a firm grasp on world trends, serve the national reform and speed up aviation industry reform. Business units and leadership at all levels must be very clear about that. They must become loyal supporters and model executors of international expansion.

3. 下面我讲几点意见。第一、大力加强国际化开拓，是顺应经济全球化潮流的必然选择。今天，那些在世界上叱咤风云、引领风尚的企业，几乎都是跨国公司甚至是全球公司，他们业务全球化、雇员全球化、资本全球化。统计数据显示，目前全世界6.5万家跨国公司，垄断着全球60%以上的贸易额、80%以上的投资额和30%～40%的GDP。

4. 跨国公司高居于产业链的顶端，调配全球资源，组织产业发展。在经济全球化的时代背景下，任何企业已经不可能关起门来求发展，小国寡民的企业注定不能成就大事业，甚至连生存都成问题。企业要有所作为，必须到世界经济大潮中去打拼，参与全球竞争与合作，凝聚全球资源，发展全球产业，分享全球市场，实现事业成功。

5. 第二、大力加强国际化开拓，是国家改革开放事业的必然选择。党的最近全会为逐步发展我国大型跨国公司和跨国金融机构，提高国际化经营水平、开拓提出了更高的要求。作为中央企业，集

I now want to raise several points. Firstly, international expansion is an inevitable choice to make in keeping with the trend of economic globalisation. Today, those that call the shots and set the trends are almost all multinational corporations or even global corporations. Their business, their employees and their capital are all globalised. Statistics show that there are currently 65,000 multinational corporations, controlling over 60% of the total world trade, over 80% of total investment and 30% to 40% of GDP.

Multinational corporations are at the top end of the supply chain. They use global resources in industrial development. Against the backdrop of economic globalization, no company can develop behind closed doors. Small-scale companies won't be able to do big business, and can even have problems surviving. If companies want to make it big, they must battle it out in the world economy and compete and seek cooperation globally. They must consolidate global resources, develop global industry and take up global market share to become successful.

Secondly, international expansion is an inevitable choice to make in our national reform. The party's most recent plenary meeting has raised the bar for the development of China's large multinational corporations and financial institutions, and for their international operations. As a central government owned company,

团公司必须坚决贯彻落实中央的决策部署，加快推进国际化进程，促进经济领域的对外开放，进而为我国改革开放事业做出更大的贡献。

6. 第三、大力加强国际化开拓，是支撑民族复兴的必然选择。有数据显示，在100个最大的发展中国家的跨国公司中，中国只有12家，其中跨国指数超过50%的只有两家。航空工业作为国家的战略性产业，集团公司作为中国航空工业的骨干企业，我们必须勇敢地走向世界，立志成长为跨国公司、全球公司，对国家战略形成有力支撑。

7. 第四、大力加强国际化开拓，是加快集团公司改革发展的必然选择。在庞大的世界航空产业中，我们所占的份额微不足道。为此，党组提出把国际化开拓作为重要的战略方向。希望同志们从战略和全局的高度，深刻认识国际化开拓对集团公司加快改革发展的重要意义，在各自战线为加快推进国际化做出不懈努力。

we must implement decisions by the central government, accelerate internationalization, work for an open economy and contribute more to the Reform of our country.

Thirdly, international expansion is an inevitable choice to make in supporting national rejuvenation. Statistics show that of the 100 largest multinational corporations in developing countries, only 12 are Chinese. Of those, only two have achieved more than 50% in their multinational index. The aviation industry is of national strategic importance. We are one of the backbone enterprises in China's aviation industry. We must walk onto the world stage with courage, determined to grow into a multinational and global corporation. We need to be able to underpin China's national strategy.

Fourthly, international expansion is an inevitable choice to make in speeding up the reform and development of our group. In the vast global aviation industry, our market share is insignificant. Therefore, the party committee has set international expansion as our strategic direction. I hope, you'll take a strategic view of this and understand fully the significance of international expansion in our group's reform and development. I hope you will each, in your own businesses, drive internationalization.

8. 国际化开拓是集团公司发展的重要战略方向。希望大家充分认识这项工作的重要性、紧迫性，认真落实党组的工作部署，勇敢地到全球市场上去闯荡、去打拼、去历练，掀起新一轮国际化开拓的浪潮，深刻认识国际化开拓的战略意义，切实增强使命感、责任感和紧迫感，为早日把集团公司打造成世界一流的跨国公司而努力奋斗。

International expansion is the strategic direction for the development of the group. I hope that everybody is fully aware of the importance and urgency of this work, and that you will implement the plan of the party committee. I hope you will venture into the global market to work, to fight, to gain experience and to create a tide of international expansion. I hope you are fully aware of the strategic importance of international expansion, and increase your sense of mission, of responsibility and of urgency. I hope you will help to develop our group into a world-class multinational cooperation at the earliest possible date.（来源：中国航空工业集团公司时任总经理林左鸣的讲话。）

注 释

诚挚的问候
当代汉语里经常用说："向你问候"的方式向人问候。当代英语里的问候是说 Hello, how are you？所以，无法安插到英语的译语里，只好舍去不译。

各单位
二十年前，商业英语里很少用 unit。过去十年里，business unit 是公司结构里的常用概念。

讲几点
英语里不说 talk about several points，但是可以说 raise several points。另外这里也可以处理成 I now want to talk about several things。

业务全球化、雇员全球化、资本全球化
一听到这样的排列就要提醒自己，汉语里重复"化"是加强语气、体现文采，而英语里的相应做法是避免重复。所以，可能的话应该想法避免

连续说三次 globalisation。

📌 小国寡民的企业

听话面意思，好像是说小国家的企业也成不了大事，但恐怕原意是指如果以小国寡民的心态去办企业就成不了大事，所以处理成 small-scale companies。还是译所指而非所言。

📌 微不足道

这个词的处理在第六课里讲解过，如果单独看，不译成 too minute too mention 就有不准确的感觉。但是在这段话里译成 insignificant 挺合适。

📌 去闯荡、去打拼、去历练

这又是汉语里排比的例子。如果逐字译成英语，会啰哩啰唆，汉语里的力度荡然无存。必须按照当代英语的惯例，以话语简练产生力度，取得类似效果：to work, to fight, to gain experience。

28. 中远讲话

1. 非常荣幸应邀来到享誉国内外的清华经管学院、来到"中国企业管理最佳实践讲坛"介绍中远集团的经营管理、改革发展情况。下面，我以"中远集团：以创新促发展赢未来"为题，就我国远洋运输业及中远集团发展总体情况；中远集团实现可持续发展的情况；和中远集团与"中国式管理"的简要情况进行介绍。

2. 在世界经济全球化不断深化的影响下，各国经济联系越来越紧密。由于地理因素的原因，海上运输在国际贸易中一直具有不可替代的作用。目前，远洋运输更是承担了全球约75%的货物贸易总量，海上运输已成为支持经济全球化和一国外贸事业发展的生命线。从我国的情况来看，我国更是90%以上的外贸物资依靠海运。

I'm honoured to be invited to the School of Economics and Management, Tsinghua University. You're well known at home and abroad. I feel honoured to attend the Chinese Enterprise Best Practice in Management Forum to talk about the operational management and development of Cosco Group. My title is, 'Cosco Group: Innovation, Development and the Future'. I'll talk about China's ocean transportation industry and the development of Cosco Group, the sustainable development of Cosco Group and 'Chinese-style management'.

With the increasing globalization of the world economy, countries are linked ever more closely economically. Due to geographical factors, maritime transportation has always had an irreplaceable role in international trade, accounting for around 75% of global cargo trade. Maritime transportation has become a lifeline to globalization and the foreign trade of any nation. As for China, over 90% of goods for foreign trade rely on maritime transportation.

3. 作为世界海运需求总量、集装箱运量、铁矿石进口量最大的国家、第二大原油进口国，海运作为我国社会经济发展的战略通道具有特别重要的意义。在战略地位日益重要的同时，我国海运业对外开放也达到了前所未有的程度，可以说，海运业是我国现在最具市场竞争性和开放性的行业之一。

4. 据统计，我国批准国外公司到国内设立独资船公司已近四十家。据世界贸易组织秘书处和我国交通运输部专家的权威分析，作为发展中国家，我国的海运业对外开放度已经超过了WTO成员方的平均水平。产业的对外开放度与其竞争力成高度正相关。由于持续对外开放及不断深化改革，我国海运业的整体实力迅速增强。

5. 我国以中远为主要代表的国际海运企业的竞争力则有了大幅提升和长足发展。作为我国国际海运业的排头兵，中远从1961年诞生到现在，已经走过了近半个世纪。经过近50年的发展，中远现在已经发展成为船队规模稳居世界前列、远洋

China is number one in shipping demand, container transportation and iron ore imports. It is the second largest crude oil importer. Shipping has great significance in China's strategy of social and economic development. As its strategic importance increases, the shipping industry in China is now more open than ever before. In other words, shipping is one of the most competitive markets and one of the most open industries in China.

According to the statistics, we have approved almost 40 foreign companies to establish wholly-owned shipping companies in China. According to the authoritative analysis of experts from the World Trade Organisation Secretariat and the Chinese Ministry of Transport, as a developing country, the degree of openness of the shipping industry in China has already exceeded the average of a WTO member. There is a very high degree of positive correlation between the openness of the industry and its competitiveness. Due to continued openness and reform, the overall strength of China's shipping industry has increased rapidly.

The competitiveness of the international shipping of China, spearheaded by Cosco, has increased significantly. We're the leader of China's international shipping industry. Since our birth in 1961, Cosco has grown for almost half a century. We now have one of the largest fleets in the world with ocean routes across the globe. We have become a multinational

航线覆盖全球的跨国航运物流企业集团，正加快从跨国经营向跨国公司进而向全球公司转变。

🎧 6. 在合资合作经营方面，近些年来，中远也迈出了重大步伐。中远首先加大了与国内大货主合资合作经营的步伐，先后与中石油、中石化、中海油等大型资源能源电力企业，与宝钢、鞍钢、首钢等大型钢铁企业，与海尔、长虹、TCL等大型家电企业签署了战略合作伙伴关系协议，为下一步可持续发展奠定了坚实基础。

🎧 7. 作为国际海运企业，中远一直积极支持国际海运界的环保、节能减排和海上反恐等行动。中远现经营着600艘现代化商船，为确保安全和环保，我们按国际规定对油轮安全进行严格管理。在企业快速发展、燃油消耗总量增加的同时，我们通过调整船队结构、优化航线设计、使用经济航速，减少碳排放，发展"绿色航运"。

shipping and logistics group. We're transforming from a transnational operation to a multinational business on its way to becoming a global company.

🎤 In terms of joint venture and cooperation, in recent years, Cosco has made significant progress. We first increased joint venture and cooperation with major domestic customers. Some of them are large resource, energy and power enterprises like PetroChina, Sinopec and China National Offshore Oil Corp. Some are large steel enterprises like Baosteel, Angang Steel Company Limited and Shougang. Others are large household appliances enterprises like Haier, Changhong and TCL. We've signed strategic partnership agreements with them, laying solid foundations for the next stage of sustainable development.

🎤 As an international shipping enterprise, Cosco has always supported the international shipping community in its work in environmental protection, energy conservation and emissions reduction as well as maritime anti-terrorism. Cosco operates more than 600 modern cargo ships and tankers. To ensure safety and environmental protection, we manage the safety of oil tankers in strict accordance with international rules. As we continue to develop at high speed, our fuel consumption is increasing. We're restructuring fleets, optimizing routes, using economic speeds, reducing carbon emissions and developing 'green shipping'.

8. 我今天的介绍就到这里。最后，我衷心希望，在中远推进全球化发展和打造"百年企业"的过程中，能够继续得到清华经管学院的积极关注和支持，我们特别欢迎清华培养的具有开拓创新精神的优秀学子加入到中远的大家庭中，为将中远建成世界一流的全球公司做出你们独特而重要的贡献！谢谢大家！

That's the end of my talk today. Finally, I hope in the process of driving forward our global development and of building a '100 year old enterprise', Cosco can continue to receive the support of your school. We would very much like your graduates with a pioneering and innovative spirit to join Cosco. We would like to see you make your own unique and important contribution to our ambition of becoming a world-class global company. Thank you!（来源：中远（集团）总公司时任总裁魏家福的讲话。）

注 释

无主句、主语漂浮

汉语里经常使用无主句，往往因此出现同一句子里几个谓语的主语并不一致的情况。在译成英语时一定要重新组织，明确主语和谓语关系。本单元第三段开始就是这种情况。

大幅提升和长足发展

这是汉语里重复表达的例子之一。从话面上看，似乎"大幅提升"和"长足发展"不是一回事，但实际上是用不同表达法形成前后呼应，产生强调的作用并且留下语言的韵律和美感。但是在英语里，只要译成二者之一则足以。两者均译就会听上去有些啰哩啰唆，失去力度。所以，处理成：has increased significantly。

企业

把中远集团译成enterprise挺合适，因为中远规模庞大，业务范围广泛，气势磅礴，用任何其他词，无论是company还是business都有点不够分量。

29. 青岛招商

1. 青岛位于中国山东半岛南端。东、南濒临黄海，西、北连接内陆，总面积10654平方公里。属暖温带半湿润大陆性气候，最热的8月份平均气温25℃，最冷的1月份平均气温1.3℃，是著名旅游避暑胜地。境内有石老人国家旅游度假区、崂山国家级风景名胜区和马山国家级自然保护区，市区海滨风景区景色优美。

2. 众多欧陆古典风格建筑保存完好，东部新区海滨雕塑园和雕塑一条街，成为青岛新的观光旅游景点。全市有2处专业高尔夫球场，三星级以上酒店39家，去年接待海内外游客1836.7万人次，其中海外游客41.7万人次，旅游外汇收入2.4亿美元，分别占山东省总量的43%、51%。青岛也是中国著名的海洋科技城。

Qingdao is at the southern tip of the Shandong peninsular. It faces the Yellow Sea to the east and south. To the west and north, it is connected with the interior. It covers an area of 10,654 square kilometers. Qingdao is in a temperate zone with a semi-humid continental climate. In the hottest month of August, the average temperature is 25 degrees Celsius. In the coldest month of January, the average temperature is 1.3 degrees Celsius. Qingdao is a renowned tourist destination particularly during the summer. Within its borders there is the National Shilaoren Tourist Area, Laoshan National Scenic Area and the Mashan National Nature Reserve. The landscape of the city beachfront is a particular attraction.

Qingdao has many classical continental European buildings that have remained intact. In the new eastern district, the coastal sculpture garden and sculpture road have become Qingdao's new attraction. There are two professional golf courses in the city and 39 hotels of three star quality or above. Last year, the city received 18,367,000 visitors. Of those, 417,000 were foreign tourists. Foreign exchange earnings from tourism were 240 million US dollars, which represented 43% and 51% of the total for Shandong province respectively. Qingdao is also a renowned marine science and technology city in China.

3. 青岛的电子信息技术、新材料技术和生物技术具有较强的优势。在青岛的中国科学院、中国工程院院士34位，其中客座院士12位。现有独立研究机构48家，高校科研机构44个，国家级企业技术中心9家，大中型企业研发机构159个，高新技术企业522家。青岛高新技术产业开发区是国家级高新技术产业开发区。

4. 青岛口岸是我国重要贸易口岸之一。拥有集装箱码头、矿石码头、原油码头、煤炭码头，是全国第二大外贸口岸和第三大集装箱大港，有通往世界130多个国家和地区450多个港口的70多条国际航线。去年港口吞吐量1.22亿吨，列全国第五位。外贸进出口货运量8236万吨，列全国第二位。口岸外向度67.43%，列全国第一位。

5. 通车里程5381公里，公路密度50.5公里/百平方公里，高速公路通车里程287公里，居全国副省

Qingdao is strong in information technology, new materials technology and biotechnology. There are 34 academicians in Qingdao from the Chinese Academy of Sciences and the Chinese Academy of Engineering. Of those, 12 are visiting academicians. Qingdao has 48 independent research institutions and 44 university scientific research institutions. It has 9 national level enterprise technology centres, 159 large and medium sized enterprise research and development organisations, and 522 high and new technology organisations. Qingdao's high and new technology industrial development zone is a national level zone.

The port of Qingdao is one of China's major trading ports. It has a container terminal, ore terminal, crude oil terminal and a coal terminal. It is the second largest foreign trade port and the third largest container port in the country. It has more than 70 international shipping lines to more than 130 countries and regions in the world and more than 450 ports. Last year, the port throughput was 122 million tonnes, ranking fifth in the country. The cargo throughput from import and export was 82.36 million tonnes, number two in the country. 67.43% of the port's business is export related, number one in China.

Qingdao has 5,381 kilometres of roads. Its highway density is 50.5 kilometres per hundred square kilometres. Qingdao has 287 kilometres of motorway, the highest figure for any

级城市之首。青岛市全面完成主要污染物排放总量控制计划并实现达标排放,城市地表水和环境空气中主要污染物年均值达到相应功能区标准。青岛被授予国家"环境保护模范城市"称号,成为中国国内最适宜居住的范例城市之一。

6. 截至去年底,经工商注册登记的各种类型企业共有72463家,其中,中国驰名商标企业有:海尔集团、海信集团、青岛啤酒集团。全市万米以上零售网点40余个,各类商品交易市场915处,引进14家世界500强企业和著名跨国公司,其中佳世客、家乐福、麦德龙、第一百盛、普尔斯马特等5家已开业运营。

7. 去年青岛市进出口总额140.96亿美元,占山东省的42%,目前与世界上192个国家和地区有贸易关系。截至去年底,全市累计批准外商投资项目13183个,合同利用外资243亿美元,实际利用外资122亿美元,已开工外资企业3315家,就业人员50万。

sub-provincial city in the country. Qingdao is fully compliant with pollutant emission controls. Its emissions are compliant too. The annual mean values of pollutants in the urban surface water and air have reached their respective functional area standards. Qingdao has been awarded the national title of 'Environmental Protection Model City', and has become one of the cities in China that is most suitable to live in.

By the end of last year, there were 72,463 registered businesses. Among them, there were leading brands including Haier Group, Hisense Group and Qingdao Beer Group. In the city, there were more than 40 retail outlets of over 10,000 square metres in size and 915 markets. 14 of the Fortune 500 and leading multinationals are operating in Qingdao, including Jusco, Carrefour, Metro, Parkson and Price Smart.

Last year, the total import and export for Qingdao city was just over 14 billion, which was 42% of the total for Shandong province. Qingdao has trade relations with 192 countries and regions worldwide. By the end of last year, Qingdao had approved 13,183 foreign investment projects. The contractual value was 24.3 billion US dollars, of which 12.2 billion was already paid up. There are 3,315 foreign-owned businesses operating in the city, employing 500,000 people.

8. 据最近统计数据，国内生产总值年均增长12%以上，一、二、三产业的比例为 8:48:44。外贸出口年均增长 13.5%，实际利用外资年均增长 20%，高新技术产品产值占工业总产值的比重达到 40-50%。人均国内生产总值达到 27000 元，城市经济总量争取进入全国前 10 名，初步建成北方国际航运中心和区域性贸易中心。

According to the latest statistics, the city's average annual GDP growth is over 12%. The ratio of primary, secondary and tertiary industries is 8:48:44. Export is increasing by an average of 13.5% every year. Paid up foreign investment is increasing 20% every year. The total value of new and high technology products is 40% to 50% of the total industrial output. Per capita GDP is 27,000 RMB. The city is on its way to becoming top ten nationally for its total economic output, and an international shipping centre in the north of China as well as a regional trade centre. (来源：青岛投资网。)

注释

位于
经常被译作 to be located in/at。而英语里的常见说法是 to be in/at。

列、名列
往往被译作 rank, ranking，没有错，但是汉语里往往连续说几个，在英语里听上去就有些啰哩啰唆。可以在第一次译过"名列"之后直接说 number so and so。

实现达标排放
可以直译为 emissions meet the standards required。也可以采用英语里的常见概念而处理成 emissions are compliant。

佳世客、家乐福、麦德龙、第一百盛、普尔斯马特
很多中国学生都知道外商投资在中国业务的名称，但是不知道人家的原文名称。应该赶快补上这一知识。

实际利用外资
可以有两种处理方法。一种是按照中国政府采用的版本，译作 actual utilisation。另外一种是按照英语商业用语处理成 paid up 或者 already in place。

30. 成都招商

1. 成都，四川省省会，位于中国西南，地处成都平原腹心地带。总面积1.21万平方公里，其中中心城区面积283.86平方公里。成都市辖9区4市6县，户籍人口1149.1万。成都平均海拔高度500米，属亚热带湿润季风气候，年平均温度17.5摄氏度。成都是国务院确定的中国西部物流和商贸中心、金融中心、科技中心和交通枢纽。

2. 近年来，成都全面遵循落实科学发展观，着力推进城乡一体化统筹发展、可持续发展，正在努力成为中国中西部地区创业环境最优、人居环境最佳、综合竞争力最强的现代化特大中心城市。当前，成都将进一步转变经济增长方式，着力推进地域经济结构调整和产业升级，大力发展现代服务、高新技术、先进制造等重点产业。

Chengdu is the capital of Sichuan province. It's in the southwest of China, in the heart of the Chengdu plane. It covers an area of 12,100 square kilometres. The inner city covers an area of 283.86 square kilometres. Chengdu includes 9 districts, 4 cities and 6 counties with a registered population of 11,491,000. It has an average altitude of 500m with subtropical humid monsoon climate. The average annual temperature is 17.5 degrees Celsius. Chengdu has been designated by the State Council as the logistics and commercial trade centre, financial centre, science and technology centre and transport hub of western China.

In recent years, Chengdu has been pursuing scientific development, promoting integrated development of cities and countryside, and sustainable development. Chengdu is striving to become a modern megacity in the mid and west of China with the best environment for starting a business, the best living environment and overall competitiveness. Chengdu will continue with the transformation of its model of economic growth. It will drive regional economic restructuring, moving up the value chain. Its priority industries are modern services, high-technology and advanced manufacturing.

3. 根据世界银行最近发布的全球投资环境调查报告，成都已经成为"中国内陆投资环境的标杆城市"。去年，国家信息中心发布的研究报告——成都已经成为西部大开发中的引擎城市、中国内陆投资环境标杆城市、新型城市化道路的重要引领城市。同年，美国知名财经杂志《福布斯》发布报告——未来10年发展最快城市，成都排全球第一。

4. 西部大开发为成都联通世界、融入国际舞台创造了良好的机遇和条件，成都已经成为广泛参与国际交流与合作、在国际舞台上逐步显示其作用和地位的重要城市。现有来自125个国家和地区的近2万名外籍人士在成都长期居住，这个数字正以每年20%的速度增长。成都是中国中西部最受外籍人士喜爱的城市。

5. 成都作为中国西部最大的贸易中心，市场覆盖四川省并辐射西部地区8个省3亿人口。社会消费品零售总额1950.0亿元，比上年增长20.3%。成都现代服务业发展迅速，各类专业市场配套完善，

According to the Global Investment Environment Survey Report published recently by the World Bank, Chengdu has already become the 'Model City for China Inland Investment Environment'. Last year, in the study report published by the National Information Centre, Chengdu has become the driver city for development in the west, a model city for China inland investment environment and a leading city for new urbanization. In the same year, in a report published by Forbes on the fastest developing cities in the next 10 years, Chengdu is number one in the world.

Developing the West has provided opportunities for Chengdu to link up with the world and to enter the international stage. Chengdu has become an important city for participation in international cooperation. Its role is felt increasingly on the international stage. There are almost 20,000 foreigners from 125 countries and regions that live in Chengdu long-term. The number is increasing by 20% each year. In the middle and west of China, Chengdu is the city most favoured by foreigners.

Chengdu is the largest trading centre in the west of China. The market sits in Sichuan province but radiates across 8 provinces in the western region with a population of 300 million. Retail sales of consumer goods is 195 billion RMB, 20.3% higher than the previous year. The modern services industry is developing fast. There

30. 成都招商

市内拥有众多的生产资料、产权交易、金融、技术、劳动力要素等市场，城市的对外的吸引力、辐射力和城市综合服务功能日益增强。

is a cluster of markets, including production material, property trading, finance, technology, and labour. The city's international attractiveness, outreach and overall service functionality is increasing daily.

6. 去年，成都新引进澳大利亚澳新银行、日本钢铁、法国电力等12家世界500强境外企业，数量为近年来最多。同时，摩根大通、汉高、GE等已落户世界500强企业纷纷扩大投资，升级驻蓉机构级别。截止去年底，落户成都的世界500强企业已达189家，位居中国中西部首位，其中境外企业149家，中国内地企业40家。

Last year, Australia and New Zealand Banking Group Limited, Nippon Steel Corporation, EDF, a total of 12 Fortune 500 foreign enterprises moved into Chengdu, the highest number in recent years. At the same time, those of the Fortune 500 that are already in Chengdu, such as J.P. Morgan, Henkel and GE, are increasing investment or upgrading their presence. By the end of last year, there were 189 Fortune 500 companies in Chengdu, making it the number one location in the middle and west of China. Among them, 149 are foreign companies and 40 are domestic businesses.

7. 成都已成为中国西南地区科技综合实力第一强市，同时也是中国西部重要的人才汇聚地。与全国其他主要城市相比，成都不仅具有人才数量的相对优势，同时人力成本低于沿海地区，具有流动性低、稳定性高的特点。目前，成都地区各类人才总量已近230万人。其中：专业技术人才82.46万人，经营管理人才17.64万人，技能人才72.71万人。

Chengdu has become the top city in terms of overall scientific and technological strength in the western and southern regions of China. At the same time, it is an important nucleus of talent in the west of China. Compared with other principle cities in China, Chengdu not only has a comparative advantage in terms of numbers of talent, but also the cost of labour is lower than in coastal regions. Staff turnover rate is low. There are now almost 2.3 million people either in, or suitable for, employment. Of those, 824,600 are specialist technicians, 176,400 are operation managers and 727,100 are skilled workers.

8. 成都是中国内陆最大的航空枢纽，截至去年底，通航城市达126个，国际及地区直飞客运航线13条；至欧洲和香港的国际及地区直飞货运航线2条。距市区16公里的成都双流国际机场是国内第五个、中西部第一个拥有双跑道的机场，旅客吞吐量和货运吞吐量均居中西部机场第一位。去年成都双流国际机场航空货邮吞吐量达到43.2万吨。

Chengdu is the biggest aviation hub in China hinterland. By the end of last year, there were direct air links to 126 cities, with 13 international and regional direct passenger flight routes. There were two international and regional direct cargo routes to Europe and Hong Kong. Chengdu Shuangliu International Airport is 16 kilometres from the city centre. The city is the fifth city in China and the first in mid and western China to have a dual runway airport. Passenger and cargo throughput are highest amongst airports in the middle and west of China. Last year, Chengdu Shuangliu International Airport aviation cargo throughput reached 432,000 tons.（来源：投资成都网。）

注 释

城乡一体化统筹发展
也可以处理成 balanced development of cities and countryside。

融入国际舞台
汉语原话里如果本身有词汇搭配不合适之处不应给交传带来障碍，本来汉译英时词汇搭配就经常需要调整。本句里处理成：进入国际舞台。

辐射、辐射力
"辐射"可以译作 radiates，因为英语里也有此一说，指的是扩散开来。但是辐射力可不能译作 radiation，那会成为原子能的辐射力！

流动性低、稳定性高
汉语的特点是把两头的话都说了，很对称。但是这不符合当代英语的习惯，两头都说容易听上去显得啰嗦。所以只译前半部足以。

专业技术人才，经营管理人才，技能人才
之前的注解已经讲过，这种情况下要避免在英语里的重复。而且"人才"在这里还是"总结词"，之前的话已经把需要的信息都讲清楚了，完全可以省去。